MODERN
NEW YORK

Steve
Hope you enjoy + love
working with you

MODERN NEW YORK

THE LIFE AND ECONOMICS OF A CITY

[signature]

GREG DAVID

palgrave
macmillan

First published in 2012 by PALGRAVE MACMILLAN® in the United
States—a division of St. Martin's Press LLC, 175 Fifth Avenue, New
York, NY 10010.

Where this book is distributed in the UK, Europe and the rest of the
world, this is by Palgrave Macmillan, a division of Macmillan Publishers
Limited, registered in England, company number 785998, of Houndmills,
Basingstoke, Hampshire RG21 6XS.

Palgrave Macmillan is the global academic imprint of the above
companies and has companies and representatives throughout the world.

Palgrave® and Macmillan® are registered trademarks in the United
States, the United Kingdom, Europe and other countries.

ISBN 978-0-230-11510-1

Library of Congress Cataloging-in-Publication Data
David, Greg.
   Modern New York : the life and economics of a city / by Greg David.
      p.   cm.
   ISBN 978-0-230-11510-1 (hardcover)
   1. New York (N.Y.)—Economic conditions.   2. New York
(N.Y.)—Economic policy.   3. New York (N.Y.)—Politics and
government.   4. New York (N.Y.)—Social conditions.   I. Title.
HC108.N7D38   2012
330.9747'1—dc23

                                                              2011036164

A catalogue record of the book is available from the British Library.

Design by Letra Libre, Inc.

First edition: April 2012

10 9 8 7 6 5 4 3 2 1

Printed in the United States of America.

For my daughter Elizabeth and my son Eric

CONTENTS

CHAPTER 1

THE CITY TOO BIG TO FAIL

ON A WET AND DEPRESSING WINTER DAY IN FEBRUARY 2009, over 1,000 New York executives crowded into the ballroom at the Grand Hyatt in Midtown. They were anxious, their once resolute confidence in the city's future shaken by the events of the preceding four months as the city and the nation plunged first into what became known as the Financial Crisis and then into the Great Recession. They had come to hear the chief executive of the city's biggest bank and their mayor reassure them that New York would survive.

If anyone could restore their confidence it was Jamie Dimon, the plainspoken chief executive of J.P. Morgan Chase, who uneasily carried the title of "President Barack Obama's favorite banker." He was one of the few bank executives to have emerged from the crisis untarnished. His bank had not engaged in the most dubious lending practices that had caused the crisis, and it was as solvent as any other financial institution. He had been mobbed by people seeking a word as he waited to take the stage and open the conference.

"I am very optimistic about the future of America, New York and the financial business," he began in his usual direct and resolute way. "I am going to begin by saying that and I am going to end by saying that." But he also made it clear that he was going to deal with the harsh realities of the economic crisis. "In between I am not going to be so optimistic," he said.[1]

Worry over the prospects for the city had emerged in March 2008, when the sixth-largest investment bank in the country, Bear Stearns, was acquired by J.P. Morgan Chase in a deal orchestrated and financed by the federal government. This acquisition was the only thing that prevented Bear Stearns from imminent collapse. Doubts continued to grow even as an uneasy calm prevailed for the next six months. Then, in a single week in September, the even larger investment bank Lehman Brothers failed, filing for bankruptcy when Treasury Secretary Henry Paulson refused to back a Bear Stearns–like rescue. The most well-known name in the securities business, Merrill Lynch, sold itself in a shotgun wedding to North Carolina–based Bank of America, unsure whether it could survive. Meanwhile, the giant insurer AIG needed a $185 billion rescue to avert collapse, and the government took over the mortgage giants Fannie Mae and Freddie Mac by placing them in conservorship.

The result was panic. As the crisis escalated, the Dow Jones Industrial Average plunged from 11,600 in early August to 8,451 at the end of the first week of October, a drop of 37 percent. The failure of Lehman made it clear that no institution was immune from the financial conflagration taking place, and credit froze since no one would lend anyone else money. Soon even the city's strongest investment banks—Paulson's former firm, Goldman Sachs, and Morgan Stanley—were worried that they couldn't raise the cash they needed. In one weekend, they hastily converted themselves into bank holding companies so they could have access to Federal Reserve loans.

With the exception of the mortgage lenders Fannie Mae and Freddie Mac, which were based in Washington, the financial firms at the forefront of the crisis were mainstays of the New York economy. Bear Stearns had recently built a new headquarters adjacent to Grand Central Station, and Lehman Brothers occupied a gleaming office tower in Times Square, as did Morgan Stanley. Goldman Sachs was well along on construction of its new headquarters downtown, adjacent to the World Financial Center, the place Merrill Lynch called home. AIG anchored the northern edge of the Financial District.

Dimon not only insisted that the city's most important industry would rebound; he defended it against the critics who claimed it was to blame for the crisis. He tackled the issues one by one.

"You hear all the time banks aren't lending. It's not true. It's fundamentally not true," he said. "In the last 90 days, J.P. Morgan has lent $10 billion—yes, in the last 90 days."

There were some legitimate complaints about Wall Street bonuses, he admitted, but they were so exaggerated. "Not everyone in those companies was responsible for the parts that lost so much money," he insisted. "I wish the President of the United States did not paint everyone with the same brush. After all that's what he asked us not to do when he was running."

And he said it was time to stop vilifying businesses and the executives who ran them, who played a vital role in the life of the country and the city he called home. "We do wonderful things for this country and the world," he said. "We need to keep these companies healthy and vibrant so they can do their job for the country and the world."

Later that day, Mayor Michael Bloomberg took the stage in the ballroom to add his assurance that the city was prepared for any eventuality, in large part because of his leadership over the past seven years.

He had used the crisis as his rationale for overturning the city's two-term limit for mayors so he could seek another four years in office. He claimed that his experience on Wall Street, his unchallenged status as the city's most successful entrepreneur, and his seven years of strong and disciplined leadership as mayor made him far and away the best choice to lead the city through the tough times ahead. Although term limits had been imposed through referendums, he took advantage of a legal loophole that allowed the city council to change the rules without any action by voters, and he marshaled all his clout as the mayor and one of the richest people in New York to win approval from a sharply divided council. His official announcement that he would run and Lehman's failure came within hours of each other.

Laying the groundwork for his reelection campaign and knowing he was speaking to a sympathetic crowd, he took up where Dimon left off. "As bad as things are, they have been worse before," he said. "We in New York seem to have an instinct for catastrophe and each time we have roared back stronger than before. The financial crisis has revived the doubts that afflicted the city in the 1970s. And remember the Cassandras who after 9/11 said the city had no future."[2]

There were fundamental differences between those two crises and today, the mayor claimed. City government was fiscally responsible and much better managed, crime was at an all-time low, neighborhoods had been revived, and even the city's education system had improved. Most of all, New York contained the talent to lead the revival—including the people certain to lose their jobs on Wall Street—if they would follow his example to come up with innovations that would create new companies and maybe even new industries.

Jamie Dimon and Michael Bloomberg were right. New York survived the economic crisis in large part because the federal government simply could not allow the financial industry to fail. New York was also affected less than most parts of the country because of the transformation of the city's economy orchestrated by the city's businesspeople— rarely getting the notice Dimon insisted they deserved—and three of its recent mayors.

Washington bailed out the city's big banks and Wall Street firms in two steps. Major New York institutions received $197 billion in capital from the Troubled Asset Relief Program (TARP), $114 billion of which went to the five most important—Citigroup, J.P. Morgan Chase, Goldman Sachs, Morgan Stanley, as well as Bank of America for Merrill Lynch. Citi would have certainly failed without the money, and others would have had to radically reduce their operations without the infusion. Then the Federal Reserve Board cut interest rates to near zero, at least for these companies, and Wall Street profits soared to $61 billion in 2009, three times the previous record set in 2006. Not only did that allow thousands of people in New York to keep their jobs, it also emboldened the firms to pay billions of dollars in year-end bonuses that were so crucial to the city's economy.

The Wall Street rescue was not the only reason for the city's good fortune. The executives who ran the city's hotels saved the tourism business, as they had after the September 11 terrorist attacks.

As Dimon and the mayor spoke at the Grand Hyatt, thousands of hotel rooms were empty because both business travelers and tourists had disappeared. A boutique called the Kimberly in the heart of the Midtown business district on the East Side saw its occupancy rate fall to a disastrous 30 percent. It began handing out pink slips to its workers. The story was the same at virtually every hotel.[3]

The hotel executives couldn't just wait for conditions to improve. They had mortgage or rent payments to make and utility bills to pay. They could never recapture the revenue from a room night not sold. So they took the only step they could—they cut prices and sacrificed profit for revenue.

Luxury hotels led the way with deals like the one at the city's priciest hotel, the Mandarin Oriental, where a $1,800 suite was available for $800. The city's biggest hotel followed that example. The Times Square Marriott Marquis offered members of the AAA club 30 percent off already reduced prices if they stayed three nights.[4] Facing the same economic equation, airlines cut fares, too, and Broadway did the same. New York was suddenly a bargain vacation that travelers could not resist, and they returned in surprising numbers.

By the fall, occupancy rates had returned to a robust 85 percent. When the numbers were added up for the year, slightly more than 45 million visitors had come to New York, putting the decline from the previous year at a mere 4 percent. The city was the number-one tourist destination in the country, displacing Orlando and its theme parks. Not only had widespread hotel layoffs been averted, but those who did lose their jobs in the winter were soon recalled. Restaurant workers, museum staffers, Broadway actors, and backstage help all kept their jobs, too. The hotel owners didn't do as well. Most barely broke even, since the average room rate had declined by almost $100 a night.[5]

The city was also insulated from the cycle by structural changes in its economy. After World War II, New York's economic base was manufacturing with about 1 million people working in factories that made cosmetics, machine tools, and especially clothes, more than one-quarter of all the jobs in the city. Even in 1966, when John Lindsay became mayor, factories still employed 850,000 people. As Bloomberg spoke at the Grand Hyatt, only 95,000 jobs remained in manufacturing, which would be hurt again in the coming months. Instead, the health and education sector employed the most people in the city, with more than 700,000 workers—and it was historically not much affected by economic ups and downs.

Nationally, the United States lost 8.4 million jobs, or about 6 percent, during the 27-month Great Recession, which was the longest downturn since the depression of the 1930s. In New York, it was the Great Recession That Wasn't. Employment declined by about only 140,000, or 3.5 percent, and the downturn lasted only 17 months.

By comparison, the city's great recession had occurred between 1969 and 1977, when a stock market crash devastated Wall Street and the city's manufacturing sector collapsed as its competitiveness waned and the city hiked its tax burden. Some 620,000 jobs disappeared over those years, and the population fell by almost 1 million people, two little-discussed factors that were as important as budget chicanery in creating the Fiscal Crisis that almost sent the city into bankruptcy.

A second major recession followed the 1987 stock market crash. It was about half as bad—325,000 jobs—but lasted six long years. The precipitating cause was the Wall Street contraction that followed the market crash, worsened by a soaring crime rate—especially murders—that made New Yorkers as pessimistic as they were in the 1970s.

The third downturn of the modern era had its origins in another Wall Street crash—this one the end of the Internet bubble—which was exacerbated but not caused by the fallout from the terrorist attacks. The 2001–2003 downturn was the least severe, with the loss of 225,000 jobs, and the shortest until the most recent downturn.

While New York City was affected less and recovered faster than the rest of the country from the latest recession, its future remains far from assured. Whether it continues to be the business and economic capital of the nation if not the world, or whether it is entering the final chapter of the New York era remains to be determined.

One answer to the city's fate will come at the corner of 46th Street and Broadway in Times Square, where the Marriott Marquis sits proudly as New York's largest hotel. The Marquis reflects the problems of the

1980s, when it was built. The lobby was located on the eighth floor, where it was safe from invasion by the prostitutes and drug dealers who dominated Times Square. Today, the neighborhood is virtually crime-free and the Marquis is usually jammed with more than 5,000 people—3,000 overnight guests, 1,500 theatergoers, and 1,000 New Yorkers attending an event in its cavernous ballroom. The hotel is the symbol for the city's crucial tourism industry, which has taken the role once played by manufacturing, hiring immigrants like Constance Williams as housekeepers and providing economic opportunity for the newcomers who have swelled the population and saved New York neighborhoods. Its health is crucial in providing a counterweight to Wall Street.

The overcrowded offices on the fourth floor of 2 Park Avenue South will provide another clue, showing whether the city can create a viable tech industry. Here Kevin Ryan, who built the city's most important Internet company in the last tech boom, the online ad pioneer Double-Click, is rapidly expanding his latest venture, the online shopping site Gilt Groupe. As another burst of Internet start-ups takes hold in the city, Gilt is already the largest, valued at about $1 billion. In a sign of a promising future, Gilt has been able to lure Silicon Valley veterans East. Chris Maliwat, a specialist on personalization, had always been attracted by the pulsating rhythms of the city. He finally accepted Ryan's offer because he believes the Internet revival will last, assuring him of opportunities no matter what happens to Gilt. The Internet companies are creating thousands of well paying jobs that along with higher education and film and TV production are well on their way to bolstering the city's middle class.

Another test of the city's prospects will come at the rail yards located on 10th Avenue between 30th and 33rd Streets, in the middle of an area once home to factories and warehouses. Vastly underutilized, it symbolized for Dan Doctoroff, Mayor Bloomberg's most important aide, the shackles that the myth of manufacturing had imposed on the city. He picked it as the site of the stadium that was the centerpiece of his plan to bring the 2012 Olympics to New York and develop so many similarly fallow areas of the city. Doctoroff's Olympic dream died, but not his plan. His partner in the stadium effort, Jay Cross, is now in charge of efforts to develop the site for the Related Cos., which has approval to create a completely new neighborhood, with 4.5 million square feet of office space, 6,000 apartments, a hotel, a cultural center, a park, and a school. Real estate has always reflected the strength of the city's economy and if Cross can lure the companies he needs to anchor such a speculative project, the city will be thriving. If he can't, it will be a sign that its most important industry—financial services—has faltered.

Nowhere will the future of Wall Street be clearer than at the new, 43-story office tower at 200 West Street where Goldman Sachs CEO Lloyd Blankfein struggles to fend off a growing legion of critics. Goldman, the last of the large securities firms to abandon a partnership for public ownership, dominated the last Wall Street boom and produced profits and handed out bonuses on an unprecedented scale. It escaped serious harm during the Financial Crisis but new regulations and an outcry over the bailout of Wall Street continues to resonate and may make his business permanently less profitable. The growth of tourism and emerging industries like the Internet and higher education have diversified the city's job base, but its wealth—and the taxes that fuel its government—still is largely dependent on Wall Street and its well paid traders and investment bankers.

The forces shaping the city's economy will collide at City Hall, where the three most important mayors of the modern era—Ed Koch, Rudy Giuliani, and Michael Bloomberg—have helped spur New York's extraordinary gains by putting the needs of the city's economy at the top of their priorities. They represented a sharp break with earlier decades, exemplified by John Lindsay, who saw the economy as a source of revenue to help those in need. Troubled by the growing gap between rich and poor, the Koch-Giuliani-Bloomberg philosophy is under increasing attack from a list of Democrats determined to recapture the mayor's office for their party and their philosophy in the next election. All of them would represent a decisive shift toward using city government to right economic inequality in the city. Taking that path amid a permanent downsizing of Wall Street would repeat the missteps of an earlier decade.

Whatever the future holds, the era of New York began to take shape in 1965 with the election of John Lindsay.

CHAPTER 2

LINDSAY AND THE GREAT RECESSION THAT WAS

LIKE MANY NEW YORKERS, THE PUBLISHER OF THE *NEW York Herald Tribune*, John Hay Whitney, approached the middle of the turbulent 1960s with increasing anxiety. He worried about the demographic shifts that saw middle-class whites flee to the suburbs and poor African-Americans and Puerto Ricans arrive to take their place. He feared rising crime rates. He was convinced that the traditional political leadership tied to the Democratic clubhouses was inadequate to deal with the city's problems.

Whitney followed the path of other crusading newspaper owners and decided to use his newspaper to focus attention on the city's dire condition and to lay the groundwork for sweeping change in the 1965 mayoral election. He had revamped the paper, making it livelier in an effort to compete with his larger rival, the staid *New York Times*. While the *Times* specialized in direct news stories sourced with government officials and other experts, the *Herald Tribune* offered its readers broader and more analytical stories.[1]

He launched "New York City in Crisis" on January 25, 1965, and detailed every ill that afflicted New York in almost 200 stories over four months. Crime played a prominent role ("Widow, 81, Raped"), the growing number of poor people was explored repeatedly ("Puerto Rican Poverty Trap"), and city government's incompetence was always on display ("City Armed with Popguns in War on Slumlords").

The economy played a secondary role in the *Herald Tribune* portrait of New York, but its stories were bleak. It focused on the troubling loss of factories and the blue-collar jobs they had always provided. Since 1958, noted its first major piece on the subject, "Businesses Come—but Mostly Go," New York had lost some 80,000 factory jobs, 30,000 in the crucial garment industry. "For a city whose unskilled and semiskilled population continues to increase, the loss is significantly critical," the story suggested.[2]

The problem was primarily one of space, the *Herald Tribune* argued. The city's manufacturers, which had existed for years in crowded streets and multistory buildings, needed bigger sites, and lots of them, to build efficient, modern one-story factories with loading docks and easier truck access. The city hadn't delivered on promises to create industrial parks. Worse, it had allowed urban renewal programs to eliminate more than 3 million square feet of industrial space.

Even when space was available, the economics of the city didn't work. "Construction costs in some boroughs of New York are more than $1.75 a square foot higher than New Jersey," said James Rice, an executive of a construction firm that was thriving by building new facilities for companies fleeing New York. "Taxes are double. Land is more expensive. It can't even be a warehouse city because the transportation pattern is so fouled up."[3] One subsequent article put the yearly loss of factory jobs at 10,000; months later, the figure was revised to 12,000. The series spurred a meeting of the city's most important business leaders and the formation of a committee to seek solutions to the plight of the factories. Even unions agreed to cooperate in the effort.

Whitney's campaign had provided a rationale for the mayoral candidacy of John Lindsay, a photogenic, liberal Republican East Side congressman who pledged to save the city with new ideas and new people, including stemming the loss of jobs.

However, as far as the economy was concerned, the *Herald Tribune*'s series told only half the story. While factory jobs were disappearing, developers had completed an impressive ten new office buildings in 1964 containing some 6 million square feet at a cost of $175 million. These new towers were quickly occupied, since New York housed the vast majority of America's most important corporations. Volume on the New York Stock Exchange hit a record 1.2 billion shares in the first great Wall Street boom of the postwar period.[4] Sixteen million visitors ignored the headlines of rising crime to visit the city. In all, New York had added almost 100,000 jobs in the previous eight years despite the leakage of industrial jobs.

The Democrats nominated the lackluster Abe Beame, and since most reporters and editors shared Whitney's view that change was desperately needed, the media was decisively on Lindsay's side. Known for his liberal views and as a maverick, Lindsay won the election. He took office determined to focus on the city's social problems and a growing racial divide. He was sure he could make New York a compassionate city for the poor and heal the tensions among its ethnic groups.

His determination to use city government to cure social ills was fueled in his first term by an economic boom that bolstered tax revenues. His response to a spike in rents as a result of the boom led him to propose the crippling system of rent regulation that had enormous consequences in the decades to come. His demand for ever more revenue led to an overhaul of business taxes, which exacerbated every other problem the city's manufacturing base faced and accelerated a precipitous decline in the sector in his second term. His success in winning a progressive personal income tax meant that his successors would have the money in good times to build the expansive government he wanted, although at the cost of burdening the city's private sector.

The *Herald Tribune* closed its doors the same year Lindsay moved into City Hall, and no other newspaper stepped forward to examine the impact of his policies on business or the economy.

The only anxiety on Wall Street was over how to cope with a booming stock market.

The long bull market of the 1960s, which lasted from 1963 until 1969, began as the market recovered from the shock of the Kennedy assassination. While the Dow Jones Industrial Average had surpassed its

1929 peak of 381 in the early 1950s, trading remained below that record year until 1963, when more than 1 billion shares changed hands for the first time ever. The next year, the Dow reached 900 on a speculative frenzy sparked by a major mining discovery in Canada.[5]

Individual investors, who had dominated the market for decades, usually acting through small retail brokerages in New York and through-out the country, were giving way to a new force—mutual funds. The first superstar manager, Gerald Tsai, produced spectacular profits for inves-tors in the Fidelity Capital Fund, where he pioneered rapid trading in the hottest growth stocks of the era. His success attracted investors and competitors, and by the end of the decade, institutional investors like mutual funds accounted for 54 percent of all trading, up from a third at the beginning of the decade. Turnover in mutual funds soared to 50 percent a year from 20 percent in the same period, fueling the surge in volume.

Conglomerates were the first growth stocks to dominate the era, created through rapid-fire mergers, which used rising stock prices as a currency to acquire other companies and send share prices still higher. Mergers also allowed executives like James Ling of Ling-Temco-Vought to promise they could deliver profit increases year after year. Companies like Meshulam Riklis's Rapid-American Corp. were so diversified—it owned the retailer McCrory Corp., Glen Alden consumer products, In-ternational Playtex, BVD, Lerner Shops, and RKO Stanley Warner The-atres—that CEOs argued their profits would be unaffected by economic cycles. Investors bought the concept, and Rapid American's stock in-creased tenfold between 1965 and its peak in 1967.

If conglomerates were an amalgam of real businesses, imitators of Ling and Riklis lured investors with more speculative ideas. Cortes Randolph hired 600 part-time student representatives to sell fad items, distribute samples, and conduct market research on campuses. When revenues jumped from $160,000 to $723,000 in one year, Randolph was ready to take his company public. The stock debuted in 1968 at $8 a share and soared to $30 by June. Now he could go out and acquire other businesses, imitating Ling and Riklis.

By 1968, investors were willing to buy almost any new issue in wildly speculative companies such as Four Seasons Nursing Centers and Applied Logic, both of which skyrocketed on their market debuts. It was, said one seasoned Wall Street executive, "the great garbage market." By 1967, trading averaged 10 million shares a day. Volume soared after President Lyndon Johnson announced he would not seek reelection at the end of March and reached a record of 20 million shares on March 31, 1968.

In an era of fixed commissions, trading volume should have meant soaring profits. But Wall Street was simply unable to handle the crush of paperwork the surge generated. Stock exchanges tracked "fails," or transactions that were rejected or never completed. An acceptable level was considered $1 billion worth of trades. In 1968, the figure exceeded $4 billion, precipitating a crisis that required shortened trading hours.

The bull market made some people wealthy—the price of a seat on the New York Stock Exchange rose from $450,000 in January to $515,000 at the end of 1968 (finally exceeding the 1929 price). It also set off an enormous hiring binge. From 1965 to 1969, Wall Street added 43,000 jobs, an increase of some 60 percent, a major factor in the economic health of Lindsay's first term.

These were not the kind of Wall Street jobs that would be so sought after in later decades. Instead, they involved mind-numbing paper-shuffling duties and offered meager pay, as John Brooks vividly described in his book, *The Go-Go Years.* "Known informally, and suggestively as the cage, the back office was an unlovely and constricting place to work in fulfillment of its sole purpose, to keep records and to move physically money and stock certificates in conformity with the transactions made in the front office. It was subdivided into a bewildering variety of departments. Merrill Lynch, the biggest broker, had about 500 separate clerical titles," he wrote.

Pay was low—$60 a week or far below that of most blue-collar jobs—with only year-end bonuses holding out the hope for sustenance. Turnover was 60 percent a year. The young, restless workers, products of the 1960s and many of whom were black and Hispanic, clashed with

old-line white supervisors wedded to 1950s concepts of company loyalty
and obedience to orders. Drugs flourished and theft soared.

While finance jobs provided the biggest boost to the economy in
Lindsay's first term, city government was not far behind. The mayor's
new and expanded programs for welfare, health care, and other assistance to the city's poor increased the city payroll by 64,000 in the first
term, a third of the total gain. Both more than offset the drain of blue-
collar manufacturing jobs, which averaged about 10,000 a year, the
same pace the city had seen for more than a decade.

John Lindsay's father, a successful lawyer and an investment banker,
had sent his son to prestigious prep schools and Yale, where he joined
one of the exclusive clubs. He even met his future wife at the wedding of
one of the daughters of the oil-rich Bush family of Connecticut.

Although Lindsay was regarded as a member of the city's upper crust,
the picture was somewhat misleading as his family was comfortable, not
wealthy. And while he had rubbed shoulders with the sons of the business
elite at school and his brother worked for one of the city's biggest banks,
he shared the attitude of mayors beginning with Fiorello La Guardia.
Business's primary role was to provide the revenue for city government
to right social imbalances. Like many mayors, Lindsay sought to help
companies so that the city would prosper, but the economy was never at
the top of his priority list. In his sixth year in office, Lindsay headed a few
blocks south of City Hall to help Merrill Lynch open a new investment
information center, a reward for the brokerage's decision to remain in
New York rather than move elsewhere.[6] The visit was unusual enough to
merit coverage in the newspapers. "I'm not sure he realized there was a
place south of City Hall," said Merrill chief executive Donald Regan. He
may have been half-joking, but it was not an introduction that anyone
would make for Ed Koch or the mayors who followed him.

The day Lindsay took office, the transit workers walked off the job
in the first of a series of bitter labor confrontations that marked the
mayor's early years in office. Lindsay had barely settled the transit strike
when he confronted an equally big problem—a gap of $633 million in
a budget of around $4 billion, despite the fact that revenues were rising.
His solution was to find new revenue. He embraced the idea of impos-

ing the city's first income tax on residents and commuters, overhauling its business tax structure, and increasing the city's stock transfer levy to take advantage of the elimination of a similar federal tax on stocks. "All these measures will be terribly distasteful to the public we know," an unnamed administration official admitted, "but the financial situation of the city is horrible."[7]

Reflecting the city's liberal political consensus, the New York Times explained that new and higher taxes were necessary to pay for a larger city government. It pointed out that in the last ten years, the number of city employees had increased from 186,000 to 237,000. The budget had jumped from $1.73 billion to $3.87 billion. It even noted that the city budget now equaled 13.6 percent of personal income in the city, up from 9.1 percent. And in an assumption fraught with consequences, the Times said that the city's businesses and residents could afford to pay more. "We are not dealing with a one horse town here," it quoted an unnamed investment banker as saying. "We are dealing with a city of enormous economic activity, enormous resources."[8]

In March, the mayor unveiled the details of his sweeping plan, which required the approval of the state legislature and governor.[9] He proposed a 2 percent graduated income tax levy on both residents and commuters, rejecting a less onerous payroll tax used by most other cities; he proposed a business income tax to replace the current gross receipts tax, a move that would raise much more money by increasing the burden on profitable financial services companies while lowering it for low-margin stores and factories; and he argued for a 50 percent increase in the city's stock transfer tax.

He needed the revenues, he told New Yorkers, to save the city and the economy. "When a city cannot provide complete safety and fire protection, and good hospitals and schools, an endless spiral downward begins. Business moves away. Jobs are lost. Less tax money comes in and even fewer services can be provided. It is time for New Yorkers to decide between a safe, prosperous future and decay," he insisted.[10]

Opposition emerged immediately. The New York Stock Exchange threatened to leave. Suburban politicians rejected the idea of taxing their constituents. The Commerce and Industry Association attacked the income tax, saying it would lead the city toward economic chaos and drive firms and taxpaying residents away, and it reiterated its support for a payroll tax. Morgan Guaranty Trust Co., where the mayor's brother was a high-ranking officer, noted that its taxes would increase by $5 million a year under the 5.5 percent profits tax.[11] A later study said the burden on all financial companies, which paid very little under the gross receipts tax, would increase by a third. One business group did have some praise for the mayor. The Economic Development Council of New York, composed of 26 leading executives, commended Lindsay for rejecting the previous disastrous policy of borrowing to pay for current expenses.

Over the ensuing months, the mayor sought the support of a reluctant Governor Nelson Rockefeller. He tried to figure out how to persuade suburban legislators to tax the commuters who lived in their districts. He won support from the garment industry trade association, which decided that apparel firms would be better off if a profits tax replaced the gross receipt tax. He repeatedly attacked the banks and insurance companies that put up the most resistance to his program. "It's about time these elements begin to give greater support to the city and its needs. Up to now they have made no contribution in business taxes. None. Zero," he charged.[12] His rhetoric became so harsh that he was forced to meet with business leaders to smooth over the disagreement.

After days and nights of bargaining, impasses, and dire warnings, a compromise was hammered out and rushed through the legislature. It featured a personal income tax starting at 0.4 percent and rising at the top to 2 percent; even today it is the only such progressive tax scheme in an American city. Lindsay reluctantly agreed to a flat 0.25 percent payroll tax on commuters, despite his fears that it would exacerbate flight from the city. A new business income tax was imposed to replace the gross receipts levy, which the mayor believed was fairer and which raised more revenue. A 25 percent jump in the stock transfer tax was approved.[13]

The budget crisis was solved, but the Economic Development Council's praise for Lindsay's fiscal responsibility proved premature. He soon reverted to many of the practices later reviled for bringing about the

Fiscal Crisis—using long-term bonds to pay for operating expenses, fudging revenues, and borrowing short term in expectation of future revenues. He did not do so secretly. All these maneuvers were covered by the newspapers, which often cheered them for closing a deficit or saving city workers from layoffs. They were endlessly criticized by the Citizens Budget Commission. They were studiously ignored by the banks that lent the city the money to finance its budget.

Within a few years, the business tax became a crushing burden on the manufacturing sector it was supposed to save. The income tax proved to be both an enormous source of revenue and an albatross that reinforced the city's reliance on the securities industry.

⊷ ⊶

AS HIS REELECTION CAMPAIGN NEARED in 1965, Lindsay moved to respond to another financial crisis—this one a result of rapidly rising apartment rents.

Rents were frozen during World War II as the federal government sought to control price increases throughout the economy. The federal rules lapsed in 1950, but New York State decided to continue them while exempting any building built after 1947. State officials soon decided that the controls were distorting the housing market and publicly committed themselves to moving rents to market rates as soon as possible. Such a policy was unpopular in the city so dominated by renters, so Mayor Robert Wagner succeeded in winning city control over the process and immediately clamped down on increases. The result was a sharp decline in vacancies in rent-controlled buildings because few occupants wanted to give up their bargains. Landlords saw their cash flow reduced as well and found it more difficult to finance needed maintenance. A 1961 re-zoning that limited areas for construction and reduced densities paralyzed construction; privately financed apartment completions in 1968 and 1969 equaled only 10 percent of the 1963 peak.[14]

Low rents in regulated housing and a space squeeze as new construction failed to keep up with demand from a booming economy led to two unfortunate results. In Manhattan, rents in market-rate housing soared. In older buildings outside Manhattan, hard-pressed landlords encouraged white flight so they could empty their buildings, carve them up into smaller apartments for the black and Hispanic newcomers, and increase their revenue.

In February, the mayor reacted to the growing anger at the rent hikes. He demanded a rollback for tenants in the 600,000 uncontrolled units, citing a report that showed that the median increase in rent was 26.5 percent and calling the figure unprecedented and outrageous.[15] He commissioned a panel of experts to suggest rent guidelines, saying that approach was preferable to rigid government regulation. When owners let it be known that they were working on a voluntary plan to limit increases to 15 percent every two years, the mayor escalated the pressure by demanding that they agree to roll back the hikes already imposed.

At first, real estate interests sought accommodation. No economist stepped forward to explain how rent controls distorted the market or that the controls themselves and the strong economy were the primary cause of the increases in unregulated units. Nor did anyone point out how restricting rents would inevitably lead to landlords cutting maintenance spending. Instead, Lindsay's harsh rhetoric allowed the demonization of landlords to intensify. The *New York Times* captured the prevailing sentiment in an editorial that began: "The need for effective action to halt gouging in uncontrolled apartments is unchallenged." The editorial went on to castigate landlords as a class: "The outrageous increases imposed on helpless tenants by many landlords have made New Yorkers at all income levels skeptical of the real estate industry's capacity for continence."[16]

By March, the mayor's panel of experts had recommended a 15 percent limit on increases, which the industry accepted. The Democratic-controlled city council balked at the plan, charging that the amount was simply too high, and began work on legislation to impose limits on all apartments in the city. When not all landlords complied with the guidelines or reduced services to compensate for the lost income, the council began drawing up a more draconian solution.

Real estate interests finally decided to fight back. A study they commissioned showed that rent control already cost the city $500 million a year in property taxes—$400 million by lowering the assessed value of buildings and $100 million by causing the abandonment of 13,000 buildings.[17] Others pointed out how extending limits to all apartments in the city would help millionaires who lived on Park Avenue as well as less fortunate residents.

The council was not deterred. In April it enacted the system of rent regulation, which more or less endures today.[18] It left rent control intact on buildings built before 1947. Rents continued to be fixed for existing tenants unless landlords undertook major improvements and could demonstrate financial hardship. If a tenant left, the rent could be increased by only 15 percent, no matter how long the rent had been frozen. Increases on all other apartments were limited to 10 percent for two-year leases and 15 percent for three-year leases.[19] Landlords were required to offer new leases to existing tenants. While ostensibly a voluntary system, it soon acquired the clout of law.

Rent control made it impossible for landlords to invest in their buildings or even operate them profitably. The housing stock in the Bronx, once the most densely populated area of the city, had consisted of five- and six-story walkups, many of which had been allowed to deteriorate. The vast shift in the city's population was partially responsible for the worsening economics of the buildings but so was rent control. Many apartments eventually became unrentable at prices sufficient to maintain them. Some landlords abandoned them as tax delinquencies, a tactic that increased fourfold between 1964 and 1974. Arson became the most viable way for owners to recover some portion of their investment, and soon the Bronx was burning. And the system did nothing to prevent a sharp increase in the percentage of their income that poorer New Yorkers paid for rent.

Meanwhile, some very rich people benefited. Author Ken Auletta, at work on his groundbreaking study of the city and the Fiscal Crisis, *The Streets Were Paved with Gold,* confronted American Stock Exchange president Arthur Levitt and asked how he could justify that his $661-a-month rent for an eight-room apartment on East 86th Street was half the market rate. "Let me think about that for a moment," he temporized, and then plaintively justified it by saying other tenants paid even less.[20]

Mrs. Otto Feurst, who spent most of the year in Palm Beach and California, didn't even blanch at the meager $440 rent she paid for a two-bedroom apartment on prestigious Central Park South. "I think a person of wealth should get anything they can get," she said. "I just spend money."[21]

By extending rent rules instead of allowing them to wither, Lindsay buttressed a system that discouraged investment in housing and created winners out of those who managed to get a rent-regulated apartment and losers out of anyone who moved to New York to seek their fortune. It also contributed to the growing sense of entitlement among the city's residents. If Levitt and Feurst could be subsidized by their landlords, why shouldn't everyone get similar treatment?

John Lindsay improbably won reelection in 1969, in part because of an effective television ad in which he apologized for the many missteps of his first term without using that word. He was also helped immeasurably by the good feelings that swept the city after the New York Mets' equally improbable World Series victory just weeks before voters went to the polls. Additionally, he had the good fortune to face two flawed candidates and to be able to take credit for an economy that added 76,000 jobs in both 1968 and 1969, the best performance in more than a decade. In all, New York had gained an impressive 183,000 jobs since he took office, reaching a peak of 3.8 million, a level the city has yet to see again.

The first sign of trouble came from Wall Street as the Go-Go Years ended in a market crash, some of the best-known securities firms failed, and workers were let go by the tens of thousands as the contraction was exacerbated by the arrival of computers to do the work of those in the back office.

The Dow Jones Industrial Average peaked at 970 in May 1969 and fell to 800 in July, stabilized, and then fell so sharply in 1970 that it plunged to 631 in May. The damage among the high-flying stocks everyone had chased was even more severe. Ling-Temco-Vought lost half its value, dropping from $135 to $62. The National Student Marketing Corporation peaked in December 1969 at $140; when investors discovered its profits were illusory, the stock plummeted to $3.50 by the middle of the next year.

Investors fled, and the volume Wall Street had staffed up to handle disappeared. The squeeze was crushing, since clerical and administrative salaries had risen 60 percent in the previous decade. Brokers had little cushion since they operated under liberal capital requirements. At first the New York Stock Exchange was able to arrange mergers for the small firms on the brink of collapse, using a special fund it had created. The fund was inadequate when larger companies ran out of money—first McDonnell & Co. with ties to the Ford family, then 80-year-old Hayden Stone, and finally Francis I. du Pont & Co., backed by the wealthy Delaware family.

Brooks estimated that some 100 firms vanished by merger or liquidation.[22] So did the back-office workers hired to cope with the bull market. By 1974, 24,000 people had lost their jobs on Wall Street. By 1977, another 10,000 jobs had disappeared.

With a city so focused on factory jobs, few connected the problems of Wall Street to the city's slumping economy. Instead, experts attributed the downturn beginning to grip New York to the national recession. Lindsay himself was more interested in the larger stage of national politics, switching his allegiance to the Democratic Party, jumping into the presidential race, sending his best aides out on the campaign trail, and returning to City Hall after his bitter defeats, shorn of his credibility and clout.

New Yorkers were loath to accept that their economy was in serious trouble. Herbert Bienstock, the director of the Bureau of Labor Statistics for New York, noted in late 1972 that jobs had fallen for the third consecutive year, but found a silver lining in that the decline was less than the previous year. A year later, he repeated the message. In part, even the experts were misled because they tracked the city's unemployment rate, which did not reflect the severity of the downturn. They didn't understand that the city's workforce was falling as a result of the population decline, holding down the jobless figure.

In 1975, the worsening trend in the number of jobs could no longer be ignored. Bienstock drew attention to the uncomfortable fact that the city was now likely to see its economy shrink for five consecutive years. The national economy was not to blame since the rest of the country was basking in a strong recovery that had begun in 1971. He called for an urgent study to find out why the city was suffering so much.

Not only had the experts failed to trace the impact of Wall Street's crash, they were unaware of the accelerating loss of industrial jobs. In the second Lindsay term, 113,000 factory jobs disappeared, three times the number of the first term. Twice as many were lost over the following four years.

Many disappeared when companies left the city for the same reasons as Schieffelin & Co., a cosmetics and pharmaceutical supplies company that had been based in lower Manhattan since the early 1930s. Its plant was located in a multistory, turn-of-the-century building on Cooper Square that was increasingly expensive to run. It couldn't find a new site in the city, and even if it had been able to find one, the cost of building would have been higher than elsewhere. Its workforce in New York was unionized, its taxes were burdensome, and the city's congested traffic made shipping difficult.

After eliminating New York at the beginning of its search, its extensive research led it to Apex, North Carolina, just outside Raleigh. Apex was within a night's drive of New York, and unions weren't welcome.

"In two ways, New York naturally has it over any place in the country," explained Edmund Mendell, the company's general manager, speaking for Schieffelin and virtually all industrial companies. "That's in general prestige and the ability to be physically where many contacts are. But when it comes to manufacturing in New York, the costs become appreciable and the operation questionable."[23]

While many firms left, others just closed their doors. The need for modern space and high costs were the primary reasons for the plight of factories, but what turned a relatively slow decline of the city's industrial base into a precipitous slide was the tax overhaul Lindsay claimed would help stem the tide.

While the business income tax was theoretically better for low-margin industrial firms than the gross receipts tax it replaced, the rate had been set so high, at 5.5 percent, that it increased taxes on those firms rather then lowered them, explained a 1974 report from the Budget Bureau.[24] Between 1966 and 1971, the tax alone was responsible for the loss of 44,500 more factory jobs than would have occurred without it. When the rate was raised to 6.7 percent in 1971, the figure ballooned to 53,400 jobs.

A third trend crippled the city, especially outside Manhattan. While experts understood that poor blacks and Hispanics were replacing middle-class whites, they did not realize that the city's population was actually declining. Fewer people meant the need for fewer stores and fewer middlemen to supply those outlets. Retail alone lost 70,000 jobs in the years 1969 to 1977, and wholesale lost almost as many—in all a quarter of the total.

When the Fiscal Crisis engulfed New York under Abe Beame, Lindsay's successor, layoffs of city workers became inevitable as well. The public payroll had ballooned under Lindsay by 64,000 in the first term and another 22,000 in the second. The city could no longer pay for a workforce that had reached 340,000 workers by the end of 1975, not counting those who worked for the transit system.

The economic decline took a back seat to the city's wrenching rush toward bankruptcy. All the maneuvers that had propped up the city's budget had led to the accumulation of massive and hidden short-term debt. When the banks realized their exposure, they refused to extend any more credit. Eventually, the state and then the federal government stepped in to keep New York from bankruptcy, and Governor Hugh Carey pushed through legislation that gave control of the city's finances to boards he controlled.

By then the disastrous state of the city's economy had become clear. While shorn of power, Beame recognized that something had to be done. He replaced his key economic deputy, sought to modernize zoning to allow mixed-use developments, and assembled experts to assess the economic impact of all new tax proposals in recognition that the highest combined city-state tax burden in the nation was an albatross for New York.[25]

In 1976, he reversed course on a just-enacted city estate tax when a storm of opposition made it obvious that thousands of well-off New Yorkers would leave to avoid it. At the end of the year, a commission he had appointed called for sweeping business tax reductions to ease the burden on industrial companies, especially cutting the business income tax in half, to 5 percent, and paring the city's unique tax on commercial rents.[26] The next year, Beame called for an end to the stock transfer tax, recognizing that it wasn't tenable to be the only place in the country with such a tax, given the changes in stock markets and computerized trading that would allow exchanges to relocate.

The Lindsay-Beame era drew to a close with some modest steps on behalf of business and the economy. Lindsay incentives and economic growth helped spur construction of much needed office space well into the second term. In return for agreeing to second the nomination of Spiro Agnew for vice president at the 1968 Republican convention, Lindsay won a commitment from Richard Nixon to transfer control of the abandoned Brooklyn Navy Yard to the city. The Yard became a key component of the city's future film industry. Downtown Brooklyn had been rezoned for commercial development, which allowed the city to compete with New Jersey as companies sought to relocate in the late 1980s. Beame at least suggested the idea that high taxes could be counterproductive.

Yet the legacy of those years was a city at its nadir precisely because business and economic concerns were given short shift. Why else would Lindsay propose a tax overhaul to aid manufacturers and then turn around and use a new tax to increase the burden on them? He had exacerbated the worst recession in the city's history, assured the rise of an enormous public sector through his income tax, and established a system of rent regulation that would pit New Yorkers against each other.

The city's future seemed bleak in 1977 except to Bienstock, the BLS official who spent his days tracking the numbers on the economy. New York City was an economic disaster area, he admitted in a speech to the New York chapter of the American Jewish Committee at the Plaza Hotel.[27] It was also, he pointed out, the undisputed center of the nation's knowledge-oriented industries, such as publishing, advertising, merchandising, and marketing, and it was filled with art galleries, theater and dance companies, and universities—all of which were destined to thrive. The result would bring an upsurge in the 1980s as sharp as the decline in its manufacturing sector.

He made the same case to Ken Auletta. The author had just spent two hours in a discussion of the economy with several of Bienstock's colleagues who were so pessimistic that Auletta was left feeling "almost suicidal." Bienstock did not share the gloom.

"Slowly, he lifted himself from a deep chair and wandered over to the wide windows overlooking Times Square," Auletta wrote in *The Streets Were Paved with Gold*. "Thirty-four stories below stretched a panorama of empty office buildings, abandoned hotels, porn theaters and massage parlors. 'Do you really feel New York is deteriorating?' he asked of no one in particular. 'It looks pretty good to me.'"[28]

Bienstock was right even as he left off the knowledge-based industry that would determine the city's fate—the securities industry. The people who worked on Wall Street and Ed Koch went to work to rescue New York.

CHAPTER 3

GREED IS GOOD

IN AUGUST 1979, *BUSINESSWEEK* MAGAZINE FAMOUSLY proclaimed "The Death of Equities,"[1] and President Jimmy Carter tapped Paul Volcker as chairman of the Federal Reserve Board. Volcker proved *BusinessWeek* wrong, and when he did, he touched off another boom on Wall Street that showered riches on New York and helped Ed Koch revive the city after the desperate years of the 1970s.

The 1970s had been devastating to New York, which lost more than 600,000 jobs and almost 1 million people. It hadn't been kind to the nation, which endured several modest recessions, little job growth when the economy recovered, and escalating inflation. It had been a trial for Wall Street as the market seesawed in a narrow trading range amid low volume that depressed revenues and squeezed profits.

The problem, *BusinessWeek* asserted, was that the nation had entered a new era in which stocks would no longer be a good investment.[2] In the widely discussed story, its editors marshaled a laundry list of reasons for their conclusion: Seven million shareholders had abandoned stocks in the decade, leaving institutional investors as the dominant force in markets. Those institutions had recently been given the go-ahead under the Employee Retirement Income Security Act to diversify away from stocks into financial products like venture capital and mortgage-backed securities as well as hard assets like real estate and precious metals. Younger investors avoided stocks given their poor performance and found alternatives like real estate more interesting.

Underlying those symptoms was the fundamental problem of inflation. Inflation led to high interest rates, which made bonds more alluring for individuals. The tax deductibility of interest payments made debt more attractive for corporations than equity. Investors fled stocks as they realized how inflation made rising profits illusory, since even once-respectable gains of 6 percent or 7 percent represented a decline in real earnings. Eventually, inflation would be so corrosive that it would lead to another and likely more severe downturn in the economy. The death of equities would be fatal for Wall Street as well.

The editors at *BusinessWeek* had no idea how decisive the appointment of Volcker as chairman of the Fed would be. Recognizing the long-term damage that inflation was inflicting on the economy by deterring investment, Volcker dramatically changed decades of monetary policy. He announced that the Fed would no longer set long-term interest rates, allowing them to change with market conditions. It would instead rely on changes in the money supply to influence the direction of the economy. He then clamped down on the money supply to precipitate an economic downturn he believed was needed to break inflation.

His change of course sent the benchmark federal funds rate soaring to 20 percent in June 1981 from 11 percent the year he assumed the chairmanship, and other interest rates rose dramatically as well. The dollar soared as money flowed into the United States to take advantage of the high rates, pummeling manufacturers that exported. Housing collapsed as well, since mortgages were simply unaffordable. A severe recession gripped the nation, with an unemployment rate above 10 percent and higher even than the peak of the Great Recession of 2008.

The pain was widespread, but Volcker succeeded in his primary goal of ending the inflationary spiral. The yearly increase in consumer prices fell to 3.2 percent in 1983, less than a quarter of its crippling 13.5 percent jump in 1981. The economy recovered rather quickly, and no sector did better than Wall Street.

Declining interest rates meant that bond prices rose, which led to increased trading. The trend of massive borrowing that had been so alarming to *Business Week* accelerated. Consumers, corporations, and governments owed $7 trillion by 1985, compared with $323 billion in 1977.[3] No longer were bonds an investment to be purchased and forgotten, the interest collected and to be replaced at maturity. They were now considered a financial instrument to be traded for big profits for their owners and for the Wall Street firms that handled the transactions. As bond profits built up, investors began to cash in some of their gains and invest in stocks. As the economy accelerated, the Dow Jones Industrial Average broke through its narrow trading range, inaugurating a bull market in stocks that sent the average soaring more than 50 percent between the beginning of 1982 and the end of 1986.

Some Wall Street firms were more eager than others to take advantage of the new opportunities presented by improved markets and lifting of many trading restrictions. Exxon had been a client of Morgan Stanley for more than 50 years, the kind of long-standing relationship built on the ties between long-serving chief executives and their investment bankers, usually cemented on the golf course. But when Exxon decided to take advantage of a new kind of floating-rate tax-exempt security to sell $78 million in bonds, it chose E. F. Hutton. Morgan Stanley simply didn't offer the type of bond that Exxon wanted.[4]

Others were even more innovative. The brokerage firm Drexel Burnham Lambert gave a bond trader named Michael Milken the go-ahead to pursue a new idea called junk bonds. These securities allowed companies with less-than-stellar credit ratings to borrow huge sums for expansion or mergers. Ivan Boesky became the face of the new risk arbitrage specialists who made millions by buying the stock of takeover targets. And the Wall Street investment bank Salomon Brothers gave a free hand to Lewis Ranieri to popularize housing bonds. Already a powerhouse in the bond market, Ranieri's creation led to Salomon dominating Wall Street in the 1980s as Goldman Sachs did two decades later in another boom.

Salomon's success was based on its skill at selling and trading bonds. It so towered over the field that the definition of a marketable bond was one in which Salomon made a market. As corporations rushed to issue more debt, they turned to Salomon to sell their issues. Once sold, Salomon profitably traded the bonds by using its own capital to take temporary positions, which it liquidated as soon as possible, usually at a profit. If it didn't make money on the trade, it at least collected a commission from the buyer and seller. In his riveting memoir of the firm in those days, *Liar's Poker,* Michael Lewis compared Salomon to a highway toll collector, taking a tiny piece of every movement on the bond highway. No unit was more profitable than Ranieri's mortgage bond operation, which made $200 million in 1983 and $275 million in 1985, almost half the firm's record profits.[5]

Chief Executive John Gutfreund had won a power struggle with a member of the founding family for the top spot as the decade began, and then in 1981 he sold the firm to Philbro Corp., a publicly held commodities firm. In this, Salomon was a pioneer, leading the early wave of securities firms that abandoned the historic partnership model to become publicly held companies. Through the sale, Gutfreund secured an infusion of capital to the firm and $32 million for himself by selling his own shares. Risking shareholders' capital instead of their own money encouraged Salomon's leadership to happily increase the size of the firm's gambles.

BusinessWeek, anointing Salomon as the King of Wall Street in late 1985, summed up its success: "Thanks to a combination of historical accident and savvy, Salomon was perfectly positioned to exploit the explosive growth of U.S. capital markets over the last decade. As a firm that has specialized in trading since its founding in 1910, Salomon knew how to maneuver in increasingly volatile markets. As a bond house, it benefited from a huge buildup in debt financing. And as a brokerage that catered to the wholesale trade, it was buoyed by a massive shift of financial assets from individuals toward pension funds and other institutions."[6]

Its profit in 1985, *BusinessWeek* estimated, would be $600 million, three times the level of the previous year. In the first nine months of the year, it had underwritten $21 billion in corporate underwritings, almost a quarter of all the money raised by Wall Street. It was twice as large as rival Merrill Lynch. If it had been a commercial bank, it would have ranked as the fifth largest in the country. Salomon's success cemented the triumph of the trader, another historic break with the traditions of the securities business. Felix Rohatyn, the banker credited with saving

New York City in the Fiscal Crisis, had been dismissive of Salomon in 1978. "They have the competence and the capital," he said then, "but they may have to buy the three-piece suits." He was forced to recant in 1985 in the *Business Week* story: "When you are that competent and have that much capital, who needs three-piece suits?"

He could have been referring to Ranieri, who owned exactly four suits, all polyester, and wore ankle-high boots like those of the football star Johnny Unitas and six-inch-wide neckties. On Fridays he switched to a tan polyester jacket and black chinos. His attire didn't matter to those who worked for him, because Ranieri looked out for them. Even when the mortgage bond unit was new and struggling, Ranieri made sure that the people who worked with him got bonuses as large as anyone else's in the firm. After all, bonuses were all that mattered as greed took hold in an entirely new way on Wall Street.

In the early 1980s, with profits scarce, Wall Street was a much less lucrative place to work. The long-established tradition of the year-end bonus had withered. In 1981, Merrill Lynch gave employees only two weeks' pay at the end of the year, and rival Bache Halsey gave a similar bonus only because Merrill did. A Dean Witter executive named Robert Stovell, famous for his weekly appearances on the widely watched PBS show *Wall Street Week,* pronounced the bonus dead in favor of a pension plan, better medical benefits, and a stock purchase plan—just like the established corporations that watched their compensation costs closely.

His conclusion was premature. Flush with profits from suddenly improving trading volumes, every securities firm reinstituted year-end awards in 1982, including Dean Witter. Some of the amounts were modest, equaling two weeks' pay. The New York Stock Exchange gave out 7.5 percent of pay, and the American Stock Exchange topped that with a 12.5 percent bonus. At Goldman Sachs, the reward was a quarter of salary.[7]

Each year pay grew, and in late 1986, bonuses set a new record. At Drexel, the benchmark reward reached 35 percent of salary for those with fewer than ten years on the job and 43 percent for those with more service. Elsewhere, the average for a junior executive right out of business school was a $25,000 year-end check in addition to a $50,000 annual salary. Somewhat more senior people averaged $200,000 on a base of $100,000. Michael Lewis, for what he was told was the best performance ever by a second-year bond salesman, made $90,000 that year, half salary and half bonus.[8]

The entire focus of the year was the day when the amount of the windfall was revealed. "Bonus day when it arrived was an enthralling reprieve from my daily routine of chatting with investors and placing bets in the markets," Lewis wrote. "Watching the faces of other people as they emerged from their meetings was worth a thousand lectures on the meaning of money in our small society. People responded in one of three ways when they heard how much richer they were: with relief, with joy and with anger. Most felt some blend of all three. A few felt all three distinctly. Relief when told, joy when it occurred to them what to buy and anger when they heard that others at their level had been paid more."

His boss, John Gutfreund, paid himself $3.1 million that year, the highest total ever for the boss of a brokerage firm, and one that generated headlines in the tabloid newspapers. The next year he must have considered himself underpaid. Michael Milken took home $550 million, a bit more than McDonald's earned that year.

New Yorkers and people across the country took note of how much money was being made on Wall Street and wanted in. Forty percent of the 1,300 members of the 1986 graduating class at Yale applied for jobs at a single investment bank. The next year, Harvard's Principles of Economics course enrolled 1,000 students in 40 sections, triple the figure from ten years earlier.[9]

Law firms in New York found that the best graduates of the nation's leading law schools were knocking on the doors of securities companies rather than vying for spots in their entry classes. The most prestigious firm in the country, Cravath, Swaine & Moore, increased its starting salary in 1986 by a whopping $12,000 to $65,000 in a desperate effort to compete. Even a clerk to a justice of the US Supreme Court gave up law for investment banking.

The money flowed into the city, beginning with the real estate market. "You could see the impact of the Wall Street boom," recalls

Jonathan Miller, who was selling new condominiums in the mid-1980s before becoming one of the city's leading experts and prognosticators on residential estate. "They were so young it depressed me. I was in my 20s and they were only five years older than I was and they were able to buy apartments for $800,000."[10] They also helped create a market for condominiums rather than the city's traditional co-op apartments, because co-op boards were skeptical of young people with so much cash to spend.

While making money may always have been the major reason for working on Wall Street, the 1980s made a new level of greed the norm, at least among the people who worked there. The conventions of what was acceptable on Wall Street were shattered in the middle of the decade during the sale of the venerable Lehman Brothers firm to American Express. Lehman had been torn apart by a power struggle between the traders led by Lewis Glucksman and the investment bankers personified by Pete Peterson. The sale netted Lehman's partners $325 million, with $15 million for Glucksman and $6 million for Peterson, which was added to $7 million he had taken out of the firm earlier.[11]

Both men had contracts specifying that they would receive 1 percent of the net profits instead of participating in the firm's retirement plan. Glucksman the trader waived that provision given the many millions he was reaping from the sale. Peterson, the refined investment banker who had been a high official in the Nixon administration, would not do so and insisted on being compensated for giving up his right to a share of the profits. In the end, Peterson extracted $18 million plus another $5 million that American Express pledged to a venture capital firm he planned to set up.

A few million dollars was simply not enough for the arbitrageur Boesky and an investment banker named Dennis Levine. Boesky made his money by buying shares in companies after a merger was announced to take advantage of the small gap between the price at which the stock traded and the price at which the merger would be completed. Levine, who earned about $1 million a year, tipped Boesky to pending mergers so the arbitrageur could buy stock before the price increased on the announcement of the deal, greatly increasing the profit, which he shared with Levine. After he was caught, Boesky agreed to pay a fine of more than $100 million, representing a rough approximation of his illicit gains, and eventually went to prison.

The idea that such unprecedented wealth was justly deserved and beyond reproach was widespread. Jim Cramer, a brash 31-year-old stockbroker at Goldman Sachs, summed up his finances with typical bravado: "There isn't anything I see in a store that I can't buy." He went on to become a famous hedge fund manager and the market guru for CNBC.[12]

The rise in pay and bonuses on Wall Street was startling. Historically, securities firms had accounted for about 3 percent of the workforce and about 6 percent of all the income in the city. By 1987, the figures had risen to 4 percent and 10 percent and had fueled much of the 1980s boom. Yet it was only a preview of what was to come. In 2007, Wall Street accounted for fully 28 percent of the income in New York, and the bonuses of the 1980s would seem like small change.

The city's political and economic calendars often coincided. Sometimes that was coincidental. The city's great economic crisis began as John Lindsay was inaugurated for a second term. New York's recovery started when Ed Koch took office in 1978. By 1977, the city's economic decline was so evident that all the candidates for mayor pledged to do something to create jobs. They weren't very specific, but the economy was almost as important as the Fiscal Crisis in their campaign speeches. Koch was elected because he said he would represent a break with the past. Nowhere was the change more dramatic than in the way he put the economy and especially development at the top of his priorities.

Gloom pervaded the city as Koch took over at City Hall. Samuel Ehrenhalt, the new local chief of the Bureau of Labor Statistics and Bienstock's successor as the oracle of the local economy, worried that the city could not thrive as factory jobs disappeared. He also argued that whatever small improvements could be detected were concentrated in Manhattan while the other four boroughs languished.[13]

New Yorkers agreed. A *New York Times* poll in late 1981 showed that half of New Yorkers wanted to be living elsewhere within the next four years, and those who thought the city was in poor shape outnumbered those who did not by a 3-to-2 margin. Forty percent said the city would be worse off in ten years.[14]

Both Ehrenhalt and the people who responded to the poll were looking backward. New York was actually well positioned as the American economy shifted from manufacturing to services. Its population, diminished as it was, was still the largest in the country and the biggest market for consumer goods and health care. While its business base had been eroded, it remained the largest concentration of corporate headquarters and therefore the nation's biggest market for business services as well. The construction sector, at half its 1962 peak of 137,000, had begun to stir. Koch built on those strengths.

The city's new mayor had served a short stint in the city council and then moved into Congress, representing the district centered on Greenwich Village. He was elected as a dedicated liberal. In the US House, he worked on a diverse array of issues, ranging from housing to transportation to foreign affairs, where he was a proponent of aid to several Latin American countries, the WIC program to provide milk to pregnant women and children, and an expansive amnesty program so that thousands of Russian Jews could enter the United States.

One early sign of his coming political reorientation was his opposition to the placement of low-income housing in middle-class areas, as Lindsay planned to do in Forest Hills, Queens. He also served as the delegation's representative on the financial control board, which served as an introductory course on city finances for him.

As he tackled the financial problems facing the city, his political thinking shifted dramatically. In a seminal speech called "The Mandate Millstone," he laid out how laws passed by Congress, many of which he had supported, made running a city so difficult and imposed obligations that meant that localities couldn't maintain their infrastructure or deal with their most pressing problems. He moved to curtail many of the social programs the city financed.

The new attitude voiced in the speech was also reflected in his approach to the economy. He believed that spurring development was the key to reviving the city, and he would make that possible through the extensive use of tax incentives. "Past administrations did not talk about jobs and profits," Koch boasted a few years later, "but how to get New York City to be the No. 1 welfare city in America. The whole business of our city is how do you get people to stay here, how do you get people to come here, how do you get business to thrive."[15]

The contrast with his predecessors was clear. "Koch did not apologize for being pro-development," says Joyce Purnick, who covered City Hall for the *Times*. "Koch never got enough credit for turning around the city's attitude toward business. This was a major shift and we now take this viewpoint for granted."[16]

The terrible Volcker-Reagan recession of 1982 proved how different New York had become. While the nation's manufacturing heartland suffered, the city lost a modest 40,000 jobs. In fact, the city passed a milestone that year. For the first time, the number of jobs in finance exceeded those in manufacturing. A more optimistic Ehrenhalt totaled up the progress between 1977 and 1981: 50,000 jobs in banking and securities, 50,000 in business services, 18,000 in culture and tourism, and 19,000 in professional fields like law, engineering, and accounting.[17]

By 1984, Wall Street's newfound wealth was spurring the city's retail sector as apparel boutiques and other specialized stores appeared in large numbers and restaurants and bars began exploding. Suddenly the experts discovered that even the boroughs were growing again. No one understood why at the time, but the liberalization of immigration laws enacted in 1965 had led to an influx of new residents, who began reshaping the city in a process that continues today.

The immigrants filled the gap created by the departure of whites to the suburbs, which had begun after World War II as the allure of suburban living beckoned the middle class and was accelerated by the city's rising crime rates. The exodus had led to a sharp decline in the city's population, which fell by 800,000, or almost 10 percent, in the 1970s.

Immigrants averted disaster for New York. If the decline had not been reversed, New York could have shrunk to a city of 6 million or even 5 million. Instead, immigrants arrived, at first in small numbers and then in larger ones than the city had ever seen. They stabilized neighborhoods by providing occupants for apartment buildings that might otherwise have been abandoned. They bought homes in depressed areas because that's what they could afford, and then they upgraded their residences and the neighborhoods. By the middle of the decade, New York could boast that it had gained more people between 1982 and 1984 than any other city in the country.[18]

Albert Ciccarelli noticed. In 1983, he bought a beauty salon in Brooklyn Heights and hired three beauticians. Soon he had a staff of 13 and planned a second shop to specialize in skin care. "A lot has happened here," he said. "There has been the addition of a few nice stores. There's a new restaurant down the street."[19]

In 1985, the same year the boroughs added more jobs than Manhattan, the city paused to take note of how New York had changed in the decade since the Fiscal Crisis. The city had balanced its budget for five straight years, and it was able to sell bonds without guarantees from Albany or Washington. Services were being restored even though there were 85,000 fewer city employees. New York had gained 218,000 private sector jobs since it hit bottom in 1977. Only the Sun Belt cities of Dallas and Houston could boast of lower percentages of jobless residents.[20]

True, more people lived in poverty, crime continued to rise, and some claimed that the gains had come at the expense of the poor, who had suffered the most from city service cutbacks and frozen welfare payments during the Fiscal Crisis. Ehrenhalt disagreed. "In some of the comments about New York, you get nostalgia for the good old days of the 50s and 60s. But this is the city's best recovery record in the post World War II era. The good old days really have been these days," he said.[21]

The most obvious sign of the city's revival was a construction boom that remade many parts of Manhattan. City tax breaks spurred residential construction. Favorable federal tax laws encouraged speculative building of offices, and the city provided additional benefits for building on the West Side. The first relocations of Wall Street firms from downtown to Midtown—First Boston in 1982 and E. F. Hutton and Paine Webber two years later—expanded the base of potential tenants.

No one typified the 1980s boom more than David and Jean Solomon, who arrived in New York as a young couple with degrees in

architecture but no interest in sticking to design. David began working as a developer in the 1970s, buying and renovating modest office
buildings and residential properties. His wife joined him in the business in the early 1980s. Jonathan Miller, who was a broker at one of
the Solomon residential projects on the East Side, remembers David as
smart and frenetic. "When he came to Astor Place to visit, he wouldn't
wait for the elevators, instead walking up to the sales office on the 18th
floor," he recalls.[22]

Their first commercial project was a 600,000-square-foot, 45-story
office building on East 49th Street between Fifth and Madison Avenues.
Others had shunned the site, believing that big office buildings could not
succeed on narrow side streets.

The Solomons proved the conventional wisdom wrong. They leased
what was known as Tower 49 at top rents and sold it in 1986 for $301
million, a record price. Suddenly, they were in the spotlight. Confident
that their success could be repeated, they began assembling land for
three major office buildings with a total of more than 2 million square
feet. Other builders were quick to follow suit. Seymour Durst, Fisher
Brothers, Tishman Speyer Properties, Bruce Eichner, and Larry Silver-
stein all joined the spree—dotting Midtown with modern office towers.
Altogether, they added almost 7 million square feet of space to the market, and their projects helped swell the ranks of construction workers to
118,000 by 1987, from 77,000 at the start of the decade. In 1985, the
downtown vacancy rate of 6.9 percent was the lowest of the nation's 16
largest business centers; Midtown was second lowest, at 7.1 percent.[23]

The economic boom created its own problems, of course, especially
an exodus of well-known companies and turmoil among established merchants in changing neighborhoods. Ever since the 1960s, employees who
had moved to the suburbs wanted to work closer to home, and rising
costs made Manhattan simply too costly for some companies. General
Electric moved to Fairfield, Connecticut, Union Carbide to Danbury,
Connecticut, and Nestle to suburban Westchester. In the mid-1980s,
some of the nation's most well-known corporate giants decided to leave
the region entirely. Early in 1987, Mobil announced that it was relocat-

ing to the Washington area. J. C. Penney said a small town outside Dallas named Plano would be a better home for a mass retailer.

As harmful as those losses were, the more serious threat was the growing interest of financial service companies in lower cost locales for their clerical and administrative workers, often lumped under the heading of back-office employees. Manhattan rents started at $30 a square foot for mediocre buildings and went as high as $55 for the best ones. New Jersey rents were as low as $15, and the best space in Westchester and Long Island cost no more than $25. New York City had the highest energy costs in the nation as early as the 1960s, in no small measure because of taxes that utilities paid. Wages were higher in the city as well.[24]

During the 1970s recession, rents had fallen sharply, and other costs rose far more slowly than in the rest of the country, easing the cost pressures temporarily. After Koch's election, the early stirrings of the economy changed that equation. In 1980, commercial rents increased about 50 percent. The increases were often huge because rents were fixed for the term of a lease. An Upper West Side landmark called Brooks TV and Radio shut its doors on Broadway after the landlord demanded an increase in the monthly rent from $1,300 to $10,000.[25]

As the boom accelerated, the push and pull of economic forces unnerved more New Yorkers, especially on the West Side, where the change was among the most rapid in the city. The first new residential towers brought better-heeled residents, which led more upscale retailers to come into the neighborhood, which encouraged even more developers to assemble land for new construction.

The dislocations were very unsettling, as Euclid Hall on Broadway between 85th and 86th Streets illustrated.[26] Built in 1900 as luxury housing for families, the seven-story building had been carved up into 300 rooms and was now a deteriorating single-room-occupancy hotel for the poor and almost homeless, with some tenants paying as little as $50 a month. A third of the rooms were empty when Rafael Aryeh and his partners paid $10 million for the building, $4 million more than the previous owner had spent only two years before. The plan was simple: wait out the remaining tenants protected by rent regulation and then convert the building into co-ops. In the meantime, Aryeh tried to cover expenses by maximizing the rent from the retail stores that occupied the first floor.

One of the casualties was Kitty Buck, who had opened a Cakemaster outlet in the building in 1941, paying $400 a month in rent. In 1985, she was paying $4,000. Aryeh demanded a huge increase that would bring it up to $10,000. "I told them to shove it," she said. "How can you pay that rent selling bread and rolls?" She shuttered the store, a step she had taken at stores located elsewhere in the area as she slowly dismantled her company. Another similar bakery was happy to take her place. Mrs. Field's Cookies, a Utah-based chain that was in the forefront of an invasion of national companies that remade retailing in the city, took a spot four doors down in Euclid Hall. "The reason is simple," a spokeswoman explained. "We were doing very well right up the street before we had to close for a construction project. We like the area. We like the people."

As much as residents enjoyed Mrs. Field's and bought its cookies and muffins, they felt under siege by all the construction and the changes it was bringing. Two major projects from two of the city's most important real estate tycoons galvanized the opposition to development. Developer Mortimer Zuckerman won a competition for a government-owned site at the corner of Central Park, offering the city's transit agency $455 million and promising to create a new home for none other than Salomon Brothers. His office, retail, and residential complex featured two towers: one 68 stories high and the other 58. Donald Trump proposed to build what he called Television City on a former railroad yard along the Hudson River between 59th and 72nd Streets. The name came from the commercial part of the plan, which was positioned as a way to keep the NBC television network from leaving the city. Trump, New York's most publicity-hungry businessman, also planned the world's largest office tower and a series of residential buildings that would house 70,000 people.

Robert Caro, the famous writer whose book on Robert Moses convinced an entire generation that big developments were suspect, led the opposition. "These projects mark a turning point for New York," he argued. "Over the last few years New York has been transformed into a different city and no one has paid attention."[27] Jacqueline Kennedy Onassis lent her star power to the cause, taking part in a demonstration against the Zuckerman project organized by the Municipal Arts Society where the marchers carried umbrellas to symbolize how the towers might put the park into shadows.

Ed Koch wasn't thrilled about Trump's project, which even he regarded as excessive. He was a firm supporter of Zuckerman's soaring towers at Columbus Circle, which he saw as a way to bind Salomon to the city and which would generate millions in tax revenue. The critics were challenging the central tenet of his administration that new construction was crucial for the city, and he would have none of it. "The vision of some of these people is the status quo," he retorted. "You know, the last one out close the door."[28]

Caro was right: the city had changed. Tax collections had doubled to just over $13 billion in Koch's decade as mayor, fueled by the threefold increase in revenue from Lindsay's city income tax, which topped $2 billion. New York had regained two-thirds of the jobs it lost in the downturn of 1969–1977, an even more impressive accomplishment since it had to overcome the disappearance of 259,000 factory jobs. In a way, the opposition to the Zuckerman and Trump projects was a sign of how much the city had recovered. No one would have raised their voices in 1977, when any sign of economic activity that would create jobs was eagerly embraced.

Fighting over the spoils of prosperity was soon to end as the city plunged into another deep, long downturn.

CHAPTER 4

THE MYTH OF
MANUFACTURING

IN RIC BURNS'S FAMOUS PBS DOCUMENTARY ON NEW York, author Pete Hamill speaks for many New Yorkers when he longs for the era when manufacturing was the city's most important industry:

> The core of it was it was still a manufacturing town, which meant that people like my father, with an eighth grade education, an Irish immigrant, could first of all form a family, and then support it. And that sense that you would get from a workingman permeated the city. I remember one of the things I missed the most was what it felt like in the subway between the hours of five and seven with working men. Guys stained with sweat, the smell of perspiration, the raw-knuckled hands, toolboxes, heading home. Nobody would mess with guys like that. And they were proud in the fact that they were working in the biggest city in the United States. They were functioning people.[1]

This nostalgia for an economy based on making things was so powerful that it influenced city policy for decades, as mayor after mayor spent hundreds of millions of dollars in a futile effort to stem the loss of manufacturing jobs. Meanwhile, with much less extensive help from city officials, the tourism industry rose to take manufacturing's place in the economy, eventually growing so large it helped protect New York from the ravages of the Great Recession.

Hamill was right that manufacturing made New York. Having an export industry—that is, producing a product or selling a service that people from elsewhere buy—is what makes a city or a country rich. Factory jobs that required little education, few preexisting skills, and only the most rudimentary knowledge of English allowed the city to absorb millions of immigrants. At the end of World War II, New York was home to more than 1 million manufacturing jobs, and as late as 1960, the total was still around 950,000. The most prominent sector was apparel manufacturing. Since the 1840s, the garment industry had been the fastest-growing segment of the city's economy, and just before the Civil War, it was believed to employ as many as 32,000 people. In the 1900s, it continued to thrive in the tenements of Lower Manhattan, spurred by the influx of immigrants, especially Russian Jews who already possessed the skills to make clothing.[2]

Several factors—including laws outlawing manufacturing operations in residential buildings, the need to be close to the new, large department stores opening in the center of Midtown, and the completion of the subway system, which allowed workers to travel easily from other boroughs into Midtown—sparked the creation of the garment district between 34th and 40nd Streets on the West Side. Some 120 high-rises were built in the 1920s to provide space for thousands of manufacturers and showrooms to display the ready-to-wear clothes that they made. As the 1960s building boom remade other areas of the city, the Garment District seemed ignored until it was discovered by Aaron Gural, whose family would become as integral to the neighborhood as the fashion firms that made it their home.[3]

Born in Manhattan in 1917, Gural learned about business selling ice cream near the George Washington Bridge. He attended New York University, where he earned a degree in accounting. Real estate seemed the obvious career choice, since his uncles were already in that business. He joined one of them at Spear & Co., where his first job was reading electric meters. He quickly became one of the firm's best salesmen and left when they lowered his commission so he would not outearn other employees. He joined Newmark & Co. Real Estate because he believed it was small enough that he would eventually be able to buy it, which he did in 1956.

He began buying buildings in the 1960s, not because he intended to resell when they had increased in value, but because he wanted the fees for managing them. The real estate community was primarily Jewish and very tight-knit in those days, recalls his grandson Eric Gural. Aaron thought it futile to compete with his friends like the Rudins and the Helmsleys for properties on desirable streets like Fifth Avenue. So he went to the Garment District, where there was no competition and property was cheap. He acquired a building on 38th Street, now home to an incubator for fledgling fashion firms, for $15,000 in the 1960s.

He understood the tenants, many of them also descendents of Eastern European Jews. When buildings got into trouble, bank presidents would call him to take over properties. Eventually, the Gurals owned 40 buildings in Midtown, most in the garment district. The uncertain future of the apparel firms that occupied the space didn't worry him. "There is nothing that can happen that will mean I can't get $10 a square foot rent in the buildings," Aaron told his grandson one day. "At $10 a square foot, I can make a good living."

By the mid-1980s, however, it was clear that the forces undermining manufacturing were affecting apparel as much as any other sector. Jobs had declined by 20 percent since 1977, and Ed Koch came under increasing pressure to do something to stem the decline. The issue came to a head over the long effort to revitalize Times Square, which was now known worldwide as a haven for drug dealing, crime, and pornography. A $2 billion plan called for demolishing the buildings on a 13-acre section between Seventh and Eighth Avenues and replacing them with a massive merchandise mart, four office buildings, and a hotel and rehabilitating nine theaters.[4]

Opposition was fierce. Critics claimed the city was "cleaning up" Times Square by destroying it, that hundreds of low-income residents would be forced to move, and that developers would reap millions in unnecessary tax breaks.[5] The garment workers' union was at the forefront of the critics, contending that the redevelopment of Times Square would lead to rising real estate costs in the Garment District.

Needing votes to win approval from the city's Board of Estimate, Koch won over Jay Mazur, the head of the International Ladies' Garment Workers' Union, by promising to launch a study of the future of the apparel district to see what steps the city could take to preserve manufacturing there. Shortly after 1 a.m. on November 9, 1984, the Board of Estimate approved the plan.[6]

Alair Townsend, Koch's top aide on economic development, says that the mayor knew manufacturing was in a long-term decline. Some voices tried to point out the economic realities. "We can't go back," argued George Sternlieb, a specialist on the city at Rutgers University's Center for Urban Policy Research. "The city's future is as a world financial capital. Manufacturing here has been in decline since the 1920s and attempts to bring it back are mostly politically motivated gestures to the waterfront and garment workers' unions who are locked into the past."[7]

Koch's compromise on Times Square officially locked the Garment District into the past. The study he set in motion was released in late 1986. It recommended the creation of special zoning that would limit property owners' ability to convert factory space to offices by requiring them to replace the manufacturing space lost on the side streets, although it provided more flexibility on the avenues.

Louis Harris & Associates had determined that the garment industry occupied 8 million square feet of space and employed 25,000 people in the area. Apparel companies also told Louis Harris researchers that they could not afford rising rents. They said that the future of fashion in the city hung in the balance. Designers needed to be in close proximity to belt makers, embroiderers, button manufacturers, and a host of other companies to actually make their products. If they left, so would the designers.

The theory did not go unchallenged. Aaron's son Jeffrey, now president of Newmark, insisted that the rezoning would reduce the value of properties. When that happened, owners would stop investing in their buildings, leading to a cycle of deterioration. Others pointed out that the restrictions would prevent the development of another thriving commercial area in Manhattan that would be needed by the firms of the future. Tellingly, the head of Conway Co., which had assessed the real estate pressures facing the area, rose at a public hearing to say the city had distorted his findings to reach the conclusion that zoning protections were needed.[8]

At the time, a city official involved in developing the concept privately told an angry group of building owners that the idea was to allow an "orderly decline" in apparel manufacturing.By not setting a time when the zoning expired, the Koch plan preserved manufacturing space long after there was sufficient demand.

Apparel manufacturing in the city declined every year after 1987, averaging a loss of 3,000 jobs annually until 2000, when the rate of decline accelerated as the unprotected apparel makers in Chinatown disappeared with the disruptions of the September 11 terrorist attacks. Just as the critics of rent regulation had foreseen its harmful consequences in 1969, Jeffrey Gural proved to be prescient about the Garment District. Landlords refused to upgrade buildings where they could not produce reasonable profits; it is the only place in Manhattan where air conditioners still protrude from office windows. Millions of square feet of office space were suddenly underutilized. The law was often ignored, but given the precarious legal situation, only some companies would relocate their offices there. Rents in the area were always the lowest of the city's major business districts.

Twenty years after the restrictions were put in place—when 15,000 apparel factory workers remained, of which only 3,000 were in the district itself—the Bloomberg administration's repeated attempts to update the zoning failed. Total factory jobs fell below 80,000 in 2009 and the number of people employed by colleges and universities surpassed those working in factories for the first time. Yet the myth of manufacturing persists, as the Bloomberg administration continues to roll out programs to save jobs under a tweaked concept that substitutes the word "industrial" for "manufacturing" and includes construction and warehouse workers.

As manufacturing withered, tourism rose to take its place in the economy, although no Pete Hamill stepped forward to glorify the people who worked in it. The lack of a champion was ironic since the people who fill the jobs in tourism are similar in many ways to those who went to work in the factories in the early 1990s. Many are immigrants who take jobs in hotels and restaurants because their English isn't very good, and skills can be learned on the job. Because most hotels are unionized and others need to match the pay scale and benefits, these jobs tend to pay decently and provide upward mobility as workers improve their English proficiency. Tourism also boosts the city's economy just as manufacturing once did. It thrives because people bring the money they made elsewhere and spend it in New York, conferring the same economic benefit as making a shirt and sending it somewhere else to be sold.

While tourists have always come to New York, their numbers in the 1970s and early 1980s were relatively modest—around 16 million a year. Many visited the Crossroads of the World in Times Square, which was an urban adventure. Carl Weisbrod, who spent most of his early career trying to clean up the area, remembers the police in the early 1980s setting up barriers on Eighth Avenue to separate the theatergoers from the prostitutes. The area's two subway stations were hotspots for crime. The vast majority of people traversing the area were men; women stayed clear of the seediness.[9]

Even in the 1970s, government officials realized that city government would have to find some way to ignite real development. In 1973, John Lindsay announced plans for a 2,000-room hotel to be built by architect John Portman, who had gained a reputation for flashy structures featuring atriums. The area was rezoned for a hotel, but the project languished amid the city's economic and fiscal problems. A decade later, Bill Marriott decided to build that hotel.[10]

Marriott had joined the company his father had founded in 1956, when it was known for its Hot Shoppes restaurants, and spearheaded its move into hotels. A devout Mormon, he had a very strict upbringing. Even as an adult and the boss of the company, his father made sure to praise his work once a year—and only once a year. Marriott came to New York occasionally to check up on the company's Essex House, its only property in the city. One day, he recalls, he was told that the Taft Hotel in Times Square boasted an average occupancy rate of 90 percent. He was intrigued because few hotels anywhere operate at such efficiency.[11]

"It was a unique opportunity," he says. "All the zoning issues had been resolved. I figured that we would have tourists on Friday and Saturday and business travelers Sunday through Thursday. And while December is the worst month for the hotel business everywhere else, New York is wall-to-wall in December."[12]

His father wanted no part of Times Square and opposed the project. Others fought it as well. While big Broadway producers, such as the Schuberts and Nederlanders, supported the hotel because they thought reclaiming Times Square would breathe new life into industry, others in the theater community lined up behind producer Joseph Papp and actor Christopher Reeve, saying the hotel would replace three older theaters on the site. They felt that the modern theater proposed to be built within the hotel was not in keeping with the Broadway they wanted to preserve.

Many architecture critics and urban planners despised the hotel as well, claiming it turned its back on the street. Their criticism became even more pronounced when designers eliminated a plaza that had been planned for the front of the hotel. The builders and the city had decided that such an area would be taken over by prostitutes and drug dealers, dooming the hotel. Bill Marriott forged ahead. Each year, the stakes mounted as construction costs soared to $400 million, double the original estimate. Marriott couldn't find partners to share the burden; it eventually owned 89 percent of the hotel, an unusual percentage since it generally preferred to manage rather than own real estate. Its balance sheet sank under the weight of the debt. "I bet the ranch on that hotel," Marriott says.[13]

He also had to overcome his strict Mormon sense of propriety. One day a taxi driver took him on a tour of the area as the hotel was rising, to show him how Times Square was improving. They stopped at a traffic light on 45th Street and Eighth Avenue, a few steps from where the hotel was soon to open. "A hooker in pink tights walked out of a drugstore," he recalls. "I said to the cabbie, 'I guess it hasn't improved that much.'"[14]

In October 1985, the hotel opened with 1,876 rooms and plans to charge more than $200 a night for each of them. Its presence increased the number of rooms in the city to 46,500.[15] While it had once been envisioned as a convention hotel, with the majority of visitors attending shows at the convention center being built farther to the west, Marriott had decided on a more diverse approach. He had moved every wall he could to create the city's largest ballroom, to attract both local and out-of-town groups. He targeted tourists, of course. And he expected business travelers to fill the rooms during the week, although it took several years for them to get used to the idea of staying so far west in Midtown.

The hotel struggled at first, although the risk Bill Marriott had taken already had an impact. "The Marriott Marquis was the first crucial event in the development of tourism in New York," says Jon Tisch, CEO of the Loews Hotel chain and longtime champion of the hospitality industry in the city. "It sent a message that it was right to make a big investment in New York."[16] By the late 1990s, the Marriott Marquis consistently filled 90 percent of its rooms every year, the figure that had lured Marriott into taking such a big risk in Times Square.

The year the Marquis opened, the city attracted about 20 million tourists. Twenty-five years later—after Disney broadened the city to welcome families and Middle America, and after the sharp fall in crime made many more neighborhoods safe for hotels—New York attracted just shy of 50 million visitors. In 1988, the city's tourism industry estimated that travelers were responsible for 143,000 jobs. Today, that number is more than twice as large, at 310,000.

CHAPTER 5

STRUCTURAL NOT CYCLICAL

NEW YORK CITY REACHED ANOTHER MILESTONE IN early October 1987. The US Bureau of Labor Statistics announced that the unemployment rate had fallen to 4.5 percent in September, the lowest it had been in 17 years. Commissioner Sam Ehrenhalt noted that "help wanted" signs were replacing unemployment lines as the symbol of the economy. Mayor Ed Koch claimed that the news showed "the city's economic boom not only has strength, it has endurance."[1]

Both men chose to ignore other warning signs that pointed to trouble. The commercial office market was weakening. Fifteen major companies had announced plans to move some or all of their operations to the suburbs in the coming year. Numerous office buildings, spurred by a federal tax break and zoning bonuses for building on the West Side, were nearing completion, and the additional space caused asking rents to drop by 10 percent in Midtown. The few tenants who had agreed to move into the new buildings were undercutting rents in existing buildings by offering their old space for sublease at cut-rate prices.[2]

New residential construction created a similar glut. In early 1986, more than 1,000 new condominiums sat empty; another 10,000 were about to hit the market along with 8,000 rental units. Experts predicted that many would remain empty.[3]

The stock market got off to a strong start in 1987. The Dow Jones Industrial Average passed 2,700 in August, up 57 percent over the past year. Then it faltered, sliding over 500 points by the fall. Profitability for Wall Street firms was declining as well. Salomon shocked its rivals by shuttering its municipal bond business and jettisoning 800 people despite its dominant status in the business.[4]

In mid-October, fear began to take hold. On October 14, the Dow dropped 96 points, the largest one-day loss ever. Only two days later, on a Friday, the Dow plunged 108 points on record trading and stood at 2,246. Something fundamental had changed. The editors of *Crain's New York Business* arrived for work on Monday and added space to the next week's issue for an in-depth report on what a weakening market would mean for the city.

They would need that space and much more. On Monday, the Dow Jones Industrial Average plunged 508 points, or 22 percent, still the largest one-day percentage decline ever. Steve Malanga, the managing editor of *Crain's,* sat transfixed that day in the newsroom before a just-installed television set turned to the fledgling CNBC. His father had died unexpectedly of a heart attack a few months before, and Malanga had just finished investing the life insurance proceeds for his mother. After the market closed, his mother's future no longer seemed financially secure, a feeling shared by millions of Americans that day.

The impact on New York was eventually severe—the second-worst downturn of the modern era. The recession revealed the city's ever-increasing reliance on Wall Street and its whims, which affected virtually all sectors of the economy. It also revealed how dependent city government had become on the revenue generated by Wall Street, further amplifying the economic swings. And it again showed the crucial connection between the city's political leadership and the economy. Whereas the 1969–1979 downturn was worsened by John Lindsay's acts of commission, this recession led to a similar loss of faith in the future due to David Dinkins's acts of omission.

The exact cause of the market collapse is still debated. Both the American and world economies were slowing. Monetary disputes created uncertainty, and fears of inflation were gaining credence. Improvements in computers had led to program trading as sophisticated investors tried to take advantage of small discrepancies between prices of a stock and the options traded on that stock. A similar innovation called portfolio insurance exaggerated swings in prices, and program trading had the same impact. Just as in the 1960s, the back-office systems at the exchanges hadn't been updated to keep up with the higher volume.

A week after the crash, a worried Ed Koch ordered a hiring freeze for city government, deferred a planned wage increase for managers, and put off a $64 million contribution to bolster the city's pension fund. Alair Townsend, deputy mayor for economic development and finance, remembers that she really didn't know what the impact of the crash would be on the city. "At this point the best thing we can do is preserve our options," she said at the time.[5]

Unlike in the 1960s, City Hall understood the importance of the financial sector. Wall Street employed 157,000 people in the city and accounted for 25 percent of all the private sector job growth in the past decade. Financial services companies leased almost one-third of the office space in Manhattan. Ehrenhalt suggested another 250,000 people—accountants, lawyers, and computer programmers—owed their jobs to the activity generated by the securities firms.

Within months, alarming news was streaming out of brokerages and investment banks. By year-end, Kidder Peabody announced 1,000 layoffs, and E. F. Hutton had agreed to be bought by Shearson, where estimates of the number of people to be let go after the merger was completed ranged from 3,000 to 9,000. It was one of six firms to close or seek new owners in the aftermath of October 19. "The old rules are off. We are in a new mode," said Donald Nickelson, the president of Paine Webber. Peter Cohen, chairman of Shearson Lehman Brothers, said a 50 percent reduction in bonuses would be appropriate.[6]

As 1988 wore on, the toll mounted. In January, First Boston announced major reductions, putting the total jobs lost at more than 8,000.

By May, the number climbed to 15,000. By year-end, the estimate had reached 17,000, and in January 1989, Merrill Lynch said it was likely to eliminate another 3,000.[7]

Firms had no choice but to react to the plunge in activity. While average daily volume was off only 8 percent, trading by individual investors dropped by a quarter, and they were the ones who paid the high commissions that bolstered profits.[8]

More damage was done as infighting tore some firms apart, including First Boston, whose leading investment bankers, Bruce Wasserstein and Joseph Perella, left to start their own, soon to be famous, boutique. The investment bankers at Kidder Peabody warred with executives at their parent, General Electric, over how to cope with changes, paralyzing the company.[9]

The crash intensified the focus on costs, making it even more difficult to keep companies from moving their headquarters or large numbers of workers elsewhere.

For most of 1988, Deputy Mayor Townsend was preoccupied with Chase Manhattan Bank, as its top executives considered relocating 4,600 employees to New Jersey. As significant as the economic impact might be, the psychological damage would be far worse. This was the Rockefeller Bank. David Rockefeller, the man who had done so much to save the city during the Fiscal Crisis, remained an influential figure there. If Chase was willing to leave, who would stay?

Townsend's best hope for keeping Chase's jobs in the city was to persuade the bank to move those employees to an underutilized parcel in downtown Brooklyn, where she, the borough president, the chief executive of Brooklyn Union Gas, and the developer Bruce Ratner had conceived of a new office park called MetroTech. If built, it would offer a less costly alternative for back-office jobs still located in Manhattan. A package of tax breaks available in the boroughs outside Manhattan also narrowed the gap with the cheaper rents and money-saving incentives available across the Hudson River in New Jersey.

For a while the cause looked hopeless, and a September *Wall Street Journal* story reported that Chase had decided to move to Jersey. The news mobilized political and civic leaders. The mayor lobbied Chase officials furiously, and the city and state scrounged up every dollar it could for an incentive plan to make MetroTech as attractive as possible. It worked. In early November, Chase announced that it would stay, promising to put 5,000 workers at MetroTech in return for $235 million in tax breaks and energy subsidies. The Chase jobs green-lighted MetroTech, the crucial project that jump-started Brooklyn's own revival in the next decade.

Keeping Chase was a major victory, and city leaders began to wonder if the dire warnings that followed the stock market crash were exaggerated. In January, a poll by *Crain's* found New Yorkers saying that they had sharply cut back on spending, but there were few signs of such a retrenchment.[10] The Zagat survey showed that only 16 percent of New Yorkers were eating out less, and the average for dining out was still an eyebrow-raising four times a week.[11] Some Wall Street castoffs were finding spots at expanding foreign banks. The decline in tax revenue was estimated at $10 million a month, a tiny fraction of the budget.

The *New York Times* was ready to call a "soft landing" for the city.[12] Mr. Ehrenhalt said, "So far, it looks like we've had a traumatic non-event."[13]

As the 1989 mayoral election approached, the economic signals became increasingly confused. The office vacancy rate moved above 13 percent.[14] By midyear, 31 prominent restaurants had filed for bankruptcy.[15] Tourism slid as both airline passenger arrivals and hotel rooms sold dropped 10 percent.[16] Tax collections weakened, with business payments down 17 percent to the level of 1985, real estate transaction fees off by a quarter, and sales taxes failing to keep pace with inflation.[17]

Linda Barbanel, an uptown psychoanalyst, reported that her own practice had declined as her clients decided that therapy was a luxury they could no longer afford. In response, she was taking her silk blouses to the cleaner less. Her dry cleaner complained that business was down a lot.[18]

Yet the total number of jobs in the city held steady, and the unemployment rate rose only modestly. An angry Lew Rudin, one of the city's foremost landlords, called Alair Townsend, now publisher of *Crain's New York Business,* to complain about the prominence the paper was giving to bad news stories. "Are you trying to talk the city into a recession?" he asked.

All eyes in the city were on the mayoral election campaign. Koch decided to run for a fourth term even though voters had clearly tired of his style, once regarded as boisterous and now as arrogant. A corruption scandal that caused one of his political allies to commit suicide and landed another in jail had hampered virtually his entire third term. Three opponents jumped into the Democratic primary, certain that he was vulnerable.

The economy received scant attention. When asked their views, Koch's challengers, not surprisingly, saw bad times ahead and claimed that the best way to meet them was to protect city services by finding more revenues. Even Republican Rudy Giuliani said that rising crime was more important to tackle than the city's heavy tax burden. Koch was more optimistic, of course, and made it clear that preserving the fiscal gains of his mayoralty was his top priority when he said he would raise taxes to balance the budget.

All these issues disappeared in late August when an African-American youth named Yusef Hawkins was killed by a mob in the white enclave of Bensonhurst, Brooklyn, sparking fears of racial turmoil. In the September primary, voters chose the African-American Manhattan borough president David Dinkins in hopes that he would heal the racial divide. Passions had cooled somewhat by the general election in November, but Dinkins edged out the politically inexperienced Giuliani by two percentage points.

Shortly after the election, Dinkins and campaign research director Doug Muzzio sat down for a briefing on the economy from Ray Horton, the head of the Citizens Budget Commission. "I don't know who would want to be mayor now," Horton told them.[19] He had grasped something business leaders like Lew Rudin had missed: the city's economy had appeared to be holding its own only because government jobs were offsetting private sector losses.

Despite the hiring freeze, Koch had allowed the city payroll to increase by 20,000 since the crash. Nonprofit social service jobs, virtually all funded by government, rose by 5,000; health care jobs, also primarily financed by government, jumped by 15,000. With tax revenue now weakening and the mayor unable to turn to the fiscal gimmicks of the 1970s, the city could no longer be the employer of last resort.

The securities industry continued to contract, and the ripples now engulfed the city. Although the Dow recovered the ground it had lost in the crash by December 1989, that was of little comfort to securities firms. Individual investors had no stomach for equities except through investing in mutual funds.

"The calls just don't come in the way they used to," said New York Stock Exchange floor broker Robert Bradley. "I'll spend time reading the newspaper or wandering around and checking stock prices."[20] Institutions accounted for 80 percent of trading, and commissions on that business averaged just six cents a share, reducing revenue by a third. Merger and acquisition activity declined sharply.

Less than two months after Dinkins took office, Drexel Burnham Lambert suddenly closed its doors, and the reordering of Wall Street and its depressing impact on the city became crystal clear.

Drexel's fate had been in doubt since early 1989, when a federal grand jury indicted the pioneer of junk bonds, Michael Milken, on 98 felony counts for cheating clients and stockholders, manipulating stock prices, tricking one company into being acquired, and helping another cheat the government on taxes. Drexel itself pleaded guilty and agreed to pay a $650 million fine. Milken protested his innocence, but the damage had been done. Clients fled; worse, the junk bond market froze up because of the scandal and because many of the companies that had used the financing tool for acquisitions collapsed.

When Drexel closed its doors in February, 5,000 employees were suddenly jobless. Rudin's firm had 200,000 square feet of empty space at an aging downtown office building at 55 Broad Street. Drexel's law firm let 25 associates go. Financial printers cut staff as well.[21] Milken pled guilty to six counts later in the year and was sentenced to ten years in prison, of which he served only two.

The cutbacks continued as business stagnated. Merrill Lynch pared its management ranks in 1990, Prudential Bache abandoned investment banking, and Morgan Stanley undertook the first-ever layoffs in

its investment banking unit. Prudential, Shearson Lehman, and First
Boston all needed bailouts by corporate parents to survive. Prudential
Bache, Smith Barney, and, most importantly, Morgan Stanley launched
studies to see if they should leave New York altogether.[22]

The securities industry now employed 145,000 workers in the city,
down 18,000 from the 1987 peak. Outside analysts and Wall Street
CEOs both proclaimed that this shrunken Wall Street would be permanent. "What's going on right now on Wall Street is a change that is very
much structural, and not cyclical at all. The Wall Street that is rebuilt
after this hurricane is going to be a much different kind of animal than
we have seen in the past," said Thomas Carroll, an industry specialist at
the accounting firm Peat Marwick.[23]

The city could no longer deny the economic toll.

The statistics were even worse in hindsight. In 1991, the number of
jobs lost the previous year was revised sharply higher. The huge business services sector, suffering from the ripple effects of Wall Street, shed
almost 40,000 jobs, and two large regional accounting firms—Laven-
thol & Horwath and Spicer & Oppenheim—shut their doors with little
warning. Law firms were slimming down, too.

The national retail giant Macy's teetered under huge debt, and three
local chains—electronics outlet Newmark & Lewis, Seaman's Furniture, and Sterling Optical—filed for bankruptcy. On Christopher Street
in Greenwich Village, retailers that catered to a mostly gay community
tried to hang on, their economic woes worsened by a troubling crime
wave. While the police denied any spike, Bob Kohler of a clothing store
named The Loft stopped selling leather jackets because thieves would
enter the store, grab them, and run. On successive days in July, a man
was stabbed to death on a nearby pier and several gay men were as-
saulted. Street traffic declined, and no one would rent vacant stores except sex shops, which only deepened the area's aura of decline.[24]

David and Jean Solomon were desperately trying to lease the three
speculative office buildings they had built on the West Side. In mid-1990,
they and their bankers at Citibank agreed to $15 million in incentives to
lure the law firm Olwine Connelly O'Donnell Chase & Weyher to 750
Seventh Avenue and waived a standard requirement that the partners

guarantee the lease. Eighteen months later, that law firm dissolved, and the Solomons lost the last of their holdings. They fled the New York real estate scene.[25]

Not only were tax revenues down, but property tax delinquencies soared, up 38 percent in the 1991 fiscal year ended in June. It was the highest level since 1980, although only half the 7.5 percent figure from 1976.[26]

The bottom line, said Ehrenhalt of the Bureau of Labor Statistics in a glum Christmas wrap-up, was that Manhattan had lost every private sector job it had gained in the 1980s. "There is more fear out there than I saw in the 1970s," said economist Rosemary Scanlon, a veteran of the Fiscal Crisis.[27]

Like Ed Koch, David Dinkins had no real executive experience when he took charge of the city in January 1990. He was a leader of the African-American political establishment in Harlem—a member of its Gang of Four, which also included former top city officials Percy Sutton and Basil Paterson and Congressman Charles Rangel. Dinkins had served a brief stint in the state legislature and a long tenure as city clerk before finally being elected Manhattan borough president, in what he hoped would be a stepping stone to City Hall. In sharp contrast to Koch, he was calm, reserved, and careful in his public statements, traits that undoubtedly helped him defeat Koch amid the racial tensions of the previous fall.

Spurring the city's recovery from the Fiscal Crisis proved a stiff challenge for Koch. The 62-year-old Dinkins faced equally daunting problems—namely, falling tax revenues as the economy contracted, demands for higher pay from the city unions, and pressure to expand city programs from the African-American community, two groups that had been crucial to his victory. Most of all, he confronted a soaring crime rate and a wave of murders that panicked the city.

Throughout 1990, murders dominated the news. Seventy-five children under the age of 16 were killed that year, ten of them by stray bullets, and many more wounded. Thirty-two drivers of livery cars operating in neighborhoods far from the central business district were murdered, as well as three medallion cabbies. Twenty-one police officers were wounded, and they shot 106 people, of whom 41 died. In September, 22-year-old tourist Brian Watkins from Utah was stabbed to death on a subway train protecting his mother from a gang of youths. The story riveted the nation as well as the city.[28] The mayor's failure to attend the funeral fueled more criticism. The decline in tourism was largely blamed on crime.[29]

Dinkins finally felt compelled to act. New Yorkers who had tired of Ed Koch's combativeness now longed for his decisiveness. On consecutive days in October, Dinkins announced a new contract for teachers with an unexpectedly large 5.5 percent raise, unveiled a plan to add more than 4,000 new police to the force (financed by a new payroll tax and increased property taxes), and revealed he was considering laying off 15,000 city employees because of budget problems.

The tabloids erupted in dismay at the seemingly contradictory policies. The city council objected to the $500 million in new taxes for the added police, which would come on top of the $800 million in new revenue they had grudgingly agreed to in the budget approved the previous June.[30]

At least everyone agreed that action was needed on crime, although negotiations with the council, governor, and state legislature dragged on until the end of the year. In December, the council and the legislature agreed to add about 3,500 cops, paid for by an increase in the property tax, the extension of an income tax surcharge, and a new lottery game.

Three months later, the mayor faced another revolt. In an unprecedented move, the New York City Partnership issued a stinging public rebuke to the mayor for failing to deal with the city's budget problems. Partnership chairman Robert Tisch, who ran giant Loews Corp. with his brother Laurence, was determined to deter the mayor from simply continuing to raise taxes and force him to cut spending instead. When the mayor didn't heed them in the new budget proposed in May, businesses directly lobbied the council to reject his new taxes and emphasize ways to make the city more efficient.[31]

It wasn't just the biggest companies that felt the impact of the mayor's decision to raise taxes in a weak economy. Smaller firms and homeowners felt the burden of Dinkins's insistence most acutely.

In Brooklyn, Best True Value owner Neil Frank's property tax bill had doubled to more than $12,000 in three years, which represented half the profit he eked out on the store's $1.2 million in annual sales. The budget proposal the New York City Partnership was contesting would push his tax to $15,000, and he said he was ready to move to the suburbs.[32]

In Dinkins's own Harlem neighborhood, 42-year-old single mother Helen Daniels faced an increase in her water bill from $150 to $500 and similar jumps in the property tax on her brownstone and her city income tax. Her $47,000 salary was stretched to the breaking point as she struggled to keep her two children in college.[33]

While the candidates of 1989 had argued that city services would need to be maintained if the economy weakened, the mood had shifted. Heeding the cries of residents and businesses alike, the city council balked at the Dinkins plan, forcing some cutbacks in spending and agreeing to smaller-than-requested tax hikes.

Dinkins remained mayor for two more years without ever convincing New Yorkers or even members of his own administration that he was firmly in command. Barry Sullivan, a top banking executive who became deputy mayor for economic development, complained to confidantes that long meetings often ended with no decision. He couldn't understand how one could run a city that way.

"David Dinkins was not a manager or a leader," says Alair Townsend, who led the drumbeat of criticism of the mayor in her columns in *Crain's*. "He would not make decisions and he didn't know what to do. The lack of decisiveness created a damaging sense of drift. Why wasn't there more panic in 2008 and 2009 when the Financial Crisis hit and everyone knew the city faced severe job losses? Because Bloomberg was in charge, and people thought he would get the job done."

In early 1992, economist Rosemary Scanlon traced how the recession kicked off by the market collapse of 1987 was now paralyzing the rest of the economy. With tax revenues falling, city government was shedding jobs. Retailers had hunkered down as their sales dipped year after year. Manufacturing was continuing its decades-long contraction. In all, she warned, the city was likely to lose 100,000 jobs that year.

Even venerable firms, many of which had weathered the 1969–1979 period, were disappearing. Business failures doubled in the first half of 1992.

Laurent, a classic French restaurant in Midtown that catered to Salvador Dalí, Jackie Onassis, and National Football League commissioner Pete Rozelle, closed its doors suddenly. It had failed to adjust as recession-weary diners opted for simpler fare.[34] The electronic firm Newmark & Lewis liquidated, its demise hastened by banks' skittishness on extending loans.

Many were casualties of the outsized ambitions sparked by the boom of the 1980s.

Harvey Russak began selling jeans on the street in the 1960s, and he opened Unique on dingy lower Broadway in 1971 to lure young people who saw themselves as part of the counterculture. In the booming 1980s, Russak became a trendsetter and undertook a costly expansion of his building. In the tough times of the 1990s, style wasn't as important; the arrival of national chains on Broadway lured away his customers, and his business failed.[35]

The soaring crime rate, the AIDS epidemic, and the lack of confidence in the city's leadership and future made businesspeople wary. Some considered leaving, including the leading securities firm Morgan Stanley. Civic leaders mounted another effort like the one to keep the Chase jobs, convening a meeting of top business leaders and the brokerage firm's CEO Richard Fisher where a succession of CEOs and Cardinal John O'Connor, the archbishop of New York, beseeched Fisher to stay in the city. He called off the search for a new home.

The unavoidable contraction of city government made matters worse. John Lindsay's 1969 income tax had bound city government's revenues closely to Wall Street. While most cities relied on the relatively stable property tax for as much as three-quarters of their revenue, personal and corporate taxes in the 1980s and 1990s accounted for a third of New York City's income. Sales and similar taxes provided another 27 percent. Lindsay's income tax had produced $130 million in its first year; in 1993, it generated $3.5 billion.[36]

The pattern was set. Since New York was the only city with both a progressive income tax and high corporate tax rates, revenues soared when Wall Street thrived and declined sharply when it did not. The city eliminated 12,500 jobs in the last years of the Dinkins administration. Public works spending was slashed so severely that contracts plunged 33 percent in the first six months of the year, from the already depressed level of the year before. Some 42,000 construction jobs had been lost, or a third of the total.

By now, everyone in New York understood that the city was in much worse shape than the nation, which had shaken off the stock market crash quickly. The city's unemployment rate was 11 percent; the nation's, 7.4 percent. Holiday sales in 1992 were projected to decline 7 percent in New York, even as they increased 4 percent nationally. The city lost 325,000 jobs during the Dinkins administration—about 9 percent.[37] Even in the Great Recession of 2008–2009, the United States saw only 6 percent of jobs disappear.[38] The idea that the city was so diversified that it could shrug off national downturns, as it had in 1982, was shattered.

Rudy Giuliani, who had narrowly lost to Dinkins four years before, was determined to try again. However, he was persona non grata in parts of Wall Street over lingering resentment from insider trading prosecutions he had launched while US attorney, especially his public handcuffing of traders. He couldn't be certain other executives would support him either. Business people—especially developers and landlords whose business is at risk if they alienate city officials—usually line up behind incumbents. In 1989, the city's leading developers had backed Ed Koch in the primary. When Koch lost, they threw their support to Dinkins instead of Giuliani, led by the enormously influential Jerry Speyer of Tishman Speyer. They were sure that a Democratic victory was inevitable.

Giuliani wasn't deterred by the obstacles. While officially a partner in a law firm, he had spent the years after his defeat improving his knowledge of the city and wooing opinion leaders across the city. He cultivated the business community in particular, appearing twice at *Crain's* forums that featured the city's civic leaders. The success of his efforts was clear by mid-May, when Giuliani quit the law firm to campaign full-time. He had raised $3 million, compared with $200,000 at the same time four years before—primarily from executives who felt that the city's future hung in the balance.[39]

Giuliani campaigned on two issues—attacking the crime rate and fixing the economy, primarily by cutting 35,000 more city jobs and reducing taxes. He drew a sharp contrast with Dinkins when he called for a reduction in hotel taxes.

In 1990, desperate for more revenue, the state had imposed an additional 5 percent occupancy tax on hotel rooms costing more than $100 a night, and the city piled on by increasing its own tax to 6 percent—bringing the total to just over 21 percent. A national association of meeting planners reacted by organizing a boycott of the city; other visitors also recoiled and went elsewhere. Hotel occupancy dropped sharply.[40]

While Dinkins had supported repeal of the state tax, he objected when Giuliani said he would cut the city tax in half and challenge the state to do the same. The $68 million in revenue could not be spared, said the mayor. Giuliani believed that eliminating the tax would spur enough new business to offset the loss. Giuliani attributed the city's woes to the mayor's lack of leadership and repeated tax hikes.[41] Dinkins said the decline was not his fault, and he proposed a range of city programs to bolster key sectors of the economy and small businesses.[42]

Giuliani won as the Republicans swept the white neighborhoods in the boroughs outside Manhattan. While his margin was only the same 2 percentage points he had lost by four years before, Giuliani had won 51 percent of the vote. Lindsay had never won a majority in either of his two races, and if Lindsay represented a continuation of the city's liberal political consensus, Giuliani represented a sharp break with it.

The new Republican mayor took office amid pessimism that rivaled the gloom of the Fiscal Crisis. A *New York Times* poll taken a month before the election found that 65 percent of those questioned said the economy was bad or very bad; 59 percent believed the city was less safe than four years before; and 67 percent complained that race relations had worsened, even though Dinkins beat Koch because voters thought he could improve the racial climate in the city. Forty-five percent said they were so fed up that they would leave the city immediately if they could.[43]

Economic experts were just as pessimistic. "The jobs problem in New York is a structural one, not a cyclical one," said Anirvan Banerji, an economist at Columbia University. "New York remains a high-cost environment and companies are finding fewer reasons to keep low-cost jobs here."[44]

Of course, like the predictions that the securities business would never regain its pre-crash profitability, these dire forecasts were wrong. In fact, the recession hit bottom that very month of the *Times* poll. Business was reviving on Wall Street, and neighborhoods outside Manhattan were stirring as well.

In 1991, investors finally shook off the caution induced by the 1987 crash and returned to stocks, in part, because interest rates were so low that bank CDs and bonds were no longer attractive. The industry had changed—the nonfinancial companies had sold or spun off the securities firms they owned. The number of brokerages and large investment banks had been pared. But the remaining firms benefited from improving markets and reduced competition.

Securities firms' profits hit a record that year, and bonuses increased anywhere from 25 percent to 40 percent.[45] Wages on Wall Street jumped 45 percent to $17 billion and suddenly constituted 17 percent of all the income in the city, up from 12 percent. Industry consultant John Keefe put the total compensation at $21 billion, up 18 percent, and the average salary at a record $98,000.[46] Bidding wars broke out as firms raided each other for the best talent. The securities industry also sparked a revival in the real estate and construction industries when Goldman Sachs, Morgan Stanley, and Lazard Frères had finally added enough new workers to need more space.[47]

While some New Yorkers moved to the suburbs or other parts of the country during the downturn, their loss was more than offset by arrivals from around the globe. Their ranks were confirmed by the city's school system, which reported in early 1992 that it had absorbed

120,000 immigrant children from 167 countries in the previous three school years. These immigrants stabilized downtrodden neighborhoods that would thrive again in lockstep with Manhattan when the recovery gained speed.[48]

The third boom of the modern era began slowly, but by the end of the decade, New York was richer than ever before.

CHAPTER 6

MAKING NEW YORK
SAFE FOR COMMERCE

MANY NEW YORKERS REGARDED THEIR NEW MAYOR
warily, unsure that he could fix a city anxious about crime and mired
in a severe recession. Small business owners and major business leaders,
however, had no such doubts.

The day after the election, the president of Fairchild Realty Group
made an offer on an office building on 46th Street in Manhattan and
eyed the purchase of two more properties in Midtown. Sam Klein's company already owned a half million square feet of office space in the Long
Island City area of Queens; the arrival of Rudy Giuliani made him confident enough to expand into Manhattan.

In Brooklyn, the owner of Bay Welding and Bay Boiler Rentals
shared this optimism. Chris Fountoukis shelved a plan to move to New
Jersey and instead bought a nearby building to expand his 15-employee
firm. "I believe things will get better. I think the mayor and others will
look at the issues that are important to us," he said.[1]

As far as Rudy Giuliani was concerned, only two issues mattered—
putting the city's finances in order by reducing spending and cutting key
taxes, and finding some way to reduce the city's appalling crime rate.

While newly installed police commissioner Bill Bratton worked out the anticrime strategies, the mayor took on the budget.

Giuliani was 49 years old, a Brooklyn-born Roman Catholic who had settled on law after abandoning the idea of the priesthood. He had graduated from Manhattan College and NYU's law school and then joined the US Attorney's Office for the Southern District, a prized job for anyone seeking a career in law or government. He landed a position with the Justice Department in Washington during the administration of President Gerald Ford. He became a Republican one month after Ronald Reagan became president and climbed the career ladder at Justice. He won appointment as the US attorney for the Southern District in 1983, seemingly a step down from his position as associate attorney general.

However, no office is better suited for an ambitious prosecutor. The Southern District, which includes Manhattan and the Bronx and a group of suburban counties to the north, holds jurisdiction over most of the country's leading crime families, Wall Street, and the nation's biggest companies. The Mob was Giuliani's first target, possibly because his father had been convicted of armed robbery and acted, at least for a short time, as an enforcer for a relative in the mob. He indicted and won convictions of the heads of the city's organized crime families in what came to be known as the Mafia Commission Trial. He led the investigations of the insider trading abuses of the 1980s, putting both Ivan Boesky and Michael Milken in jail.

He welcomed the publicity his actions brought, meeting with reporters over drinks, staging highly publicized arrests, and making extensive use of the "perp walk," where defendants were paraded before reporters and, more importantly, photographers and TV cameras. In some cases, his efforts backfired. He became despised in parts of Wall Street when he condoned the handcuffing of Wall Street executives during an arrest. The man was never even indicted.

When he first ran against David Dinkins in 1989, Giuliani had emphasized his law-and-order background, in part, because he had not yet developed many strong views on other city issues. He placed himself in a popular framework for Democrats, saying that he was an admirer of the Kennedys. After his defeat in 1989, he discovered the Manhattan Institute.

The Manhattan Institute, founded in 1978 by a former CIA director for Ronald Reagan, had emerged as a source of ideas for a series of conservative reform mayors in places like Indianapolis, where it provided the rationale for making municipal departments compete against private firms to maintain their work. It emphasized reducing the size of local governments, especially by slashing the tax burden and privatizing services. It attacked liberal positions on welfare and other social issues. Since Giuliani's inner circle was made up entirely of lawyers from the US Attorney's Office and a few old friends, the Manhattan Institute was his brain trust in remaking the city.

He followed the prescriptions of the Institute to the letter in tackling a $2 billion budget deficit. He demanded an immediate 1 percent reduction in spending and announced he would cut 15,000 people from the city's workforce, which David Dinkins had allowed to increase to a record 250,000. Despite the shortfall in tax revenue, particularly acute owing to a decline in property values in the city, he fulfilled his campaign pledge to pare the city's hotel tax, hoping to shame Albany into eliminating its crippling surcharge. He also announced that he would trim taxes particularly resented by businesses—the nation's only tax on commercial rent payments, for instance, and an unincorporated tax on partnerships and the self-employed.[2] In all, his plan reduced the $31 billion budget by $500 million. However, he refused to trim the police budget, and he reacted angrily when state monitors of the city budget suggested he do so.

Dinkins had reluctantly cut the budget—although the budget cuts he implemented meant that he spent less than expected, not less than had been spent in the previous year—because his hand was forced by falling tax revenues. Giuliani wanted to reduce absolute spending because, he said, city government was strangling the economy. Democrats and their allies claimed that "the poor would bear the brunt of the pain," and city union leaders warned that they "were not in business to give up what we fought so hard for."[3] The city's business community rallied to support the mayor.

Ken Giddon, owner of a clothing shop named Rothman's, lined up behind the hotel tax cut because his store was seeing far fewer out-of-towners than before.[4] Real estate tycoon Jerry Speyer, who had given David Dinkins large campaign contributions in 1989, said the mayor's actions were absolutely necessary and described New York as in a "war-time situation."[5]

Apartment builder Samuel LeFrak, once known for his developments in Queens and now the driving force behind a similar project across the Hudson River in New Jersey, was even more enthusiastic. "When was the last time a big city-mayor said he wanted to cut taxes?" he asked. "It's like man bites dog. If it serves as a wakeup call to the banks to start lending again, it's enough to get me to start building again."[6]

The election and Giuliani's determination to stick to his promises convinced business leaders that New York still had a middle class that shared their values, notes Steve Malanga, who covered the election and its aftermath for *Crain's*.

The city council read the election returns the same way, and a major-ity was prepared to let the mayor forge ahead. At just $32 billion, his first budget represented the first decline in spending since the Fiscal Cri-sis of the 1970s and the first time the city's payroll was pared since the 1980s. Despite the opposition, Giuliani's decisive action on the budget gave New Yorkers hope. "The mayor is the chief mental health officer of the city. If people feel good about the future because of what they hear from the mayor they make decisions to remain in the city, both indi-viduals and businesses," explained Mitchell Moss, director of New York University's Urban Research Center, in the days after Giuliani swept into City Hall.[7]

The mayor's tackling of the crime rate lifted spirits in the city even more.

Four years earlier, Bill Bratton got a stark introduction to the fray-ing fabric of New York as soon as he walked off his plane at LaGuardia Airport, on his way to an interview for the top job at the city's transit police.[8]

Four limo drivers harangued passengers at the baggage claim looking for a fare; his licensed yellow cab was grimy and dilapidated; abandoned cars lined the expressway into Manhattan; squeegee men double-teamed the cab when it exited the Queens–Midtown Tunnel, looking for a handout. His tour of the subway system was equally depressing. It began with a deliberately jammed turnstile that forced riders to file past a scruffy-looking man demanding the tokens of anyone passing through the slam gate to reach the trains, which themselves were crowded with sleeping people stretched over several seats.

Bratton had come to New York because a pending reorganization of the Massachusetts state police was likely to cost him his job and his place on the fast track. He had been the number-two cop in Boston at the age of 32, a meteoric rise that reflected his combination of street-savvy policing, an academic bent that put him in touch with emerging theories of crime, and an unerring sense for self-promotion.

He was inspired by a 1982 *Atlantic Monthly* article by criminologists James Q. Wilson and George Kelling called "Broken Windows," which argued that neighborhood disorder created fear in citizens and must be dealt with in order to attack serious crime. Responding to minor or quality-of-life offenses was required if police wanted to win public support and assistance.

Bratton moved quickly after taking over the transit police in 1990. Told that he had to act to reduce fare-beating, he moved to arrest the offenders rather than try to deter them with police standing in every station, which was impossible to sustain. The transit police soon discovered that many of those detained were wanted on more serious crimes. His efforts resulted in a 22 percent decline in felony crime and a 40 percent drop in robberies. When the political appointees who ran the transit system denied him a raise amid a budget squeeze, he returned to Boston, where he became the police commissioner. He was happy until the election of a new mayor made it uncertain how long he could hold the job.

No appointment was more important to Rudy Giuliani than police commissioner. He considered retaining Ray Kelly, who had made a dent in the city's high crime rate under Dinkins. In the end, though, he chose Bratton, who came back to New York with two advantages. He could build on the strategies he had implemented in the city's transit system. He would take advantage of the rapid growth in the police force, which reached almost 40,000 after the NYPD merged with the transit and housing police.

He moved quickly in early 1994, overhauling the Dinkins–Kelly Safe Streets, Safe City plan that emphasized community policing to make cops a more visible presence. In Bratton's view, the Kelly approach was flawed because it would send young and inexperienced police officers into rough neighborhoods without a clear mandate of what to do. Instead he said he applied the broken-windows concept by demanding arrests for quality-of-life crimes, which, as in transit, led to the arrest of many people wanted for more serious offenses. He reversed the long prohibition on street cops making drug arrests, put in place years ago due to fears of corruption. He used the additional manpower to flood high-crime areas. The most important innovation, conceived by trusted aide Jack Maple, established the use of computerized statistics to track crime in each precinct as a tool to hold commanders accountable for reducing crime.

In the first year of Giuliani–Bratton, major crimes in the city declined by 4 percent, and there were 12 fewer murders, a trend that mimicked both the preceding years and what was happening nationally.[9] But the next year the results were far more dramatic. Giuliani announced a 19 percent drop in murders, the largest on record. Robberies and auto thefts declined by 15 percent; every one of the 76 New York precincts showed a decline in crime; and the biggest reductions came in the poorest and most dangerous neighborhoods.[10] Thus began a remarkable trend that continued after Giuliani forced Bratton out of office to install more dependable loyalists and even after Ray Kelly returned to lead the department for Michael Bloomberg.

Giuliani's critics, as well as some criminologists, say he deserves little credit for what occurred. They noted that it was Dinkins who boosted the size of the police force, although it was political pressure that forced him to do so. They say that broad national trends were primarily at work—the reduction in the use of crack, the nationwide movement to sharply increase the number of criminals incarcerated, and a decline in the number of young people, statistically the most likely group to break the law. After all, crime declined in cities across the country.

Certainly those trends played a role in New York. But they do not account for the differences between New York and other cities. Between 1993 and 1995, the FBI's national index of reported violent and property crime declined by 3 percent. New York's violent and property crime index plummeted by 25.9 percent. New York accounted for fully one-third of the more than 432,000 fewer crimes in the country, although it contained only 3 percent of the nation's population.

The day Rudy Giuliani left office, the city reported that violent crime in 2001 had fallen another 12.3 percent, while cities like Chicago, Los Angeles, and Boston had seen increases. Over his eight years as mayor, the overall crime rate had fallen 62 percent, including a two-thirds reduction in murders and robberies. Some 81,000 fewer cars were stolen in 2001 than in the year when he took office.[11]

James Q. Wilson has no doubt about why crime fell so dramatically in New York, and the reason is not national trends or Rudy Guiliani's leadership or Bratton's adoption of broken windows. Rather all the strategies Bratton implemented were designed to change the way the police saw their job. "The biggest change in policing in this country that's occurred is usually associated with Bill Bratton," he said in 2011. "And that's a correct association. He made a huge difference. But people misstate what the change was. They say he adopted the 'broken windows' theory. Well, I'm not sure he did and if he did, I'm not sure it made much difference to the crime rate. What he really did—his fundamental contribution—was to persuade the police that your job is not to make arrests. Your job is to prevent crime."[12]

One of Giuliani's closest aides, first deputy mayor Peter Powers, has no doubt about the link between crime and the economy. "We knew if we didn't deal with crime the economy would never come back," he says.[13]

Yet the city's economy had boomed throughout most of Ed Koch's tenure even as crime rose relentlessly, in part, because the city's business districts were insulated from what was occurring in the more dangerous neighborhoods. Two decades later, when the Great Recession struck in 2008, criminologists told skeptical reporters that economic hard times would not necessarily lead to an increase in crime, and they were proven right when the FBI reported crime declined in both 2009 and 2010 across the country.

Even tourism's relationship to crime was not direct. In late 1994, a 31-year-old tourist from Hamburg was wounded while on a Circle Line tour boat by a random gunshot fired from shore, immediately recalling the famous subway murder of Utah tourist Brian Watkins four years before. The city saw an increase in visitors that year to more than 25 million.[14]

The indirect effects of the decline in crime were enormous. No matter what economic swings occurred, never again would an opinion poll of New Yorkers show the pessimism of 1977 or 1993. The steady influx of young people, especially college graduates, swelled as parents no longer thought New York was too dangerous for their children. The fact that the biggest decline in crime occurred in the poorest areas laid the foundation of the gentrification that swept the city over the next 20 years. Tourism benefited most of all, as hotels could now be built in every neighborhood of Manhattan and in Queens and Brooklyn, providing the necessary beds to accommodate 50 million tourists a year.

Bill Bratton was not around to take credit for what happened. At the end of Bratton's first week as police commissioner, the *New York Daily News* plastered him on the tabloid's Sunday cover with the headline, "Top Cop Bratton: I'll End the Fear." Giuliani was not amused. Bratton was summoned to City Hall that evening to be dressed down by Powers, and the message was clear: only the mayor should get credit for the decline in crime.

Bratton was not the kind of person who would comply with such a demand. He wanted to make sure his cops got the credit for the gains because it would lift morale and make them even more effective. He had no intention of fading into the background. After all, publicity had helped make him a star at such a young age.

But Giuliani, who believed that Dinkins's unwillingness to command center stage had doomed his four years, was not about to be eclipsed. He forced Bratton out after 27 months, replacing him with a longtime friend, the self-effacing fire commissioner Howard Safir. Safir in turn was succeeded by Giuliani's onetime police driver, Bernard Kerik, who would be sent to jail for allowing a contractor seeking a city license to pay for work on his home while he was commissioner.

As Bratton departed, the economic recovery was beginning to take hold. The owners of the Chicago steakhouse Morton's opened a location in New York despite being warned against the city. They were immediately deluged with reservations despite an average $60-per-person tab. A survey of local retailers showed them expecting the 1994 holiday to match the sales increases in other cities for the first time in several years. An investment boutique named Odyssey Partners paid $205 million, or about $200 a square foot, for the iconic IBM headquarters building on Madison Avenue. It was the highest price paid for a building since the real estate collapse during the last years of Koch. At the same time, word leaked that the Durst family, who had been such bitter opponents of the Times Square development plan, were seeking to refinance three of their existing buildings to raise the money for a speculative office building right on 42nd Street between Sixth and Seventh Avenues.[15]

Private companies added 30,000 jobs in 1995, and the city's prospects looked brighter, although no one imagined the dizzying heights the next boom was about to bring.

CHAPTER 7

IMMIGRATION SAVES
THE NEIGHBORHOODS

THE CENSUS BUREAU HAD A SURPRISE FOR NEW YORK-ers in late August 1990. Despite the economic boom of the preceding decade and neighborhoods that seemed to be bursting at the seams with new arrivals, the bureau announced that it had counted 7,033,179 New Yorkers, some 40,000 fewer than it had found ten years before.[1]

Mayor David Dinkins called the number "unadulterated nonsense."[2] Governor Mario Cuomo claimed the Republican administration in Washington was deliberately trying to erode Democratic seats in Congress. Demographer Emanuel Tobier of New York University pointed to a 28 percent increase in births in the city in the last decade. "It is inconceivable to me that this type of increase could take place without an increase in the population," he said.[3]

Five months later, the Census Bureau admitted that it had failed to do a good job counting people in cities, especially in New York, and revised its figure up to 7,322,564. While city officials continued to insist that some 300,000 people had still been missed, the revision represented a historic milestone.[4] The increase of 3.5 percent closed the chapter on the disastrous decade of the 1970s, when the population had declined by about 800,000 people. The new count also made New York one of the few urban areas in the Northeast or Midwest to see its population grow.

Demographers all pointed to the same reason for the city's resurgence—immigration was reshaping New York. In 1970, the number of foreign-born New Yorkers had declined to just over 1.4 million, or only 18 percent of the population, the lowest figure in the century. Now more than 2 million residents had been born elsewhere, 28 percent of the total. Without the surge in immigration, New York's population in the 1980s would have declined by another 9 percent instead of growing. New York would have been on the road to the kind of city Detroit became. "Is there anything wrong with a city of 5 million?" asked Lou Winnick, who had studied the role of immigration for many years. "No. But a city that goes from 8 million to 5 million—there would be cobwebs all over."[5]

Instead of abandoned blocks, neighborhoods were repopulated by the immigrants, who first crowded into existing housing stock and then invested to improve it. The new arrivals reinvigorated the local economies where they lived. They provided the manpower to bolster the city's key industries; after all, the primary reason they came was for the economic opportunities the city offered. And while New York became known as an immigrant-friendly city, it achieved that reputation only after a decade of conflict.

New York's good fortune resulted from the landmark 1965 Immigration and Nationality Act, which replaced the national quota system imposed in the 1920s. The 1920s law not only limited the number of immigrants, it favored Western European nations where there was little interest in coming to the United States. The 1965 reform eliminated those quotas and opened the country to the rest of the world by creating four pathways: immigrants could be reunited with other family members, they could come to fill the need for specific jobs, they could qualify under a program designed to diversify the countries of origin, or they could claim refugee status.

This dramatically affected the nationalities of the immigrants who flocked to New York. In 1970, Italy was the largest source of foreign-born New Yorkers, followed by Poland, the Soviet Union, Germany, and Ireland. In 1990, the Dominican Republic was by far the largest source of immigrants, followed by China, Jamaica, Italy, and the Soviet Union. Washington Heights in northern Manhattan, where many Dominicans decided to settle, was one of the first areas to show the enormous benefits that immigrants brought to the city.[6]

Named for Fort Washington, constructed by the Continental Army in its vain effort to hold New York during the Revolutionary War, the neighborhood was most well-known for the George Washington Bridge, the busiest motor vehicle span in the world. The neighborhood had long been a destination for new arrivals—the Irish in the 1900s, European Jews in the 1930s and 1940s, and Greeks in the 1950s and 1960s. Dominicans came because conditions on their homeland were so dismal— the average salary in the early 1990s was $40 a month—and often took jobs in the city's service industries, such as driving livery cabs. Some became business owners and bought out the Puerto Ricans who owned bodegas that supplied food and other necessities to poor neighborhoods. The Dominicans could afford to send somewhere between $300 million and $600 million a year back to their homeland in the early 1990s, second only to tourism in economic impact on the country.

This success story received little attention. Instead, Dominicans soon came to be associated with the crack-cocaine drug epidemic sweeping the city. Part of the problem was the bridge, which allowed suburbanites to easily enter the city, buy drugs, and make a quick getaway. Another problem was corrupt cops, who allowed the activity to flourish so they could rob the dealers and make some sales themselves with the drugs they stole. Violence engulfed the neighborhood. In 1990, the 34th Precinct, which included Washington Heights, accounted for 103 murders, the second highest in the city.

The corrupt police officers were arrested in the early months of the Giuliani administration, and the Bratton tactics eventually made the neighborhood safe again. The stigma faded, and the presence of Dominicans spread throughout New York, fitting for the largest immigrant group in the city.

The impact in Queens was even more pronounced, especially in Flushing, the last stop on the No. 7 subway line, which became known as the International Express. Originating in Times Square, the 7 train's

Queensboro Plaza stop was adjacent to the Greek and Italian communities of Astoria; then it reached Sunnyside, a neighborhood populated by Koreans and Colombians; Jackson Heights followed, a South American enclave led by Colombians; and it ended in Flushing, where Taiwanese Chinese and other Asians created one of the most thriving areas of the city—and sparked resentment for their success.

The four-square-mile area had suffered like so many neighborhoods in the 1970s. Its buildings were deteriorating and many stores were shuttered, although its schools continued to be regarded as among the best in the city. Their attraction was irresistible for Taiwanese who had come to the United States to get a college degree and decided to stay, often getting married and looking for a place to raise their children.

By the early 1990s, 40 banks, 200 small shops, and hundreds of restaurants had made the area home. The Sheraton LaGuardia East, which opened in early 1992, offered a menu written in both English and Chinese, with dishes for both tastes.[7] Visitors from Asia accounted for half its customers, occupancy had climbed to 85 percent, and it charged rates similar to Manhattan hotels. The recession was hampering Flushing, but less so than elsewhere in the city, with office space costing $25 a square foot and three-bedroom apartments renting for $1,100 a month.[8]

Despite the influx of Asians, Flushing continued to be represented in the city council by 75-year-old Julia Harrison. Once an insurgent Democrat who worked for Eugene McCarthy in the 1968 presidential election, Harrison resented the changes taking place in Flushing. She drove to another neighborhood, College Point, to do her grocery shopping; she called the new arrivals "colonizers," and she claimed they were very different from immigrants like her grandparents since they seem to have arrived with loads of money. She disparaged many of them as schemers and criminals. "It's all very discombobulating, very upsetting," she said. "We all recognize that change is part of life, but it doesn't sit well."[9]

Despite her well-known antipathy to so many of her constituents, she won reelection in 1997 with 48 percent of the vote over four challengers, including a Taiwanese accountant named John Liu, who got 20 percent of the vote.[10] Four years later, Harrison was unable to run because of term limits and was succeed by Liu, who became the first Asian member of the city council.[11] Eight years later, he was the first Asian-American to win citywide office when he captured a very competitive race for city comptroller, and he emerged as a front-runner for mayor in 2013. With Asians accounting for more than 1 million New Yorkers, any mayoral campaign by Liu would begin with significant advantages.

If Dominicans revived Washington Heights and the Chinese reinvigorated Flushing, the influence of Koreans could be seen throughout the city. Many of those who had left South Korea were highly educated college and professional school graduates unable to pursue their chosen fields in the United States because of their inadequate English and because of licensing laws. Many decided to become small business owners, opening greengrocerers throughout Manhattan and in the other boroughs.

The havoc wrought by the 1970s economic crisis and the soaring crime rate eased their way, since there was relatively little demand for the small, narrow storefronts that were ideal for greengrocers.[12] Signing a lease and stocking the shelves required as little as $5,000 in some neighborhoods of Brooklyn or the Bronx. The Koreans' work ethic made the stores economically viable because they were often operated by a husband, wife, and other relatives, some of them working without pay. While currency controls prevented Koreans from bringing much cash with them, they did transplant the institution known as the *kye*. A group of Koreans contributed on a regular basis to a pool of capital, which members of the group could use to start a business.

The stores were an immediate success with their long hours (often open 24 hours a day) and fresh produce, which was attractively arranged on the sidewalks at a time when grocery store selections were sparse. In the early 1990s, some 1,400 Korean greengrocers dotted the city.

While welcomed in most of Manhattan, the Koreans faced racial tensions in some poor neighborhoods. Many Korean storeowners viewed their mostly black and Hispanic customers as untrustworthy and as likely to steal as pay for their food. African-Americans saw the Koreans as intruders who took advantage of them.

The tensions exploded in early 1990 when the owner of the Red Apple greengrocer in Flatbush was accused of striking a black patron, who he believed was stealing. A boycott of that store and another Korean-owned greengrocer nearby riveted the city. Residents picketed the two locations, and confrontations inflamed racial tensions. Mayor Dinkins refused to take sides and tried to end the boycott through negotiations, although the public was clearly on the side of the storeowners. His ambivalence was widely criticized, and it took him more than a year to visit the stores.[13] While the boycott eventually ended, Giuliani revived the incident during the 1993 election to claim that Dinkins was too weak to run New York.

Ironically, the early 1990s were the high point for Korean greengrocers. As the city's economy improved and crime declined, national retail chains discovered the city, driving up rents. Koreans found that the higher rents eroded their profits. The combination of the capital they had accumulated in the United States and easier currency restrictions in South Korea allowed them to buy businesses in other sectors. They moved into the dry-cleaning business—a big improvement since they were open only six days a week and only during daytime hours. Women gravitated to nail salons, a skill that could be mastered in about six months and didn't require a state license like barbering or hairdressing. The racial tensions subsided in calmer, more prosperous, and gentrifying neighborhoods.[14]

The children of the newly arrived Koreans were never steered toward small business ownership by their educated parents—they were pushed to get high grades and attend college. An analysis showed that 28 percent of Korean immigrants were self-employed but only 5 percent of their children were. That was half the rate of American-born Caucasians.

"There are two stories behind the Korean greengrocers disappearance," summed up Laura Vanderkam. "One involves a changing New York economy. The other is a story of how immigration can work in America—a testament to how far these new Americans have come in a single generation."[15]

The steady stream of immigrants in the 1980s turned into a torrent in the 1990s. With the influx, the 2000 Census showed New York had grown 6 percent, or by 456,000 people, exceeding 8 million people for the first time. The city accounted for two-thirds of the population gain for the entire state, a reversal of previous trends. The number of immigrants rose from 2.1 million in 1990 to 2.9 million in 2000, a 38 percent increase. Over 1 million of them lived in Queens, just under half the population, and among neighborhoods it came as no surprise that the largest numbers were in Washington Heights and Flushing. Hispanics became the largest ethnic group in the city, not surprising because the Dominican Republic and Mexico were two of the five largest countries of origin.

The newcomers were younger, they came as families, and their goal was to work. Immigrants who arrived from English-speaking countries took advantage of their language proficiency, and other groups climbed the economic ladder as they learned English.

According to the 2000 Census, 79 percent were between 18 and 64 years of age, compared with 56 percent of the native-born Americans. The youngest were Mexicans, who had arrived in large numbers in the last decade; 80 percent of Mexicans were between ages 18 and 44.

Even when men came first, their families followed. Immigrants from Trinidad and Tobago were a notable exception. The women came first and their husbands followed. The same pattern repeated itself for Filipino women, who took advantage of a special waiver for nurses to enter the country.

The census found that 73 percent of the foreign born lived in family households, compared with 62 percent of all New Yorkers. Since so many women were of childbearing age, these families grew. The statistics didn't reflect that growth because the children were counted as native born, so the median age of that group was 29 compared with 39 for the foreign born.

As had so many immigrant groups before them, they crowded into the available housing. A quarter lived in overcrowded conditions, three times the rate of those born here. The most severe conditions were among Mexicans (five persons per household), followed by Bangladeshis and Pakistanis.

The overcrowding was in part a necessity because many of the jobs they took did not pay very well, a reflection of their limited English proficiency. In 2000, the median household income was $39,900 for the native born versus $35,000 for foreign born, with the gap for women substantially less than for men. Even when the deck was stacked against them, immigrants found ways to survive economically. Just one-third of Mexicans possessed a high school diploma, so they earned just 42 percent of the city average. They compensated by having the largest number of workers per household, which brought their household income to 85 percent of the city average. Virtually all came to work. The labor participation for every group, except for Dominicans, was higher than average.

More important, the longer they lived in New York and the more their English improved, the better off they became economically. The census found that half of those who arrived before 1990 now spoke English proficiently, their household income was sharply higher, and their poverty rate, 20 percent, was lower by 5 percentage points than more recent arrivals'.

Despite the strident claims of some anti-immigrant groups, they did not come to take advantage of welfare and other social programs even before rules were tightened to make benefits more difficult to obtain.[16] There was one exception—refugees from the former Soviet Union, the major source of European immigration. The 1990 Census counted one in four on welfare. Despite the popular misconception, immigrants did not impose extraordinary demands on city services, especially considering their economic and tax contributions, except for the school system, where their children enrolled in large enough numbers to result in overcrowding, especially in Queens.

The Dominicans who bought bodegas and the Koreans who established greengrocers were in the vanguard of a trend that encompassed many other groups. The 2000 Census suggested that half of all the self-employed people in the city were immigrants, although they accounted for less than 40 percent of the population. In Queens, 10 percent of immigrants were self-employed compared with 6 percent of native-born Americans.[17]

Most of those businesses stayed close to the neighborhoods where their owners lived. Between 1994 and 2004, the number of firms citywide increased by 10 percent. The numbers were much higher in immigrant neighborhoods: 55 percent in Flushing, 47 percent in Sunset Park, 34 percent in Sheepshead Bay–Brighton Beach, and 18 percent in Washington Heights. New York boasted the most Hispanic and Asian businesses of any city. Only four states could count more Hispanic firms than New York City.

Business creation led to more jobs. Between 1994 and 2004, New York City's employment increased by 7 percent while the number of workers in Jackson Heights increased 28 percent, in Sunset Park 23 percent, in Sheepshead Bay–Brighton Beach 13 percent, and in Flushing 12 percent.

Transportation became a mainstay. Immigrants owned about one-third of the city's taxicabs, a far better economic proposition than just driving one. Others owned livery car services and created commuter van companies to supplement poor bus service. Day care became another immigrant-dominated business, albeit one that offered only a modest living, and professional service firms like travel agencies thrived, as did an ethnic press to cater to the needs of the new communities.

Thomas Chen and his wife were making metal window gates in their Flushing basement in the early 1980s to supplement his income as a garment factory worker.[18] He had bigger ambitions and graduated to making custom windows for neighborhood contractors and then invested in the equipment needed to mass-produce windows for the wholesale market. Sales soared, and in 2001, he amassed the capital to build a new 165,000-square-foot factory in College Point, Queens, a location he chose after deciding that his workers—three-quarters Chinese and Hispanic immigrants like himself—were unlikely to follow him if he relocated to lower-cost sites he looked at in New Jersey. The company continued to grow until it operated three plants, including one in China, and passed the $50 million mark in annual revenues.

Lowell Hawthorne replicated that experience in the Bronx.[19] He came to New York in 1981, graduated from Bronx Community College, and worked as an accountant until he and six siblings pooled their savings to open a bakery selling Jamaican patties, baked goods, and curries to the West Indian population on East Gun Hill Road in the Bronx. It was a business they knew well, since their parents had produced the same products back in Jamaica.

Success came quickly, and Hawthorne moved beyond West Indians to the mainstream market by signing a contract with the city school system, opening stores in Manhattan, and franchising the operation when he ran out of relatives to join the business. It now operates 120 stores, 70 in the city.

The economic success of immigrants—and the city they saved—was clear from a series of reports issued on the eve of the Great Recession.[20] They accounted for one-third of the city's economic activity, a figure that had increased by 61 percent in the period from 2000 to 2008. Household income reached $45,000 in 2008, rising 15 percent faster than inflation and nearing the figure for native-born New Yorkers. They bolstered the city's middle class. Fifty-five percent lived in families with incomes between $20,000 and $80,000, compared with 44 percent of those living in families where everyone had been born in the United States. The number who owned homes rose 50 percent during the 2000–2008 period.

By the middle of the decade, they were most numerous in service industries, but they were a force throughout the economy. One-quarter of all chief executives in the city were from elsewhere, as were half of the accountants and a third of office clerks and receptionists. In finance, a quarter of sales agents were immigrants and a third of financial managers. In real estate, they represented almost half the property managers and architects and a third of the brokers. Half the doctors were born elsewhere.

Mayor Michael Bloomberg, who not surprisingly became one of the leading spokesmen for new laws to encourage immigration, summed up the city's experience for a US Senate committee in 2006. Without immigrants, he said, New York City would collapse.[21]

CHAPTER 8

ALL THAT GLITTERS: THE DOT.COM BOOM

NEW YORK ENTERED THE INTERNET ERA WHEN THE husband-and-wife team of Bob and Aleen Stein moved their pioneering company Voyager from Santa Monica, California, to New York. The city's place in the tech boom of the 1990s would be defined by two classmates from Yale University—Kevin Ryan, who built the city's most important Internet company, DoubleClick, and Henry Blodget, whose reckless hyping of risky stocks made him a fortune and cost those who followed his recommendations far more.

It all began with the development of the CD-ROM, an improvement on the audio CD that offered more capacity than the computer hard drives of the early 1990s and the ability to create interactive programs.

The Steins founded Voyager in 1985 to work on converting films into some sort of interactive experience. Their breakthrough came in 1988 with the release of Beethoven's Ninth Symphony, considered the first consumer CD-ROM. By 1993, finding themselves spending more time in Manhattan, the Steins moved to New York, and the CD-ROM boom was on.

New York, after all, was home to the talent—artists, writers, and marketers—required to produce content and to find ways to sell it.

"California is focused on making movies, which we don't do," Stein said. "We needed to be where all the skills that go into making our products are."[1]

Small companies like Voyager sprang up, and big publishers and media companies jumped into the new market as well. Philips Electronics, which made its hardware products in Knoxville, Tennessee, established its multimedia division in New York and put 100 people in an office building on the city's West Side. Virtually every other major publisher and media company followed.

A software industry had always existed in the city—primarily specialists in applications for Wall Street and banks. A New York City Partnership study found 800 of them in 1993 employing what seemed to be an impressive 6,700 people. "We might not overtake Silicon Valley but we're creating a giant new Silicon Alley that will have enormous impact on the local economy," said a Partnership executive.[2]

The new media companies, as they were called, began clustering in Midtown South in the 20s on either side of Park Avenue. When Prodigy Services Inc., one of the pioneers of online access, relocated from suburban White Plains to the area, the idea of Silicon Alley as a geographic concentration took hold.

Meanwhile, in Atlanta, an engineer named Kevin O'Connor was trying to create software that would place ads online in a way that would maximize their exposure. An ad agency executive suggested he put together a network of websites that would compliment that goal.

Atlanta may have been O'Connor's home, but it was thousands of miles from the ad agencies, media companies, venture capitalists, investment bankers, and tech-oriented lawyers and accountants that his fledgling company needed. O'Connor, an experienced executive who had already created and sold one software company, considered California but decided he would be lost among the thousands of technology companies already there. New York seemed intimidating yet more promising, especially since it was the home of those advertising agencies and media companies that were his customers. In 1996, he took his three employees with him, and they settled into a cramped office on 23rd Street, in the heart of Silicon Alley.

O'Connor had doubts about New York's supposed cumbersome regulations, high taxes, and generally anti-business attitude. His biggest surprise was that the city wasn't ready for companies like his. He couldn't find a law firm that would represent it, so he had to hire one on the West Coast. Job offers were routinely rejected by potential recruits who preferred the security of established companies to the risks of a start-up. And while some people thought New York would be a good place because of all the money in the city, local venture capitalists weren't all that interested in helping the tech companies in their backyard.[3]

DoubleClick was on to something important. While it competed against search engines like Yahoo! and online services like American Online, it soon put together a network of 75 sites and used cookies, a new software code, to figure out the best ad for a visitor in 15 milliseconds. One person who saw the possibilities was Kevin Ryan, an investment banker who had jumped to the media business and launched a website for the comic strip Dilbert. "I knew the Internet would be the biggest thing in my lifetime and I wanted to be part of it," he recalls.[4]

Not everyone receiving attention in New York had the experience of the Steins or O'Connor. In upstate Ithaca, two juniors at Cornell University decided one night that they, too, should start a company. Stephan Paternot, a computer science major, and Todd Krizelman, a biology student, thought there would be an opportunity to offer online chat rooms focused on specific topics, and they named their company WebGenesis. They moved from their dorm room to a tiny office in Ithaca before decamping for Silicon Alley.

They burst into the spotlight three years later in 1997 when Cornell alumnus Michael Egan, the former owner of Alamo Rent a Car, invested $20 million in the company in what was believed to be the largest investment ever made by an individual in an Internet company.

He sometimes called them "the kids." Other investors in WebGenesis admitted that they did not exactly understand what the company did. Mr. Egan didn't care. "They were self-starters who had a vision," he said. "It was like walking in and finding Willie Mays and Mickey Mantle looking around and asking if they could join their team."[5]

Not everyone was so impressed. Executive recruiter Gregg Grossman specialized in Internet and other tech companies but decided not to do searches for Paternot and Krizelman. "There was this cool factor about them. The idea was that no one wanted to surf the web alone but wanted to do it with other people," he remembers. "The only real thing they had going was that they had created the company in a dorm room. There were lots of really smart people in Internet companies. These guys weren't that."[6]

Paternot and Krizelman said they would use the money they had raised to improve their technology and add staff. More than a quarter, or $5 million, was budgeted for brand advertising to establish their website, then called the Globe, among users. Many other Internet start-ups opted for the same strategy, spending money from venture capitalists and later public offerings on big-ticket advertising campaigns that benefited the old media far more than the new.

While Silicon Alley established a foothold in New York, Wall Street realized the riches to be garnered from tech companies in the Valley, Alley, and virtually anywhere else.

The two-year bear market resulting from the October 1987 crash finally hit bottom in November 1989 with the Dow Jones Industrial Average at a little over 1,800. By the end of 1994, the Dow had topped 3,800 and the Street was healthy again. In addition to the money made from stock trading, higher share prices spurred a surge in investment banking deals like mergers and acquisitions. The firms rebuilt their workforces, with total employment reaching 165,000 in 1994, and pay began to rise as well, topping $27 billion or an average of $120,000 per employee.

As the market continued to rise and merger-and-acquisition activity accelerated, Wall Street kept expanding. Profits in 1997 topped $12 billion, up $1 billion in the last year and more than double the best performance in the 1980s. Pay kept rising, too. An executive recruiter who tracked compensation claimed that 1,000 people received bonuses of more than $1 million in 1996. The following year he estimated that 1,500 people broke into seven figures. It was only the beginning of the riches created by the Internet–Wall Street connection.[7]

In 1995, Netscape decided to tap the public markets only 15 months after two veterans of the tech business, James Clark and Marc Andreessen, created a browser allowing people to easily navigate the Internet. The company produced only $17 million in revenues in the first half of the year and lost a little more than $4 million in the same period. No matter. Underwriter Morgan Stanley priced the 5.75 million shares at $28. The stock opened at $71 and surged above $74 amid heavy trading as those lucky enough to be allocated shares rushed to cash in their big profits. At the end of the day, the stock closed at $58.25, up more than $30—the best opening day ever for a stock in a big public offering. The total market value of Netscape was now $2.2 billion, more than many well-established software companies. The tech boom had begun.[8]

Kevin Ryan's classmate at Yale, Henry Blodget, was working as a fledgling investment banker at Prudential Securities. A technology buff, he had been one of the early adopters of Netscape's browser and learned as much as he could about the new technology companies.[9] With Wall Street expanding and an expertise few others could claim, he joined Oppenheimer as the junior analyst covering the tech sector for around $70,000, not far from Michael Lewis's top pay at Salomon in the 1980s. Starting to make a name for himself, Oppenheimer was forced to guarantee him at least $1 million a year when an Internet start-up tried to lure him away with a million-dollar compensation offer.

The rules of stock analysis were changing. The ability to tear apart a financial statement to assess the quality of a company's earnings no longer mattered when investors clamored for companies with "vision" and weren't put off by even millions of dollars in red ink. Soon concepts like the number of eyeballs, or visitors to a site, became paramount, and the louder an analyst cheered a company, the more they were respected. "If you come to the industry and insist on applying traditional valuation techniques you are going to miss some enormous stocks," Blodget said.

Blodget was competing against more established rivals like the Morgan Stanley team of investment banker Frank Quattrone and analyst Mary Meeker, who had handled Netscape's initial public offer (IPO). He needed to make a splash and began to focus on Amazon.com, then only an online bookseller. The company had attracted more than a few skeptics amid large losses, and short-sellers were amassing large positions in Amazon, betting on a decline in the company's stock. Blodget decided that investors didn't care about the losses and that if the stock did start to rise, the short-sellers would be squeezed and have to buy shares to cover their positions, sending the price up even higher.

He made his call in December 1998, telling the Oppenheimer brokerage force that he believed Amazon—then trading at $244—could soar to $400 a share. CNBC featured Amazon and Blodget's audacious prediction in its coverage of the market in the morning. The stock gained $46 that day, one of the largest moves ever by an Internet stock, and it reached Blodget's predicted $400 price the following month. The effect was enormous. Now every investor realized that they, too, could reap a bonanza playing the Internet game. Amazon's stock, meanwhile, peaked a few months later; it didn't trade at that level again until 2009.

Giant Merrill Lynch recruited Blodget in early 1999 in an effort to catch up with Morgan Stanley and Goldman Sachs, the leaders in Internet stock underwriting. Given the hundreds of millions of dollars in investment banking fees that Merrill expected to gain, the $3 million a year it handed Blodget seemed a small price.

Now backed by the biggest sales force in the country, Blodget had a highly visible platform to sell his theory that the Internet was changing the way every industry operated, and the Internet companies he followed would be the agents of that revolution. Not every company would succeed, he cautioned repeatedly, but those that did would prosper spectacularly. Picking those companies was the key to success.

Merrill Lynch and the other firms cared more about the money they could make now. Internet IPOs were the fuel of their profits in the late 1990s, as go-go stocks had been in the 1960s and bonds in the 1980s. Companies agreed to use Merrill Lynch to sell their first public offering and subsequent stock and bond sales because of Blodget's reputation and enthusiasm for the sector. They expected, and were frequently promised, that his research reports would recommend the stock. In 1999, spurred by the surge in investment banking he sparked, Merrill's profits more than doubled to $2.62 billion. The firm was no longer an also-ran in Internet underwriting.[10]

In 1998 and 1999, Wall Street raised more than $4 trillion in almost 35,000 stock and bond offerings. The amount raised in IPOs in 1999 was a record. That year Goldman Sachs edged out Morgan Stanley as the top underwriter, although each came close to generating $2 billion from their deals, and Merrill Lynch finished third. Morgan's profits overall increased 46 percent to almost $5 billion. Goldman Sachs, in its first year as a publicly held company, earned just shy of $3 billion.

"It is truly a reflection that this whole notion about this new economy that everyone is talking about, is, in fact, real," said Alan Sheriff, a managing director of underwriting at Credit Suisse First Boston, just three months before tech stocks began their long slide.[11]

The New York Internet sector matched Wall Street's sharp ascent. In 1995, local companies attracted modest amounts of venture capital. The companies that had gone public in New York had seen their stocks rise an average of 38 percent since their IPOs, or about half the increase of such firms elsewhere in the country. The next year, New York-area companies raised $150 million in the first quarter, seven times the figure for the first three months of 1995.[12] One didn't even need to own a computer to get millions if you were like Candice Carpenter.

A publishing executive, Carpenter decided that the Internet would be about communities of shared interests. She created Parent Soup, a concoction of expert and amateur advice about raising kids, and she announced she would replicate the effort with sites on jobs, health, and other areas under the banner of the company she named iVillage. Her idea, sketched out on a napkin during a meeting with executives from America Online, soon brought in $11 million from a group of investors that included AOL, the big cable company TCI, publishing stalwart the Tribune Co., and one of California's most important venture capital firms, Kleiner Perkins Caufield & Byers. Carpenter believed she would get half her revenue from advertisers and half from commissions on products sold through the site, but she also admitted she spent many sleepless hours at night wondering if that business plan would actually work.[13]

The industry's momentum continued to build as companies attracted money for a range of strategies. InterWorld Technology Ventures created an online payment system it promised could speed the growth of e-commerce, Netcast Communications said it would create Internet radio, Medscape provided medical information on the Internet, and N2K launched the most ambitious music site yet seen on the web. Together that had raised almost $50 million by late 1996.[14]

Two years later, *Crain's New York Business* took a skeptical look at this new industry in a story called "Up in Smoke." It surveyed the new media industry in New York, which, according to a recently released Coopers & Lybrand report, had created 55,000 full- and part-time jobs in the city, making it as large as advertising and more important than both magazine and book publishing in terms of employment. Crain's calculated that more than $1 billion had been raised by these new companies in the last four years without producing any profits or viable businesses. The story established the connection between the new media companies and Wall Street and called the frenzy taking place a Ponzi scheme.[15]

iVillage, Crain's pointed out, had burned through $70 million without reporting a profit. DoubleClick wasn't much better, losing $14 million on $51 million in revenue in the first nine months of the year. It spotlighted EarthWeb, started by Columbia graduate Jack Hidary, who had spent four years doing brain imagery research before he conceived the idea of a web design firm in 1994. Within two years, rapid changes in technology allowed companies to do what EarthWeb did in-house for a fraction of the cost, so Hidary turned to chat software. When that idea went nowhere, he turned to websites for techies. At each turn, his backers at Warburg Pincus and Co. kept opening their wallets. In October 1996, they gave him $6.7 million. Then another $10 million. Then $3.7 million.[16]

As Crain's editors worked on the story, it seemed others shared doubts about the viability of Silicon Alley. DoubleClick shares had fallen from $50 to less than $20 in July. One of its major competitors, 24/7 Media, was selling at just under $12, compared with its IPO price of $18.50. Silicon Alley favorites like the music site N2K and the online mall Cyber Shop were trading in single digits.[17]

But just days before the story was published, the venerable investment bank J.P. Morgan took EarthWeb public, raising some $29 million despite accumulated losses of $14 million and only $2 million in revenue. Seeing a window opening, theglobe.com's investment bankers at Bear Stearns rushed to market, pricing the shares conservatively at $9. Friday morning, with the issue containing "Up in Smoke" on the presses, the stock opened at $87, climbed to $97, and finally closed at $63.50. It was the biggest first-day IPO gain in history, a distinction it would hold throughout the Internet boom. The company had sold 3.1 million shares and raised $28 million. Its market capitalization was almost $700 million. Its revenues were less than $2 million a year. Its losses were several times its sales.[18]

The meteoric rise seemed ridiculous to many. Internet analysts didn't agree. They said that the company attracted 2 million people a month to its site and had the potential to grow much more quickly than others in the same business. Krizelman, now 25 years old, said he was "euphoric." If the IPO did nothing else, he insisted, it would bring the company needed attention.[19]

California cardiologist George Mitchell didn't share in the excitement. He had considered buying stock in the computer maker Dell after it had first gone public but failed to act and regretted the big gains he had missed. He was determined to buy a high-tech stock. When his wife told him over breakfast that she had heard on television that theglobe.com would skyrocket, he logged on to his online brokerage account and placed an order for 500 shares. He didn't know anything about the company or the way the IPO game was being played. The IPO shares were allocated to select institutions and other favored customers of the underwriter. The amount that was sold was only a fraction of the expected demand, practically guaranteeing a pop in the stock. When the stock soared, those allocated IPO shares took quick profits from the likes of Dr. Mitchell, whose order was executed at $92 a share. He had lost a substantial amount of money by the end of the first day. Eventually the stock would be worthless, but the Internet would own the city's spotlight for the next two years.[20]

Moviefone, a ten-year-old company that had begun by offering movie times and selling movie tickets over the phone, migrated to the web and built a business that covered almost two-thirds of the movie screens in the country and had become so well-known that it was the subject of a *Seinfeld* episode. AOL found Moviefone irresistible and bought it for $388 million in stock. The founding Jarecki family still owned 73 percent, so its members took home $283 million.[21]

Where there was that kind of money to be made, everyone followed. Companies that had already completed their IPOs created what were known as carve-outs, in which they spun off divisions in separate offerings. The market loved it. By early March, 16 more New York companies had filed for IPOs, compared with 39 for all of the previous year. iVillage was a big name, now selling itself as the only web company specializing in information for women, even though it lost $44 million in 1998 on only $15 million in revenue. Another was TheStreet.com website founded by James Cramer, the young Wall Street trader who boasted of his bonuses to the *New York Times* in the early 1980s. By the end of June 1999, 17 New York companies had completed IPOs in just the last four months. Pressure was growing on the holdouts to follow, especially larger ones like Agency.com with its 650 employees, because stock options had become the obsession of Silicon Alley when companies went public. Liberally issued to workers, the options promised easy money for everyone in the Alley when companies went public, crucial since the start-up companies were intense affairs with long hours and often poor working conditions. Top executives felt pressure, too. Since few companies were making money, a constant infusion of capital was required to cope with what was called the burn rate.[22]

Secondary offerings became as frequent as initial ones. It now was understood that the best way to exploit the market was to begin with an IPO that sold only a small percentage of the company's equity. The scarcity boosted the stock price, and secondary offerings were then sold at much higher prices. The ad firm 24/7 Media sold its first secondary offering at $46 a share, almost four times its IPO price of $14. The founders and top executives of Internet companies often used these secondary offerings to begin to cash out when restrictions on such insider sales were lifted, usually 180 days after an IPO. If no such offering was planned, the executives sold shares anyway, claiming they needed to diversify their holdings.[23]

Foreign companies rushed into the city from around the world, and venture capital firms came from the West Coast. "There is great opportunity here because there are so many old line companies that will need to be reinvented on the Internet and so many great operations people," said Adam Dell, the brother of the founder of Dell Computer, who left a venture firm in California to start his own in New York.[24] Longtime New York funds like the Rockefeller family's Venrock joined the rush for Internet deals.

The moneymen decided that with competition so intense, experienced executives were needed to manage the Internet companies, and salaries soared. The former head of California's GeoCities, a bigger version of theglobe.com, received a guaranteed $10 million package when he joined Official Payments Corp. in New York. Average cash compensation jumped by 60 percent to more than $300,000.[25]

Wall Street was no longer the most lucrative place to work in the city. A 34-year-old analyst at Donaldson Lufkin & Jenrette, Tim Weller, joined a start-up called Akami Technologies as chief financial officer. The stock options he was given were soon worth $190 million. He was far from alone. Recruiter Gregg Grossman remembers a partner at Goldman Sachs who left the firm to found an Internet company. As the partner explained to Grossman, it was simple arbitrage. So much money was flooding into the sector that one could do better running an Internet company and taking a piece of that pie than earning a big Wall Street bonus.[26]

If Grossman had doubts about many of the Internet companies he worked with, he believed in DoubleClick. When the recruiter first met executives from the online ad company in 1996, he offered to take his fee in the form of stock options, as he had with other new media companies. No thanks, he was told—they would pay in cash. They were smart, too.[27]

Advertising appeared likely to be a key component of whatever business strategies emerged for the Internet, although in 1997 the total spent on advertising on the web was about $200 million. In June, DoubleClick raised $40 million in venture capital, all from firms in Boston and on the West Coast, since New York funds remained skeptical of online ventures. A little more than six months later, it became the first New York Internet company to go public, raising $60 million. Its stock rose 57 percent in the first day of trading.[28]

DoubleClick spent the money to rapidly expand the business beyond its two mainstays—targeting and delivering online ads and representing websites to advertisers. It first bought out a key competitor for some $500 million and then acquired a treasure of database information by purchasing Abacus Direct Corp. for $1 billion. The theory was that by knowing what products consumers had purchased, DoubleClick would be able to match ads and potential buyers more effectively. It was the company's first big mistake.[29]

Although DoubleClick could not actually match up the information, consumer groups and privacy advocates reacted angrily to the idea, claiming that no one would be safe from a company that had collected so much information and could spy on consumers so effectively. The storm intensified when the company said it would merge its online and offline databases. Despite efforts to reassure regulators, led by then President Kevin Ryan, it took DoubleClick almost two years to end the controversy, when the Federal Trade Commission ruled it had not violated consumer privacy.[30]

In the meantime, Internet advertising had soared to $1 billion a year, and DoubleClick was the biggest player in the business—it represented about half of the biggest websites, placed ads for many of the nation's major corporations, provided email marketing, and sold information from its huge database. Revenue in 2000 almost doubled to $506 million, and the company claimed on a pro forma basis to be break-even, although according to normal accounting rules it lost $13 million.[31]

DoubleClick had become so much the face of the city's new media sector that its search for a new headquarters attracted enormous attention, especially when the company dropped hints that it was also considering moving to New Jersey. It zeroed in on a large office building on the far West Side known mostly for the skating rink on its 16th floor. DoubleClick signed a lease to take 150,000 square feet to accommodate its explosive growth, aided by $5 million in city incentives and tax breaks, the first such concessions given to an Internet company. It publicized its plans to make one part of the rooftop into a gathering site, which would wind up being a place to drink and unwind, and another part into a basketball court—all very New Economy perks for its workforce.[32]

"When we were at DoubleClick many people had very little experience as senior managers or executives," says Melanie Hughes, head of human resources for Ryan at DoubleClick and then again for him at Gilt. She remembers that, in its heyday, the average age of employees was about 26 and an excitement that was palpable. "There was a playfulness around DoubleClick; there were a couple of parties a week on the outdoor deck, people went out during the day to play basketball. It was all part of the irrational exuberance," she says.[33]

Other advertising-oriented Internet companies established increasingly secure footholds as well. 24/7 Media ran three major ad networks that comprised more than 100 websites, a rival to DoubleClick's original business. Razorfish emerged as one of the best web design firms. AdOne Network created a way to distribute classified ads.

Ryan, now the company's chief executive, was convinced as ever that the Internet would be the most important development in his lifetime, but the frenzy surrounding this fledgling industry made him nervous. DoubleClick's stock had soared from $40 early in 1999 to $135 later in the year and continued to be volatile. One day in early 2000, while skiing in the French Alps, Ryan learned that the firm's market capitalization had soared $1 billion without any news to drive up the stock. He decided to take advantage to raise as much money as he could to bolster the company for the shakeout he was sure would come. His belief in the Internet's future was vindicated when online ads skyrocketed to $50 billion in 2011. His fear that the stock mania could not last was also justified.

The city now had a rival to Wall Street. In a study conducted for the now well-known New York New Media Association, PriceWaterhouseCoopers reported early in 2000 that the new media industry had created almost 140,000 jobs in New York City, two-thirds of them full-time positions, up from 27,000 jobs in 1995. It counted 3,800 companies, which had raised $6 billion in venture funding and IPO proceeds in six years, boasted $10 billion in yearly revenues, and paid out more than $8 billion in salaries.[34]

Internet companies, often now labeled dot-coms, had accounted for a quarter of all the office space leased in Manhattan, surpassing finance companies for the first time. The industry spilled out from Silicon Alley into the Garment District. Landlords whose buildings were located on the avenues, and therefore not bound by the special zoning restrictions, ousted their apparel tenants paying $10 a square foot to sign up new media firms at more than double that amount. The Starrett-Lehigh Building, a former railroad warehouse on 26th Street, accelerated its conversion to office use when space-hungry Internet firms agreed to snap up more than a third of its space at rents as high as $30 a square foot.[35]

Large PR firms, accountants, and real estate brokers all established new units specializing in new media. Small firms found themselves abandoning their former specialties to concentrate on the fastest-growing sector of the economy. Nonprofits, fixated by a report that the 20 richest new media executives were worth $3.9 billion, started honoring executives like Candice Carpenter and Jon Diamond of N2K. They were disappointed with the results. Internet executives were too focused on their businesses to care much about philanthropic endeavors, and their paper wealth was not liquid enough to result in big contributions.[36]

The biggest winner of all was ironically the very traditional media companies that were supposedly going to be driven out of business by the online upstarts. Internet companies simply couldn't spend all the money they raised in venture capital, IPOs, and secondary offerings on technology or staff. So, following the example of theglobe.com, they poured it into old-fashioned brand advertising on network television, national magazines, and newspapers. A Silicon Alley company named the Mining Co. spent $10 million on ads on TV, on the radio, and in the *Wall Street Journal* and the *New York Times* to announce its name change to About.com. HotJobs received worldwide attention when it plunked down $2 million for a single ad during the 1999 Super Bowl.[37]

Wall Street was the other major beneficiary. Bonuses in 1999 rose by almost a third. Executive recruiter Alan Johnson's survey said that at least 75 people would take home more than $10 million and that the number of investment bankers and traders making $1 million would total 2,000. The people who ran Wall Street companies did even better. Merrill Lynch's David Komansky, who had linked his leadership to Blodget in a very public way, was paid $29.3 million in cash, bonus, stock, and options, a lot more than the $3.1 million that brought Salomon's John Gutfreund such notoriety in the late 1980s. The two co-chiefs of Morgan Stanley weren't far behind, at $26 million.[38]

The renowned jeweler Harry Winston decided to go where the money was. It rented a restaurant in the Financial District and invited several hundred young and single Wall Streeters—mostly men—to peruse diamond-encrusted watches, five-carat engagement rings, and $175,000 princess necklaces, hoping to convince a few to part with a portion of their bonuses.[39]

Once again, New York was booming. Rents for office space began rising in tandem with the growth of Internet firms and accelerated as Wall Street firms sought even more space. First, the costs in the city's best Class A properties moved up, forcing many firms to relocate to side streets in older so-called Class B buildings. Then the rents jumped in those buildings. The frenzied nature of the market was clear in 2000, when the average office rent for Manhattan soared 33 percent to $50 a square foot, about double where it was when Giuliani took office.[40]

The residential market reflected the good times as well. Brothers William Lie and Arthur Zeckendorf, sons of one of the city's most storied real estate builders, broke ground in 1998 for a new tower at 515 Park Avenue, where they expected to sell condominiums at $1,500 a square foot, one-third higher than the going rate for new luxury condos. The average apartment that year cost $531,000, up 20 percent in the previous 12 months. The increases were so great that even Internet entrepreneurs like DoubleClick's Kevin O'Connor decided that he wanted a more reasonable price by relocating to the less trendy Upper West Side.[41]

In the fall of 1999, more than 50 new upscale restaurants opened in Manhattan, and the famous *Zagat* survey said it would add 300 new eateries when its guide was published early the next year. The sums needed to enter the business became very large—Métrazur, an Italian eatery in Grand Central Terminal, cost $5 million to open—but the experts insisted this boom was different than the one that swept the city in the late 1980s. "In the Eighties everyone and their uncle thought they could open a restaurant. This boom is mostly professionals," said restaurant consultant Clark Wolf.[42]

The city's arts and cultural organizations thrived. More than three-quarters saw their attendance rise, and almost as many reported fund-raising gains that year. Eight new institutions were chartered to join the 106 already open in the city, with more on the way, including the Museum of Sex, a home for German and Austrian art sponsored by cosmetics heir Ronald Lauder, and a fire museum at Rockefeller Center.[43]

The boom seemed to show that President Ronald Reagan's idea of trickle-down economics could work, at least in New York. Shortages of qualified workers began appearing in 1997, and companies began increasing pay despite an unemployment rate of more than 9 percent. Restaurants were among the first to feel the pressure, and the Oyster Bar in Grand Central raised the salary of assistant managers above $30,000, up a third in just two years. Fast-food places were swept up in the competition. A recruiter said a store manager in Manhattan now could expect to make $45,000 a year; in Minneapolis, a manager would have to oversee several stores for that kind of money. Waiters at the city's best restaurants like the steak house Smith & Wollensky took home $100,000, including their lucrative tips. Placement firms reported administrative assistants had cracked the $50,000 barrier, and accounting and other professional service firms began emulating the tech companies with signing bonuses, although these were in cash, not stock options.[44]

While construction activity did not rival the tax- and incentive-spurred 1980s, it was robust, with 15 office towers and 50 residential buildings under way. Every unionized electrician was working, and contractors said they needed 1,500 more to keep up with demand. Overtime was the only solution for those workers and many other trades.[45]

In all, New York City added a record 281,000 jobs between 1998 and 2000. More New York City residents were working than at any other time since the Fiscal Crisis of the 1970s. All the losses of the 1987–1993 recession had been overcome. The total wages paid in the city soared by a third. Total Wall Street compensation rose by an incredible 68 percent over those three years, and for the first time, securities workers accounted for more than 20 percent of income in the city, even though they were only 5 percent of the workforce. Job growth would have been even larger if there had been any place to put the people needed at securities, professional service, and media-related companies.

The problem wasn't that the city, or even Manhattan, had been completely developed. Large areas along the waterfront that had once been crowded with factories were now abandoned or hopelessly underutilized. The intense effort begun in the Koch administration to develop parts of commercial areas in Brooklyn and Queens as an alternative to pricey Manhattan achieved modest success. But it was mostly stymied because those areas were only marginally cost competitive with the suburban alternatives for back-office jobs and simply undesirable for the higher-level and better-paying professional jobs.

Instead, a strip of land along the Hudson River in New Jersey emerged as the prime destination for companies that couldn't find space in Manhattan. The cost of building was lower and the tax savings were bigger. For companies whose main operations were downtown, the PATH mass transit system provided a one-stop connection to Lower Manhattan. Merrill Lynch closed on a parcel for a major office building where Colgate-Palmolive had once made toothpaste. Goldman Sachs announced plans to build the tallest building in the state. Chase Manhattan Bank, the institution that in the 1980s moved some 5,000 workers to Brooklyn instead of New Jersey, signed a lease to put thousands of employees in two new office towers at a development called Newport.[46]

New York senator Charles Schumer, who was much more active in local economic issues than most US senators, convened a group of prominent business leaders to figure out a way to keep those jobs in New York. At the same time, private equity executive Dan Doctoroff came to understand how the potential of the city's economy was hamstrung by the huge tracts still reserved for manufacturing as he developed his plan to bring the 2012 Olympics to New York.[47] Then the Internet bubble burst, Wall Street contracted, the city entered a recession, and terrorists brought down the World Trade Center towers.

CHAPTER 9

THE FORGOTTEN
RECESSION

EACH BUBBLE HAS A TRAJECTORY ALL ITS OWN, AL-
though none may ever top the Internet stock craze of late 1999 and
early 2000. The technology-dominated Nasdaq composite index, the
best measure of Internet stocks, first moved past 3,000 in late October
1999. Four months later, it broke through 5,000. In the first week of
March, it rose 7.1 percent, and an equity strategist at J.P. Morgan said
that so much money was flowing into high-tech mutual funds that the
index was likely to move higher.

Not all stocks shared in the mania, especially some of the best-
known new media companies in New York. Theglobe.com, whose first-
day IPO rise marked the beginning of the bubble, had fallen to $7 a
share in February 2000 amid doubts about its strategy and the abilities
of its two very young founders. One-third of the city's 43 publicly held
web start-ups were trading below their offering price, including iVillage,
which had lost $93 million in the previous year and had only enough
money for one more year at its current burn rate.[1]

The Nasdaq set a record on Friday, March 10, when it inched up
to 5,049. It then lost 9 percent of its value in the first three trading
days of the next week. Boosters of tech stocks believed it would be a

temporary setback—at least for most Internet companies. Thirty-four-year-old Matthew Johnson, the chief Nasdaq trader at Lehman Brothers, tried to puncture the idea of a bubble. "Nothing about the market worries me except the speculation that has been taking place within the Bulletin Board in penny stocks," he insisted. "I don't consider what has taken place within Nasdaq to be speculation. It reflects the promise of tomorrow and the belief that this is a technology revolution that will change the world economy."[2]

By the end of the month, the Nasdaq had fallen 10 percent, the definition of a correction. By the end of May, the index traded around 3,400. Tech stocks rallied over the summer but retreated again in the fall, beginning an almost uninterrupted decline that bottomed out with the Nasdaq barely above 1,100 at the end of September 2002.

The 20 New York companies that had filed for IPOs but had not gone to market now had no way to raise the capital they needed.[3] Other companies faced delisting from Nasdaq because they couldn't maintain a stock price of higher than $1 a share, including iVillage and the advertising companies Razorfish and 24/7 Media, whose stock had fallen from $50 a share in just one year.[4]

Candice Carpenter was replaced at iVillage by a veteran of the television industry. A 54-year-old former Marine and veteran of consumer product companies Xerox and Viacom took over from the Cornell whiz kids Stephan Paternot and Todd Krizelman at theglobe.com. Its stock was now worth less than $2 a share, it had lost $10 million in just three months, more than it took in revenue, and it had only $32 million left in reserve. Unfortunately, more experienced executives had no answers for the dilemma—unprofitable companies couldn't survive without more capital.[5]

Repeated waves of layoffs swept through Silicon Alley. Those let go first were able to find jobs with other Internet firms, at least for a while. In the end, few survived. Emily Liu had joined the delivery company Kozmo.com and soon found herself working directly with the company's top executives, a heady experience for someone just beginning her career. She remained loyal through five rounds of cutbacks until she lost her job in the spring of 2001, when the firm liquidated.[6] Landlords who had filled so much space with new media firms now rushed to protect themselves. They would not agree to leases until Internet companies could post two years' rent in security.

The end to theglobe.com came in the summer of 2001, when it shut down its websites, claiming to be the victim of a weak online advertising market. The stock traded the day it announced it was closing at 13.5 cents. The vast majority of Internet companies succumbed to a similar fate.[7]

A few months later, the *Silicon Alley Reporter*, which had been the chronicler and booster of the industry that shared its name, shut down. "The story's over," said publisher Jason McCabe Calacanis. With the city now focused on the aftermath of the September 11 terrorist attacks, Silicon Alley faded from view.[12]

Yet the first company to go public and the most prominent face of Silicon Alley did not disappear. Bolstered by the proceeds of the stock sale CEO Kevin Ryan had decided on the day he was skiing in France, DoubleClick persevered even as Internet advertising declined. It was forced into waves of layoffs to survive and tried to reduce its reliance on Internet advertising by developing email marketing and other sources of revenue.[8]

With Internet advertising growing again in 2005, private equity firms decided that DoubleClick, trading around $7 a share, was undervalued.[9] Ryan and other top executives opposed a sale, believing the company's value would rise sharply in the next few years, but its board didn't share their optimism and agreed to sell the company to the San Francisco buyout firm Hellman & Friedman for about $1.1 billion.[10] Almost exactly two years later, Hellman sold a revamped DoubleClick, refocused on web advertising, to Google for $3.1 billion. The deal would lay the foundation for the rebirth of the Internet sector in New York.[11]

While tech stocks sent the Nasdaq index plunging, the Dow Jones Industrial Average of 30 blue-chip stocks and the Standard & Poor's 500 index of large companies declined only modestly. Wall Street clung to the belief that nothing had fundamentally changed for it.

The few firms that did cut back—like Merrill Lynch—found themselves criticized for panicking. Offers remained plentiful for those who lost their jobs, even those who had worked in the technology sector or those caught in a wave of securities firm mergers.[13] The Swiss bank UBS paid $12 billion in the summer of 2000 to buy the midlevel securities firm PaineWebber, a shockingly high price.[14] Lehman Brothers even allocated $450 million for additional hires to take advantage of the talent available.[15]

Profits were still strong, boosted by pre-Nasdaq crash deals. Despite a weak fourth quarter, most firms reported higher profits for 2000 than the previous year. That translated into bigger paychecks. Tech analyst Frank Quattrone renegotiated his deal with CSFB so that he could make as much as $30 million a year. The number of $1 million bonuses doubled again to 4,000, said Wall Street expert Alan Johnson, who estimated average bonuses would increase by 25 percent. The first estimate of the total from an official source—the state comptroller—put the payout at $13.3 billion.[16]

Yet the warnings signs were everywhere. Mergers and acquisitions activity and stock and bond underwriting had seesawed all year. As 2001 began, the national economy seemed to be weakening. In March, exactly a year after the tech crash, investors decided it was time to get out. Both the S&P and the Dow fell sharply. The S&P hit bear market territory—a loss of more than 20 percent from its peak—on March 12. The Dow fell below 10,000 two days later, two years to the month after it first broke through that barrier on its way to 11,723.

With trading by individual investors falling fast, discount brokers like Quick & Reilly, online brokers, and their imitators at the larger firms like J.P. Morgan Chase began cutting back. Firms that were also-rans in specific businesses jettisoned whole units, as Prudential Securities did when it shut down its investment banking and institutional bond operations.[17] By the time the bear market was officially inaugurated, Wall Street firms had announced the axing of 10,000 jobs.

Some of the biggest cuts had come at Merrill Lynch, where new brokerage chief Stanley O'Neal was determined to rein in costs, a move that would convince the board to name him David Komansky's successor as chief executive. By the late summer, it was clear that Wall Street's retrenchment was far greater than anyone had expected. J.P. Morgan

Chase's layoffs climbed to 8,000, and Citigroup passed 4,700. No longer were just lower-level executives and traders let go; even top investment bankers were put out on the street.[18]

By the end of the year, Wall Street had slashed its payroll, which had hit a record 200,000 in the city in 2000, by some 33,000 jobs, a far sharper ax than had been used after Black Monday in 1987. The impact on the city followed the pattern of 1969 and 1987 once again.[19]

⊷ ⊶

WHILE TECH IMPLODED and Wall Street contracted, the turbulent tenure of Rudy Giuliani was drawing to an ironic close. Repeating the experience of Ed Koch before him, Giuliani had been unable to resist the tax revenues produced by a Wall Street boom. The once-strident conservative allowed the city's budget to increase rapidly in the year he ran for reelection and throughout the second term. The city's payroll grew again, finally passing the total he inherited from David Dinkins.

Following Bill Bratton's ouster, Giuliani installed longtime friend Howard Safir as police commissioner and then Bernard Kerik, who had once been his driver. Neither ever overshadowed their boss, although Kerik's dealings with Mob-connected contractors eventually landed him in jail and tarnished Giuliani. The strategies that had been put in place were so effective that the crime rate continued to decline precipitously. Giuliani's defense of all police actions, including the shooting of an unarmed African immigrant in the Bronx named Amadou Diallo, exacerbated his already tense relationships with minority communities.

His administration attempted to provide space for the economy to grow by rezoning manufacturing areas first for big box retailers and then for office use, but neither plan succeeded. The administration tried to stem the loss of jobs to New Jersey and elsewhere with big tax breaks for companies claiming to be considering relocation, with some success. Giuliani's development obsession was sports stadiums. He first tried to figure out how to build a baseball stadium for his beloved New York Yankees on the West Side. When opposition proved too intense, he worked to finance a new facility adjacent to the team's current one in the Bronx. He backed a stadium with a retractable roof for the Mets in Queens. He intensified his effort as his second term drew to a close, fearful that his successor might not be as passionate about baseball as he was.[20]

His once-loyal supporters in the business community had been alienated by a series of disputes that stemmed from his insistence that he control everything that happened and be the only one to get credit for the Administration's achievements. Business improvement districts (BIDs) were established when a majority of the property owners in a commercial district agreed to pay an extra real estate assessment to provide sanitation and security services. When the mayor clashed with the leadership of the largest BID, the Grand Central Partnership, over whether that BID would aid in the renovation of Grand Central, he punished that and every other BID by denying increases in their assessment. BIDs would do his bidding or suffer.[21]

To the consternation of the city's hotel and tourism executives, the mayor ordered them to name his press secretary as head of the agency, even though she had no experience. The move was prompted by a demand from the mayor's wife, who believed Cristyne Lategano had conducted an affair with the mayor.[22] The mayor feuded with the Port Authority of New York, claiming that their operation of the city's airports was inept, and he sought to find ways to wrest control back for the city. When a heat wave led to a blackout in some of the city's poorest neighborhoods, Giuliani lambasted ConEd publicly, noting that it was an entity beyond control of the mayor and claiming that it ignored city officials.[23]

Most business leaders kept their criticisms private, seeing no point in being subject to the retribution the mayor could deliver. *Crain's* publisher Alair Townsend became their voice. In a column headlined "If Budget Chief Worked for Koch, He'd Be Out Looking for a Job," she criticized Giuliani's director of the Office of Management and Budget for calling executives who underwrote city bonds to tell them not to support the Citizens Budget Commission.[24] The CBC had committed the sin of criticizing some elements of the mayor's budgets. In another piece, she defended the right of the Brooklyn Museum to show a painting of the Virgin Mary that Giuliani incorrectly described as showing excrement splattered over the image. She chastised the mayor for cancelling a city grant to the New York Historical Society when it had the gall to ask Bratton to speak at an event.[25]

The mayor's unhappiness with the CBC, the nonpartisan, business-funded watchdog group that had exposed the city's budget chicanery long before the Fiscal Crisis, was particularly illuminating. The CBC understood how much Giuliani had abandoned his promises of smaller government. With Wall Street pay soaring, personal income taxes sky-rocketed 62 percent during Giuliani's two terms in office. His final budget was just shy of $40 billion, 25 percent higher than his first. He had cut taxes modestly, $500 million in the last budget, but the city had become more competitive economically because Governor George Pataki had pushed through a much larger reduction in state income taxes.[26]

In 2000, the last year of the boom, the city added an extraordinary 102,000 jobs.[27] In all, the city had increased employment by 432,000 during the Giuliani era, and the total of 3.7 million jobs eclipsed the 1987 peak and was just a few thousand shy of the 1969 record. The city's credit was now rated A3, the highest in a decade.[28]

The national downturn that had begun after the Internet bust took a toll on other sectors the following year, when business travel weakened. By the spring of 2001, occupancy rates had fallen by 10 percent. When tourists began putting off trips as well, rates plunged, especially at luxury hotels. A room at the city's most expensive hotel, the St. Regis, was available for $390 a night, a little more than half the $714 it charged in 2000.[29]

The disappearance of tech firms had not been noticed at first as banks, securities firms, and law firms continued to seek additional space. They shelved those plans early in 2001, and worried companies put 9 million square feet up for sublease, compared with 2 million square feet the previous year, and slashed asking prices as well. Plans for three speculative office buildings on 42nd Street were scrapped. Experts warned that residential prices would be the next to fall. After all, prices in Manhattan had increased 68 percent in the last six years, while income had risen only 24 percent.[30] If Wall Streeters weren't buying, others couldn't afford the lofty prices.

Crain's New York Business even found a silver lining to the gathering dark clouds. Executives they sampled were taking off more time than usual over the summer because there wasn't as much business to attend to.[31]

By primary day, September 11, 2001, Mayor Giuliani had receded from the spotlight after a tumultuous year. It had been excruciating for him: he had challenged First Lady Hillary Clinton in a race for a US Senate seat from New York, admitted he was involved with a woman named Judith Nathan, announced he had developed prostate cancer, separated from his wife, and withdrew from the Senate race. While many were glad that his time in office was ending, he remained popular. In June, the Marist poll showed that 57 percent rated his performance as excellent or good.[32]

Four Democrats had entered the race to succeed Giuliani—Public Advocate Mark Green, City Comptroller Alan Hevesi, Council Speaker Peter Vallone, and Bronx Borough President Fernando Ferrer, the lone minority. The economy failed to get any attention, just as in 1989. Improving the city's educational system was the top issue, with several candidates endorsing various kinds of tax increases to provide more money to schools. In the last weeks of the campaign, Ferrer surged and Hevesi and Vallone faded.[33]

On the Republican side, the billionaire Michael Bloomberg loomed as the heavy favorite against a former Democrat and longtime politician, Herman Badillo. Once a Wall Street executive, Bloomberg had been fired from Salomon Brothers and invested his $10 million severance in the information and media company that bore his name. Bloomberg LP dominated the business of providing information for Wall Street and was growing as a media force as well.

The city woke up that morning to a beautiful late summer day.

CHAPTER 10
DISASTER STRIKES

THE TERRORIST ATTACKS OF SEPTEMBER 11, 2001, KILLED 2,753 people in the city's Financial District,[1] destroyed 13.4 million square feet of office space at the World Trade Center and damaged another 17 million square feet nearby,[2] disrupted the city's economy, vaulted Rudy Giuliani into the national spotlight, and shook New Yorkers' confidence in their future.

The attacks were a watershed for the country and the world, sending the United States into two costly wars on the Asian landmass and launching a permanent war on terror that fundamentally changed the nation's priorities. Ironically, this was far less true in New York, especially economically. The attacks did not alter the broad forces determining the city's future, with one important exception: the election of Michael Bloomberg as mayor.

As New Yorkers counted and mourned the dead, the most immediate economic task was the reopening of the New York Stock Exchange, which had delayed trading as the planes struck the Twin Towers and remained closed for the rest of the week. Trading became a symbol of the city's ability to recover. The work required was enormous, but the Exchange reopened on Monday, and the plunge in stock prices—7.1 percent in the Dow Jones Industrial Average—was actually cheered, since many had expected far worse.[3]

The scores of displaced downtown firms rushed to find homes for their workers. In ten days, they signed leases for 5.5 million square feet of office space, mostly in Midtown. Lehman Brothers took over the Sheraton Manhattan hotel, which didn't have any guests arriving anyway. Others went to the suburbs.[4]

The impact radiated quickly. Tom Cat Bakery in Long Island City cut its 177 employees' hours by 20 percent; four of its biggest customers were hotels destroyed or shut down by the attacks.[5] Restaurants were empty. Nonprofits not directly involved in World Trade Center relief saw donations plunge.[6]

No one knew how long the disruption would last, but many people assumed the worst. Real estate experts said that the Midtown vacancy rate would decline and rents rise as companies relocated there.[7] Developers accelerated plans for new office buildings, including work being done on the Port Authority Bus Terminal so that a 1.3 million-square-foot office building could be built above it.[8]

But New York could not recover by itself, government officials thought. Senator Charles Schumer went to President George W. Bush to ask for billions of dollars. "How much do you want?" the president asked the senator, in a story Schumer often told later. "Twenty billion dollars," the senator replied, a figure he admitted he had simply pulled out of the air.[9]

The gloom deepened. Tourism was devastated by the sharp decline in air travel. When a terrorist alert was issued six days before the New York City Marathon, foreign runners bailed out. Even some doctors and nurses who had volunteered to man medical stations failed to show up, spooked by the alert's specific warning about bridges, which were key landmarks on the course. In all, more than 5,000 runners simply didn't start the race, and only 24,000 finished the race, the lowest number since 1990.[10] Wall Street had already been retrenching as a result of the tech crash, and the market plunge shook investor confidence even more. Securities firms saw their revenues decline even as the disruption increased their costs. Bonuses were clearly going to suffer.[11] New Yorkers hunkered down, and retailers predicted a bleak holiday season.[12]

Despite the anxiety, many of the downtown area's most important institutions never considered leaving. Incoming New York University (NYU) president John Sexton addressed a meeting of the school's deans in the days after the attack. From now on, he told them, we will be known as *the* New York University. It was both his affirmation of NYU's commitment to the city and recognition that the school, whose enrollment and reputation were in ascent, really had no choice but to hope the city would survive and thrive.[13]

The most telling sign of what was unfolding came from the city's real estate market. Confounding the experts, the Midtown vacancy rate rose to 8.6 percent at the end of October, despite the fact that relocating companies from downtown had taken almost 4 million square feet.[14] It turned out that companies had overcommitted to space during the boom years. The recession, combined with the implosion of the Internet companies, meant there were still millions of square feet of available space. For all the focus on the attacks, other, more powerful forces were shaping the city's economy.

When the planes struck, voters were just beginning to trek to the polls to vote in primary elections for mayor. Bronx Borough president Fernando Ferrer was believed to be closing the gap on front-runner Mark Green, the city's public advocate. Billionaire businessman Michael Bloomberg was widely expected to defeat a weak challenge from former Democrat Herman Badillo.[15] After some initial confusion, the election was called off and rescheduled for two weeks later.

All the candidates were professional politicians except one, Bloomberg, whose rise as the city's most successful self-made man could be traced to his years at Salomon Brothers and to Paul Volcker's efforts to break runaway inflation. In a way, the most important politician of modern New York owed his success to the city's first modern Wall Street firm.[16]

Raised in Medford, Massachusetts, Bloomberg was an indifferent student, bored by his unchallenging high school, but an exceptional Boy Scout, completing the requirements for its highest level, Eagle Scout, a year before he was even old enough to be awarded it. He was so proud

of the achievement that he always brought it up when he appointed
anyone to his administration who was also an Eagle Scout. He was an
equally undistinguished student at Johns Hopkins until a late sprint to
impress graduate schools. It was at the Harvard Business School that his
already substantial self-confidence received a boost. He found his classmates, many well connected and from famous families, to be decidedly
unimpressive.[17]

Graduating as the Vietnam War raged, he planned to enter officer candidate school rather than be drafted, but he failed the physical
because of flat feet and headed off to Wall Street because it sounded
interesting. He spurned Goldman Sachs, which he thought stuffy, but
accepted a job offer from Salomon Brothers, which he joined in 1966 as
its first Harvard MBA.

Bloomberg did well enough as an equities trader, but he made some
important enemies without establishing strong ties to any equally powerful allies. He was pushed aside to the company's information services
department. Loyal to Salomon and having become a new father, he
stayed rather than seek a new job. He had already done some work
on his own time to improve the information provided by the standard
Wall Street Quotron information terminal. Now, using his knowledge of
what traders needed, he greatly enhanced Quotron's computer screens
by imbuing them with the ability to compare various scenarios for the
stocks and bonds they traded. They were called B-pages. Salomon's top
executives didn't see much value in his work, and shortly after the firm
merged with Philbro and became publicly held, he was fired—although
he walked away with $10 million in severance, which would be more
than $30 million today.

He took $300,000 of that money and founded Innovative Market-
ing Systems in 1982 to improve on his Salomon product, eventually
pouring much of his severance into the company, which was later re-
named Bloomberg LP. When Paul Volcker freed interest rates and bond
prices became volatile, traders needed easy access to the information
Bloomberg had assembled, and the company's success was ensured.

By 1997, he was bored again, divorced, incredibly rich, and full of
the same self-confidence that had served him so well. He was also in-

terested in running for mayor. The field of potential candidates seemed underwhelming. He began studying the city, much as Rudy Giuliani had after his first defeat by David Dinkins; redirecting his charitable contributions to local institutions and increasing them by millions of dollars; and cultivating personal relationships with the powerful and famous. A lifelong Democrat, he was told he could never win a Democratic primary, so he became a Republican a year before the election.

He already had strong views about the city, its economy, and the role business should play. Opening an economic forecast session that included Crain's editors at his company's then-cramped headquarters on Third Avenue, he took direct aim at the Giuliani policy of providing big tax breaks to companies to keep them from leaving. Companies that located elsewhere wouldn't be missed, he said, because they wouldn't attract the talent they needed to compete. The city shouldn't waste money on such second-class operations. It didn't seem to matter that he had built a major operation in Princeton, New Jersey, for his own company and found plenty of good people to work there. His company later arranged incentives for its move to a new office tower nearby on Lexington Avenue, which he decided to forego only after being elected mayor.

At first, he wasn't taken seriously. It wasn't until November 2000 that the *New York Times* even mentioned that he might be a candidate,[18] although he had first raised the possibility in a 1997 interview about the publication of his autobiography, and the tabloids and gossip columnists had been floating the idea for more than a year. Business people didn't line up behind him either. The city's leading real estate developers and landlords arranged to donate the maximum amount to all four of the Democratic candidates. Investment banker Dan Doctoroff, working tirelessly to bring the 2012 Olympics to the city, remembers that he gave to several of the Democratic candidates even though Bloomberg was a key member of the board of the Olympics effort. Doctoroff assumed that one of the Democrats would win. "Interesting guy, interesting life, but it's very hard for a Republican to win when there has not been a cataclysmic event," concluded the acerbic political consultant Hank Sheinkopf—a comment more prescient than he could have ever known.[19]

By that point, voters were tired of Rudy Giuliani, or so went the conventional political wisdom. With a huge registration edge, one of the Democrats would recapture City Hall. Democrats themselves acted as if Giuliani's first victory had been an accident caused by a weak Democratic candidate, and the second merely an example of the power of incumbency. But a Bloomberg focus group in December 2000 suggested that voters didn't agree. The billionaire businessman was almost as well-known as the longtime politicians running on the Democratic side. The voters wanted someone gentler than Giuliani, but still a good manager, a fiscal conservative, someone they could trust on crime. Those were not the strengths of the Democrats. Bloomberg portrayed himself as the candidate who would continue the best of Giuliani and jettison the worst. He emphasized his experience as a successful businessman and placed particular emphasis on his commitment to improve the public schools.

The attacks turned the political equation upside down. Ferrer led the primary two weeks later but failed to win the required 40 percent to avoid a runoff. It was assumed that Mark Green would win the second vote because he would inherit the bulk of the votes from the two eliminated candidates.[20] Meanwhile, Giuliani sought to remain in office for three months beyond the end of his term to handle the crisis, a request Green agreed to and Ferrer summarily rejected. The move backfired on Green, hurting him badly with African-American voters, who were Giuliani's most implacable opponents. Green did win the runoff, using increasingly harsh and racially tinged ads against Ferrer, but he was fatally weakened by his overt political calculations and his alienation of minority leaders.[21]

The campaign, when it resumed, was conducted in the shadows of the attacks and the sudden emergence of Rudy Giuliani as the city's savior. The controversial and divisive political figure who had worn out his welcome was suddenly replaced by "America's mayor," whose calm and determined response to the attacks was just what New Yorkers needed.

Carl Weisbrod, then head of the Downtown Alliance business improvement district and a key participant in the efforts to stabilize the area after the attacks, saw Rudy's appeal first hand as he traveled around the country in the next two years to discuss how New York had handled the crisis. In each city where he spoke, he would meet at least one person who would tell him that the problem their city faced was that it lacked a leader like Giuliani. "I always responded that there are different styles of leadership for different times," he recalls. "Giuliani was a great leader in that he filled a power vacuum when no one else knew what to do. He was willing to make decisions, not always the right ones, but at least he was prepared to make them. As was his wont, he pulled power into himself. That was fine for the time. It also wore thin rather quickly."[22]

It wasn't long before Giuliani's clout waned. He failed to get the $20 billion in federal aid funneled to the city rather than the state, and the rebuilding of the Trade Center was turned over to the state as well. His effort to remain in office died quickly. But when he endorsed Bloomberg in late October, his popularity was at its peak and his imprimatur indispensable. Bloomberg spent $74 million of his own money on the campaign, and his unprecedented ad buys were extremely effective. He also did particularly well in a debate in the days before the election, saying that the city itself could deal with a growing budget deficit without additional help from Washington. He said the private sector would rebuild the economy, and he ruled out a tax increase.

The 59-year-old Bloomberg won by about 30,000 votes. In many ways, his election was the most important consequence of the September 11 terrorist attacks for New York City.

Whatever went wrong in 2002—and a lot did—was blamed on September 11. It took longer to reopen damaged buildings downtown than expected. The *Wall Street Journal* didn't move back to its home at the World Financial Center, across from where the towers stood, for almost a year.[23] Getting into and out of downtown was difficult. Despite the early thought that September 11 would require new construction, building across the city plunged as project after project, including the tower above the Port Authority Bus Terminal, was put on hold because the economy was contracting so quickly.

Wall Street continued to retrench, not because of the terrorist attacks but because business was weak. Mergers and acquisition activity plunged early in the year,[24] and layoffs mounted.[25] Lehman Brothers, whose bond business had initially remained strong, joined its rivals in

the spring with its first downsizing in five years. As in previous downturns, securities firms abandoned whole areas. This time junk bond units
were first on the list.[26] The biggest worry was that the terrorist attacks
would force the industry to spread out geographically. Consultants publicly advised the firms to do just that, claiming that technology meant
that no one needed to be physically near anyone else. Federal regulators
echoed the suggestion.[27]

Hardest hit were small businesses, especially those located in Lower
Manhattan. Few had business interruption insurance to cover their losses
or cash reserves to tide them over. Emergency loans were available, especially from the Small Business Administration, but they required col-
lateral, and many business owners were not confident enough to risk
assets like their homes.[28]

Apparel manufacturing was devastated. The orderly decline planned
by city officials who instituted special zoning in the Garment District
turned into a rout. The zoning was of no help, because the transportation disruptions from the attack made life impossible for the factories
that had congregated in Chinatown, outside the protected area. Between
2000 and 2002, 19,000 apparel factory jobs disappeared, almost a third
of the total.[29]

The torrent of red ink in the city budget deepened the gloom. Tax
revenues plunged after the attacks, a fact attributed primarily to September 11 and the recession, leaving the city with an almost $5 billion deficit
to close in the budget for the year that began July 1. At first, Mayor
Bloomberg stuck to his campaign promises. He balanced the budget for
the coming year by cutting spending, paring back the capital plan in part
by eliminating the baseball stadiums Giuliani had proposed,[30] imposing new cigarette and other nuisance taxes, and borrowing $1.5 billion.
While critics pointed out the parallels to the discredited maneuvers of
the 1970s, Bloomberg's supporters claimed the move was justified as a
reasonable response to an extraordinary event.[31]

The mayor's calm and determined approach won him plaudits, even
as he took controversial steps such as banning smoking in every bar and
restaurant and in offices. The city's fiscal health did not improve, however, and despite the budget cuts and borrowing, the budget for the year

was projected to fall $1 billion short of revenues and the budget for the next year to be at least $4 billion in the red.[32] The Bloomberg who had said tax increases would drive residents and businesses to leave the city now had a new mantra. "The law requires us to have a balanced budget. Period," he said in October, when he first raised the prospect of higher taxes. "And those who think we can cut $5 billion out of expenses just have absolutely no idea how this city works. You could not do that under any stretch of the imagination."[33]

His solution shocked those who had supported him—a 25 percent increase in property taxes,[34] the largest in the city's history; a request that Albany reinstitute the commuter tax it had eliminated in 1999[35]; and a series of spending reductions.[36] In all, his proposal called for more than $4 billion in new revenue.[37] It also underscored the mayor's philosophy about how he would manage the city. The Bloomberg administration would preserve the city's quality of life, not only with the police and a commitment to stay tough on crime, but extending to other services and to the social safety net that New York provided. It was the quality of life that was the bedrock of the economy. If that meant New York taxes were high, it was a cost that could be borne. New York was a premium product, he said, and wasn't for everyone. That philosophy would be at the heart of his administration for all three terms. Anytime he or one of his aides discussed their strategy for the economy, they started off by saying a strong economy began with improving the quality of life in the city.

But whatever statewide political goodwill had existed after the attacks had dissipated, at least in the suburbs, and the state legislature rejected the commuter tax. That turned the attention to the property tax, the only major revenue source the city could increase without Albany's agreement. Real estate interests mobilized to reduce the 25 percent hike, as they had done with the Dinkins plan in 1991, but their efforts were undercut when the city's leading business group, the New York City Partnership, supported the mayor. Although some Partnership members also belonged to the Real Estate Board of New York, its membership primarily reflected the city's big financial, media, and professional service companies. They bought the quality-of-life emphasis and the idea of the city as a premium location—the first sign that the relocation battles that had preoccupied the previous administration would not be a problem for Bloomberg.[38]

The city council scaled back the increase to 18 percent. Still, it raised almost $1 billion in the first six months and twice that amount for the next fiscal year. It was the largest increase ever, and the president of the New York City Partnership said she thought it was necessary because of the impact of the terrorist attacks on the city's finances.[39]

At the one-year anniversary of the attacks, the city comptroller decided to total their economic cost. William Thompson put the figure at $83 billion. He included the decline in jobs, down 83,000 in the last 12 months, making an assumption that the city's economic downturn had reached bottom before the planes struck the Trade Center. He warned that the cost could approach $100 billion if the economy weakened further. "On one single day, the economic picture of the city changed," he claimed.[40]

It wasn't true, of course. The city's economic slide was already accelerating in the late summer, as the national recession cut into tourism and the Wall Street cutbacks reverberated throughout the economy. But blaming September 11 was what New Yorkers wanted to hear, and it guaranteed the biggest headlines. It was also vital to provide the rationale for the $20 billion President Bush had promised the city, not all of which had yet arrived.

Some economic news continued to be bleak. Prices for the millions of square feet of sublease office space continued to weaken, causing a general decline in rents, which were now 20 percent lower than the peak in 2000.[41] Space at the gleaming new Time Warner Center at the southwest corner of Central Park, built on the site of the controversial tower Mort Zuckerman had been forced to abandon in the late 1980s, simply couldn't be rented. So the developer, Related Cos., and its financial partner Apollo Real Estate Advisors simply moved their offices there to take the remaining space.[42]

Yet in the end, it was clear that New York had more than survived. *Crain's* reporter Lisa Fickenscher remembers that as early as 2002, small business owners downtown had become increasingly resentful of businesses elsewhere in the city, which were back to business as usual, if not with sales as robust as they might like. "It was as if they were living parallel lives," she remembers.[43]

The international runners who had failed to show up for the 2001 New York City Marathon were back the following November, when 31,834 people crossed the finish line, a record turnout.[44] Speculation that college students would go elsewhere proved untrue. In 2002, NYU received more applications than any other private school in the country, and the average SAT score increased to 1,340, up from 1,190 a decade earlier. The story was the same at Columbia, which was on a building and hiring binge.[45] Executives appeared to feel the same way as the students. They moved to the city for promising jobs. At first they claimed it was out of solidarity for New Yorkers; soon it was just because it was the right career move.[46]

Tourism recovered, in part, because of a determined effort by hotel owners and the city to tap into public sympathy for New York, and because of refocused marketing that targeted nearby cities in the Northeast, where people could drive or take the train to visit. Low rents attracted new retailers, especially foreign companies looking for a foothold in the United States and expanding national chains like American Eagle Outfitters, Skechers, and Forever 21.[47]

If September 11 had truly been the driving force behind the economy, New Jersey should have benefited from the relocation of companies across the Hudson. Instead, by mid-2002, vacancy rates there were soaring as well. Jersey City's jumped from 0 percent to 12.3 percent,[48] and it kept climbing. Wall Street firms had plenty of space in Manhattan, given their big layoffs, and had no need for the newly built offices across the river. Construction continued on the tower Goldman Sachs was building, the tallest in the state, but it would be more than half empty when it was completed in 2004.

It became clear that the downturn was very unlike the steep recession of the 1970s or the drop in the 1990s, because it was a Manhattan-only recession. Virtually all the jobs lost were in Manhattan; employment in the other four boroughs even grew slightly. The attacks slowed immigration only temporarily, and the population continued to grow, attracting retailers like Home Depot, which opened its first store on Staten Island and its thirteenth in the city in late 2002. The famous Swedish furniture store IKEA eyed a parcel in a Brooklyn's Red Hook neighborhood, a place known not long before for drug dealing and organized crime. It was sure the area was safe enough that people would come from all over the city to shop for the bargains IKEA offered. It was right, too.[49]

New York had steadied itself following the attacks. Wall Street rescued it yet again.

New areas of business showed great potential to rebuild profits for the big securities firms, including a new product called credit default swaps, which one early story correctly described as "complex contracts that basically insure corporate lenders and bond investors against defaults."[50] J.P. Morgan was the leader in the business, since it had essentially invented them. Proprietary trading's importance grew. While Salomon Brothers in the 1980s had used its own capital, it did so primarily to facilitate the buying and selling of bonds, while making a profit on its own trading. Now firms like Goldman Sachs unleashed its traders to gamble on markets using the firms' own capital. The numbers seemed large—Goldman's average money at risk each day reached $47 million in 2002, almost double the figure two years earlier—yet it was still only a fraction of what was soon to be wagered.[51]

Proprietary trading was an attempt by large firms to duplicate the success of hedge funds, pools of capital from wealthy individuals and institutions that used higher-risk trading strategies to outperform standard market indexes. These funds suddenly seemed omnipresent, because many were started by traders laid off in the last two years or who left when their bonuses shriveled. They headed to the city's priciest real estate, near the famous Plaza Hotel.

While credit default swaps, proprietary trading, and especially mortgage securitization gained momentum, an old-fashioned market rally lifted the securities business. The Dow Jones Industrial Average found life in March 2003 and rose by almost 3,000 points, or 36 percent, by year-end to close at 10,500. The IPO market revived when a promising tech company called Google let it be known that it was planning to go public.[52] Citigroup started hiring analysts, Credit Suisse

First Boston hired investment bankers away from Merrill Lynch, and Cantor Fitzgerald announced it would expand into asset management and foreign exchange, planning to double its staff over the next four years.[53]

Cantor's move was the most significant. Cantor's offices had been in the upper floors of One World Trade Center, and all 658 employees at work on September 11 had died in the attack, about two-thirds of its entire workforce. CEO Howard Ludnick had vowed to keep the firm alive, and he had succeeded. Pay on Wall Street rebounded too, hinting at the riches to come.

So many people were so wrong about the terrorist attacks and their impact.

In August 2002, researcher Joel Kotkin, of the Pepperdine Institute for Public Policy and the Milken Institute, published an opinion piece in the Wall Street Journal called "The Declustering of America." Weighing in on the debate of how to rebuild the site of the attacks, Kotkin argued there was simply no need for big office buildings. So-called industry clusters like finance in New York and technology in Silicon Valley were obsolete, because the dispersion of talent made them unnecessary and advances in technology made proximity less important. The terrorist attacks would speed this evolution, especially if there were more, because people simply wouldn't subject themselves to the risk. After all, weren't Wall Street companies rapidly diversifying the geographic footprint of their operations?[54]

Companies did decide that they could not have all their facilities close together. Bank of New York built an operations center outside Manhattan, although it merely crossed the East River to Brooklyn. New York Life reacted similarly, taking over a vacant IBM office building in suburban Westchester for a portion of its New York workforce, although the CEO complained about the productivity lost there every time it snowed. The biggest losses came not because jobs were moved but because they were simply eliminated, a victim of technology. The investment bankers and traders had no interest in leaving Manhattan. It was the same story in Silicon Valley and many other places in the country as other cities were reborn, most following in the footsteps of New York.

Nor was the economic impact devastating. Three years after the attack, economists at the Federal Reserve Bank of New York revisited their early work on the effects of September 11. They found that whatever employment losses had resulted had been overcome by the end of 2002, about the same time the city comptroller study was claiming dire consequences for the city. Neither residential nor commercial real estate showed any attack-related decline.[55]

A leading student of the city had predicted that outcome when he came to the offices of *Crain's New York Business* a few months after September 11 to discuss what lessons history could offer the reporters to guide their reporting. Columbia professor Kenneth Jackson recounted a series of disasters that had struck the city, which seemed almost as wrenching when they occurred as September 11. He rhetorically asked whether those attacks had altered the fundamental course of the city's history. The answer, of course, was that they had not, and neither would September 11.

Carl Weisbrod understood why years later, when he was recruited to help New Orleans recover from Hurricane Katrina because of his expertise in such disasters. Vast areas of New Orleans were rendered uninhabitable by the hurricane. By contrast, he noted, the terrorist attacks actually affected a very small area. The rest of the city soon resumed life and business activity as if the attacks had not occurred. Once New York put its psychological trauma behind it, the story of the city's modern era resumed.

CHAPTER 11

OLYMPIC DREAMS

THE MOST AMBITIOUS EFFORT TO REMAKE MODERN New York—especially to break the constraints the myth of manufacturing imposed on the city—began across the Hudson River at a soccer game.

A friend invited Dan Doctoroff to the 1994 World Cup semifinal between Bulgaria and Italy at Giants Stadium. A successful 35-year-old investment banker now doing deals for the Bass family's private equity fund, Doctoroff had attended World Series games, Super Bowls, and the NBA finals. He thought it was worthwhile since this would probably be the only time the World Cup would be held in the United States in his lifetime.

None of those other big sporting events prepared him for the experience. The fans, their faces painted, were frenzied for the entire match, never sitting down. Never the typical cynical Wall Street executive, he was completely captivated. This experience could be replicated many times over if New York could somehow host the Olympics, he thought. "It was very unlike me," he remembers. "I was usually so pragmatic."[1]

Like so many other talented people around the world, Doctoroff had been drawn to New York because of the opportunity it offered. Born in Birmingham, Michigan, he had attended Harvard, worked for a short time as a political pollster, and gone to the University of Chicago

Law School. His wife landed a job in New York in 1983 before he finished law school, so they moved to the city, and Doctoroff took classes at NYU to complete his degree. He recalls that his most important job each day was dealing with alternate side of the street parking, the New York ritual in which people without the money to garage their cars are forced to move them twice a week to clear the way for the sanitation cleaning crews. With time on his hands, he explored the city via the subway system. After getting his degree, he landed an entry-level job at Lehman Brothers, the kind where late nights are routine. After several long days, he remembers riding in a livery car up the FDR Drive, looking back on the lights of downtown, and realizing how much he had fallen in love with New York, or at least his romanticized version of it.

His knowledge of the city's government and politics was superficial, so he started reading the metropolitan section of the *New York Times*. He pored over the 1,169-page *Power Broker,* Robert Caro's classic study of the ills of New York. It was his introduction to development in the city. He spent two years quietly studying the economics and requirements of the Olympics, a relatively easy task since Atlanta was gearing up to host the 1996 games, and information was widely available. He came to believe that the most important benefit of hosting an Olympics was that it served as a catalyst for getting things done that would otherwise languish. Its deadline was unalterable, and the excitement surrounding the games generated an unusual degree of cooperation.

Enlisting the aid of a noted urban planner, he soon realized that the decline of manufacturing had left enormous tracts of underutilized land, most of it along the waterfront, that were both ideal for Olympic venues and in dire need of redevelopment. The insight gave him the vision he needed to convince New Yorkers that the Olympics were worth pursuing and would benefit the city. He drafted a plan that placed a big X over a map of the city to show where the events would be located and how the logistics would be managed. Most importantly, he zeroed in on the West Side of Manhattan for the Olympics stadium, the same area that Giuliani had once eyed for the Yankees.

The Giuliani administration had come to some of the same conclusions as Doctoroff. It had tried to rezone many industrial areas to allow big-box retail stores, then scarce in the city, but had never been able to push the proposal forward. It proposed an ambitious rezoning of the West Side, keyed to moving Madison Square Garden farther west, although its plan came too late in the mayor's second term to gain much momentum.[2] It also worked on a plan to extend the No. 7 subway line to the area, crucial to any development scheme, using a special taxing district to provide the money. The mayor himself was never forcefully behind these schemes. Like Pete Hamill, Giuliani remained nostalgic for the manufacturing jobs that had been so important in Brooklyn when he was growing up. He embraced an expensive plan to build a freight tunnel under the Hudson River to link the port in Newark to Queens, in part because he believed it would spur manufacturing jobs.[3]

Doctoroff had no such commitment to that past. While he believed there might be a role for some manufacturing that produced goods for the local market, he saw that the city's future lay elsewhere. "There was always a hope, some might say a delusion, that manufacturing—big box manufacturing that had been so common in the city through World War II—was going to come back," he recalls. "To my mind it was clear that it wasn't. When you look at classic location theory, what do you need for manufacturing? Access to markets? Yes, at some level. Transportation? New York was not designed for the transportation access manufacturing needed. Space? Cost? New York was just not a natural hub for manufacturing. It was very clear from the trends. What you had were these vast areas of the city that had been used for manufacturing or distribution that people weren't prepared to address because it would have meant that they were giving up on that delusion."[4]

With Wall Street booming and new media expanding rapidly, the need for a major boost to development seemed obvious. Doctoroff's plan received a major boost in mid-2001 from a task force commissioned by Senator Charles Schumer. The Schumer Report implored the city to create 60 million new square feet of office space to accommodate the jobs the city was certain to create. The areas it spotlighted were the West Side and Long Island City, both central to Doctoroff's Olympic plan.[5]

Not many New Yorkers were enthusiastic. They saw the games as just another inconvenience. Many business people were skeptical, too, but Doctoroff's ability to package an idea was second to none. He knew no one on the board of the New York City Partnership, the city's leading business group, when he presented his plan in 1996, yet he made such a strong impression that developer Mort Zuckerman ordered up a series of favorable articles in his newspaper, the *New York Daily News*. Doctoroff raised $15 million with relative ease, even as those who opened their wallets warned him how difficult his task would be.

He was struck by how cautious the city's business leaders were and how many scars they carried from previous development battles. "Keep it simple," warned Fred Wilpon, a developer and owner of the New York Mets.[6] Although Doctoroff had originally targeted the 2008 games, he soon realized that the time was too short to prepare a bid and the date would be too close to the Atlanta games, so he switched to the 2012 Olympics. He won the support of both Giuliani and Governor George Pataki, and he eventually joined forces with the New York Jets, who would become the major tenants of the stadium after the games. He spent the 2001 election year selling the games to the candidates for mayor. Michael Bloomberg wasn't a problem, since he was already a member of the Olympic steering committee, but neither was he likely to win. Both Mark Green and Fernando Ferrer endorsed at least the overall concept, and Doctoroff proceeded with his planning, expecting to work with Mayor Green. September 11 changed that scenario.

A few days after the election, he received a call from Nat Leventhal, a longtime city power broker, who asked him to serve on the transition committee that Leventhal was heading up for Bloomberg. He agreed. Two weeks later, Leventhal called to ask him if Doctoroff would consider becoming the deputy mayor for economic development. He said no. Leventhal called back and prodded him to at least meet with the mayor-elect. Fifteen minutes into the interview, Doctoroff knew he would take the job.

Doctoroff had made enough money to live comfortably. He decided that Bloomberg's unexpected victory presented a unique opportunity to accomplish big things. Since Bloomberg financed the campaign from his own fortune, he owed no one anything. In the interview, Doctoroff realized that the mayor-elect shared his view about the future of New

York and how it could rise to face the global competition they both saw emerging. September 11 not only motivated Doctoroff to do something for his adopted home, but created the kind of unity of purpose he had hoped to generate with the Olympics. Doctoroff agreed to work for $1 a year, although he insisted that he remain in charge of the effort to win the Olympics.

The idea to hire Doctoroff had come from Leventhal, who was among those who had originally been skeptical of the Olympics quest but was eventually won over. After years in government and the government-dependent nonprofit sector, he shared Doctoroff's frustrations with the status quo. "Dan was filled with ideas, and he wasn't a city official who would be deterred by all the reasons not to do something," Leventhal says. "He was a businessman who would get things done."[7]

While restoring the city's fiscal health fell on the mayor's shoulders, the rebuilding of the World Trade Center site was a responsibility of the state. The Port Authority of New York and New Jersey, a unique bistate agency controlled by the governors of the two states, owned the Twin Towers and surrounding buildings, making Governor Pataki indispensable in the process. The state's powers over land use were more effective than those of the city, and its procedures less cumbersome. The Bloomberg administration was consulted and periodically tried to intervene in the many disputes that plagued the rebuilding of Ground Zero, but its role was secondary.

Doctoroff launched the city's planning department on a series of efforts to reclaim the areas he had targeted for development. None was more important than the West Side, the site of his Olympic stadium. After six months in office, the outlines of his plan emerged. The city and the New York Jets would build a $1.2 billion stadium on a platform over rail yards that served as a storage area for Long Island Rail Road trains.[8] The city would rezone the area because the stadium would set off a development boom that would extend the Midtown business district all the way to the Hudson River and build the commercial office space called for in the Schumer report. The city would encourage residential development as well, creating a new neighborhood some had begun to call Hudson Yards. To make all this possible, Doctoroff proposed a tax-increment financing district to provide the Metropolitan Transportation Authority with the $1.5 billion it needed to extend the No. 7 subway line to the site, a project it was not prepared to fund on its own.[9] The stadium would have a retractable roof, allowing it to serve as an expansion of the adjacent Javits convention center. It would be a flexible facility so it could be configured as a new arena for winter sports like basketball and hockey.

In typical New York fashion, community opposition arose almost immediately. The business coalition Doctoroff had put together to support the Olympics effort was strained as well. Many downtown leaders worried that development sparked by the stadium would be a threat to the rebuilding of the Trade Center, siphoning off potential tenants. Hotel owners and others involved in tourism were cool to the idea of a stadium as a replacement for the straightforward expansion of the convention center they had long sought. The Javits Center lost out on large conventions and the thousands of visitors they would bring to the city because it was too small to accommodate them. Giuliani had blocked any efforts to improve the center because it was run by the state. The domed stadium also worried the Dolan family, owners of Madison Square Garden and its professional basketball and hockey teams. It could be a threat to the concerts and many other events that were key to the Garden's profitability.

Doctoroff brushed aside fears that his plan for the subway line was too expensive and that his overall plan would hurt downtown. Lower Manhattan appealed to financial companies tied to the area by history, like Goldman Sachs, and companies like Empire Blue Cross Blue Shield in low-margin businesses that needed lower-cost space.[10] The media, entertainment, and professional service firms that dominated the Midtown market wouldn't move downtown, could afford higher rents, and would expand outside the city if more office space wasn't created in Midtown, he insisted. His dismissive tone alienated many people. Doctoroff's staff at City Hall developed enormous loyalty to their boss because he was smart and his ambitions were challenging. But working for him was difficult, because he was demanding and knew he was the smartest person in the room. When a staffer offered an idea, it was frequently dismissed. Then a few days later, Doctoroff would revive the idea, revised and improved. Others would not be as understanding as his staff when the fight over the stadium intensified.

Throughout 2003, Doctoroff pitched his conceptual plan in meetings designed to build support. He reached a compromise with tourism interests, and the city signed on to a $1 billion–plus expansion of the Javits Center while continuing to insist that the stadium would provide a facility for events that the center couldn't accommodate. The arena configuration was eliminated in an effort to ease the Dolans' concerns. Doctoroff staunchly defended his financing plans, arguing that the Olympics would boost the city's economy by $12 billion and leave a legacy of improvements that New Yorkers would enjoy for decades.

In March 2004, he unveiled his plans in a series of well-orchestrated events. Jets owner Woody Johnson, heir to a pharmaceutical fortune, was prepared to spend millions on behalf of the stadium. He hired lobbyists with ties to both Democrats and Republicans, and they lined up key labor unions, including construction and hotel workers. Local politicians, including recently elected councilwoman Christine Quinn, vowed to fight the stadium to the end. A few business leaders objected, too, especially Broadway theatre owners worried about congestion. Doctoroff had a little more than 15 months to win approval for the stadium before the International Olympic Committee was to vote on the site of the 2012 games.[11]

The early opposition to the stadium was fairly routine for major projects. But the Dolans' decision to enter the fray and their willingness to outspend the Jets and Doctoroff were unprecedented. Never before had a coalition of community groups and politicians been given the resources to launch television ads opposing a project. The Jets countered with their own barrage of advertising. By the fall, a civic group reported that the two sides had spent $11.5 million, two-thirds of it by the stadium's opponents.[12]

On the surface, all the money was designed to influence public opinion. In reality it was designed to influence one man: Assembly Speaker Sheldon Silver. Typically, City Hall or a private developer makes a proposal to rezone a tract of land, and the idea passes through the city's painstaking approval process. The city planning department oversees an environmental impact statement, which often takes years, and then certifies the idea. Once that imprimatur is given, formal reviews begin, with a seven-month timetable. The local community board considered the proposal, although its opinion is purely advisory; the borough president also weighs in, again with no direct ability to influence the outcome. The city planning commission, controlled by the mayor, then approves the plan, sometimes with changes, sending it to the city council. The council has the power to change or kill the project but in practice, only two members of the council matter. The council member from the area can block the project because he or she is given deference by the other 50 members who expect similar deference in return. The council speaker must agree to the project as well since the speaker's control of the council is usually absolute. City officials and knowledgeable developers work their way through this minefield always knowing that they will have to make concessions—usually reducing density and adding affordable housing—with the local councilperson and speaker to seal the deal.

However, the Metropolitan Transportation Authority, a state agency, owned the stadium site. The decision on whether to allow the project to proceed would be made by an obscure board called the Public Authorities Control Board, which was composed of three people: the governor, the majority leader of the state senate, and the speaker of the state assembly. Governor Pataki's vote was assured. Senate Republican majority leader Joseph Bruno publicly insisted that he had doubts about the stadium, but Mayor Bloomberg was a crucial source of campaign funds for the GOP, and he was expected to vote yes in the end. Silver was the key. Assembly Democrats from the West Side opposed the stadium. Silver, who represented downtown, said he needed to be assured that the development to be ignited by the stadium would not hurt efforts to rebuild the World Trade Center site.

Doctoroff scrambled to present an offer that Silver could not refuse by increasing the incentives for companies to remain or relocate downtown. When that didn't work, the Bloomberg administration held up projects the speaker supported. Later it sped up those plans and showered millions more on his district. Doctoroff again offered to increase incentives to lure companies downtown. But it was all in vain. In June, only a month before the International Olympic Committee was to vote, Silver announced that he would block the stadium. An angry Bloomberg denounced him. "Without the stadium, we won't have the catalyst for the growth of this neighborhood and we'll have to revise our plans to make up for it. The delay will be measured in years, not months," he said.[13]

Doctoroff wasn't quite ready to give up on a decade of effort. Although he had steadfastly rejected Queens as a site for the Olympics stadium, he and Mets owner Fred Wilpon hastily drew up plans for a new baseball stadium there, which would be used for the Olympics as well. It was too little, too late. On July 7, about one week shy of the 11th anniversary of the World Cup game he had attended, the International Olympic Committee (IOC) summarily rejected New York's bid. It was a devastating defeat for the mayor, Doctoroff, and the business leaders who had accompanied them to the IOC meeting in Singapore. Yet the mayor remained loyal to his deputy. If reelected in November, he said, he wanted Doctoroff to remain deputy mayor. "In the world that I come from and Dan comes from, it's just another deal. You go on."[14]

Doctoroff, who had traveled 175,000 miles in the months before the vote trying to secure the Olympics, headed off for a bike ride in the Andes Mountains in Peru to purge the defeat and think about whether he wanted to continue in the job.[15] He decided that he did, and soon he was ready to tackle the West Side again. A year later, he resurrected the idea of spurring development in the area. He spearheaded a proposal for the city to buy the site from the transit agency, this time with the support of the new council Speaker, Christine Quinn. After negotiations, the city and the MTA agreed that the city would rezone the property and the MTA would solicit bids from developers who would promise to build according to guidelines, which called for 12.4 million square feet of office space, apartments and condominiums, a cultural center, and a new public space.

The lure was irresistible for the most important developers in the city. Certainly they wanted to make a lot of money, but the way real estate owners become extraordinarily rich is poorly understood. While they make millions on the fees they take for constructing and managing office buildings, their enormous wealth comes from making the right investments. In 1995, Jerry Speyer helped orchestrate a deal in which he and partners like David Rockefeller and Goldman Sachs arranged to buy Rockefeller Center out of bankruptcy for $306 million in cash and the assumption of $845 million in debt.[16] Five years later, with the help of the Crown family of Chicago, he bought out those partners for $1.85 billion, ending the Rockefeller association with the complex they had built in the middle of the Great Depression.[17] Today, Rockefeller Center is worth about $8 billion, real estate experts estimate.

Moreover, money was only part of the allure. Most of the bidders were already rich, including Jerry Speyer of Tishman Speyer and the Related Cos.'s Stephen Ross, who regularly appeared on the Forbes 400 list of the richest Americans. The West Side site offered the opportunity to ensure themselves a place in the city's history. Doctoroff appealed to their egos. "The city hasn't done anything like this before, certainly not in Midtown. We want to create a 21th century Rockefeller Center," he said as the bidding began.[18] "Someday, the rail yards will carry the winner's name just as Rockefeller Center does."

Tishman Speyer, the owner of Rockefeller Center and other landmarks like the Chrysler Building, lined up Morgan Stanley as its anchor tenant and envisioned as a centerpiece a new version of Rome's Spanish Steps. Related Cos. allied itself with Rupert Murdoch's News Corp. and designed an entertainment venue linked to that company's new headquarters. Douglas Durst, the builder of the first office tower in Times Square, partnered with Vornado Realty Trust and said it would bring the magazine publisher Condé Nast to the site. They pitched their plans to the city and the MTA, in meetings with the community, and with newspaper editorial boards. They all desperately wanted to win. At the end of a session with the editors of *Crain's New York Business,* Tishman's Speyer was asked if there was anything else he wanted to say. Yes, he replied. "No one has asked how much Tishman wanted to develop the site. We want it a lot."

Tishman won the competition, promising to pay the MTA $1 billion and spend as much as $1 billion to build the needed platform over the rail yards. In addition to the Spanish Steps, the company expected to build four or five office towers and more than 3,000 apartments, of which 10 percent would be set aside for working-class New Yorkers. It was going ahead even though Morgan Stanley had pulled out and the collapse of Bear Stearns had sent shock waves through the city.

Amid the growing financial crisis, Speyer had second thoughts, despite how much he had wanted to win. Tishman began demanding concessions from the MTA, which were refused. The deal collapsed, and it appeared that once again Doctoroff's vision of reclaiming the West Side to allow the city's economy to grow would be thwarted. Unexpectedly, one of the losing bidders stepped forward. Related Cos. had essentially withdrawn when it lost its anchor tenant, News Corp. Now Stephen Ross said he would agree to the same terms as Tishman despite the risks. "It's not often that you get a second chance at the dream of a lifetime. We will create New York's next great neighborhood," he said.[19] Doctoroff's dream remained alive.

The saga of the West Side was Doctoroff's most important and controversial initiative, but there were many others. In early 2005, he pushed through an ambitious plan to rezone the adjacent waterfront neighborhoods of Greenpoint and Williamsburg in Brooklyn. They, too, had once been home to thousands of manufacturers, virtually all of which had moved or gone out of business. An influx of artists and young people looking for cheap rents suggested that the area would be ripe for housing. The city council agreed to rezone 175 blocks to encourage large-scale residential construction, including towers of up to 40 stories along the waterfront. More than 10,000 new apartments could now be built, with more than 2,070 set aside for poor and middle-income families.[20]

The administration worked tirelessly on behalf of developer Bruce Ratner's plan for Atlantic Yards. The developer of the office complex MetroTech, which had saved thousands of jobs in the 1980s, Ratner had long thought a stretch of land near downtown Brooklyn could be redeveloped, but he, too, would need public money to reconfigure rail yards. When the New Jersey Nets were put up for sale, he was persuaded to buy the team and move it to Brooklyn, filling the psychological hole created when the Brooklyn Dodgers moved to California in 1958. His plan touched off a storm of controversy second only to the West Side fight, but in the end Silver agreed to support it. Much as had been envisioned on the West Side, the new arena was to be the centerpiece of an entire new neighborhood, with the 22 acres expected eventually to support 6,400 new market-rate and subsidized apartments and a small amount of office space.

The Doctoroff agenda continued even after he resigned in December 2007 to become president of the mayor's beloved Bloomberg L.P., a sign of his boss's undiminished confidence. In Queens, more than 200 small businesses occupied Willets Point, an area without sewers that polluted the nearby bay. Dominated by auto repair shops, these businesses had turned back all attempts to dislodge them. Even Robert Moses had given up on redeveloping Willet's Point. The Bloomberg administration finally outmaneuvered the businesses, winning council approval for a plan that called for 500,000 square feet of office space, a hotel, a convention center, and more than 5,000 apartments.

Despite the Financial Crisis and recession, the administration persevered. In mid-2009, it won approval to revive the once-thriving waterfront district of Coney Island by injecting new life into the beachfront entertainment area known for the Cyclone roller coaster while adding high-rise hotels and another 4,000 apartments.

In all, the Bloomberg administration claimed that it had rezoned up to a third of the city.

Doctoroff could not escape the myth of manufacturing completely. In early 2003, the mayor gave an interview to one of his favorite newspapers, the *Financial Times,* to defend his stewardship of the city. Two industries matter in New York, he said—financial services and tourism. Manufacturing would not help the city emerge from the recession. "If you are a pharmaceutical company or a steel company, you do not need to be here," he said with a bluntness even Doctoroff usually avoided. "New York City should not waste its time with manufacturing."[21]

The backlash was immediate, especially from Arthur Rubenstein, who ran a company that made steel stairs and other metal products. "Our company and our employees, most of whom are New York City residents, contribute significant taxes (although perhaps not by Bloomberg standards) to the city. Mr. Bloomberg should remember that the city's boundaries extend beyond Manhattan and that sectors such as financial services can't provide employment to all the city's residents," he wrote in a letter to *Crain's New York Business*.[22] This was a fight that Bloomberg could not win. So Doctoroff came up with a 36-page report that outlined an industrial policy built around preserving space in special industrial business zones. The city had deliberately replaced the word "manufacturing" with "industrial" to broaden the types of business that could be helped and to protect itself from being held accountable for the impossible goal of slowing the decline in factory jobs.[23]

While the zones may have helped some companies, they could not change basic economics. Manufacturing jobs declined every year that Bloomberg was mayor—through the difficult early years, the Wall Street–powered boom years, and the worrisome years that followed the Great Recession. In 2009, the number of jobs in higher education surpassed those in manufacturing. Today, only 75,000 people hold factory jobs, and the once-sacred apparel shops employ 15,000.

THE CITY MAY HAVE SIDESTEPPED THE WORST EFFECTS of the Financial Crisis and subsequent recession. But the Doctoroff agenda did not.

Doctoroff's many speeches in support of his plans always contained the caveat that the development he envisioned would take decades to complete. He claimed that the city's economic modeling had shown how the projects could be continued despite cyclical ups and downs. In 2008, his successor rushed to complete approval for projects like Willets Point and Coney Island, saying publicly that the mission was to make it impossible for the next mayor to reverse these plans. The mayor's decision to run for a third term allowed the last major piece, Coney Island, to make it through the gauntlet of council approval.

While sincere about the need to understand economic cycles, neither Doctoroff nor anyone else in the administration foresaw a financial meltdown so severe that virtually all financing for real estate projects disappeared.

In Brooklyn, the Atlantic Yards project was delayed for years by legal challenges aimed at both stopping the project altogether and over-turning, at least in New York, a controversial US Supreme Court decision allowing eminent domain to be used on behalf of private developments like Atlantic Yards. The last legal hurdle wasn't cleared until November 2009, when the state's highest court said that eminent domain could be used to evict the last holdout, whose apartment occupied a spot destined for a luxury box at the arena.

By then the stirring designs of architect Frank Gehry for the arena, a soaring tower called Miss Brooklyn, and numerous apartment build-ings had been jettisoned as too costly. After the final court ruling, Ratner broke ground for a scaled-down arena, scheduled to open in late 2012. He must also build the first apartment building, designed to rise 34 sto-ries and contain 400 mostly affordable units. No timeline exists for the other buildings that were part of the original plan.

The Bloomberg administration continues to fight off legal challenges at Willets Point, where it needs to evict the remaining businesses before it can begin the work, expected to cost hundreds of millions of dollars, to clean up the pollution and create the infrastructure needed. The city continues to insist that the area will create thousands of jobs, although there is no specific plan for what will go on the site or even which devel-opers will do the building.

Coney Island is in a holding pattern. The city took control of the famed entertainment area and brought in a new operator to upgrade the attractions and businesses on the boardwalk. Here, too, infrastructure needs run into the hundreds of millions of dollars, and large-scale build-ing seems nowhere on the horizon.

It is at the West Side rail yards that the survival of the Doctoroff agenda hangs in the balance and in the hands of Jay Cross, who had been Doctoroff's key partner in the Olympic stadium effort. He had been hired by the Jets in 2000 to lead the effort to build a stadium for the team, which suffered financially because it was merely a tenant in the rival New York Giants' facility in New Jersey. While Doctoroff commanded public and media attention, the unassuming Cross worked behind the scenes to make the stadium workable and often soothe feathers that Doctoroff had ruffled. When the West Side plan failed, he led the Jets team that negotiated the first professional football stadium–sharing deal with the New York Giants. Yet when Stephen Ross proposed that he join Related Cos. to be in charge of Hudson Yards in 2008, he jumped at the chance.

Cross labored for the next three years to overcome the hurdles that the Financial Crisis had added to the already complex project. The agreement with the MTA was repeatedly revised to push back the time when Related was required to begin making payments on the $1 billion it promised the transit agency. A revised zoning of part of the site was maneuvered through the city council. He had to replace financial partner Goldman Sachs, which abandoned the project in early 2010, eventually convincing the Ontario municipal pension fund that the scheme would succeed and make it a fortune.

He told potential tenants that they could pioneer the city's next great neighborhood—now targeted to contain 6 million square feet of office space, a state-of-the-art five-story, 1 million-square-foot retail complex, a luxury hotel, 5,000 apartments, a cultural center, and 12 acres of public space. His credibility was bolstered by the Doctoroff-inspired subway line extension, which was well under way and likely to be completed on time. Ross allowed him to offer the first companies willing to step forward a deal that was hard to refuse: Related would build the most modern and efficient office tower in the city at cost. Related would lease the space or sell the entire building, whatever the tenant desired. With significant tax breaks as part of the Hudson Yard package, it would be an irresistible proposition.

The only problem was that a better deal was possible downtown. Condé Nast, which had at one time committed to be the anchor tenant as part of the Durst plan for the site, considered Hudson Yards as its lease in Times Square was nearing an end. Cross simply couldn't compete with the World Trade Center site, with its own tax breaks and other incentives. With the media business much less profitable than it was when Doctoroff boldly named it as one of the anchors of Midtown, every dollar mattered, and Condé Nast took 1 million square feet in the first building to rise at Ground Zero. Cross moved on to other prospects.

The accessories company Coach agreed to anchor the first building, but it was in the corner of the property on terra firma. Cross would need one or more tenants to begin construction of the platform, the key to the ambitious plan.

If Cross could lure the tenants he needed to start construction, the Doctoroff vision of what New York could become would take a big step forward. His ambitious development schemes had opened up vast areas of the city. If the economy started growing again and if financing became available, the space would be there to allow the city to finally surpass its 1969 employment peak.

CHAPTER 12

IF YOU BUILD IT
THEY WILL COME

IF CONSTANCE WILLIAMS HAPPENED TO BE RIDING ON the same subway car as Pete Hamill when she returned to her Bronx home after her shift as a housekeeper at the Marriott Marquis, the noted author probably wouldn't look twice at the small woman who had come to New York from Jamaica. In modern New York, however, she represents the hundreds of thousands of New Yorkers who work in the city's tourism industry and, without advanced education, form families and support them. They are proud to be working and proud of the work they do.

Like the millions of other immigrants who have fueled so much of New York's success, Williams came to the city in 1971 because there was more economic opportunity than in her native country. She settled in the Bronx, primarily working as a baby nurse. When she heard that there were openings at a new hotel in Times Square, she took the trip into Midtown to apply. It took three rigorous interviews before she was hired. The pay at first was actually less than what she was making, but the job offered stability, health care benefits, and rewarding work. "The main thing for me personally is that I like my rooms to be done to the best of my ability," she says. "I like to make the guests happy. I like to talk to people and I meet some very interesting people."[1]

With pay for veteran housekeepers now more than $20 an hour, Williams has climbed into the middle class. She bought a co-op, traveled back and forth to Jamaica, and helped put her nephew and nieces through college, with a little left over to spend in the many stores she frequents near the hotel. She is one of more than 300,000 people in the city who owe their jobs to the tourism industry, which has grown from attracting 25 million people a year in the 1980s to twice as many today.

The Marquis laid the foundation for that growth by opening Manhattan's West Side for hotels and showing that national chains could succeed in the city. Rivals like the flagship Hilton on Sixth Avenue followed on the heels of the Marriott's opening in 1985. But amid the recession of the early 1990s, the future of the industry seemed uncertain. The city's tourism bureau had yet to develop sophisticated ways to count tourists, so it tracked the number of arrivals to the area's three major airports as a proxy, and that number declined early in the decade. Experts worried that after visiting New York once, visitors would seek out other American cities. The increasing number of direct flights between Europe and cities like Atlanta, Chicago, Dallas, and Washington was a particular threat. New Yorkers, especially those hosting friends and relatives from elsewhere, believed that national attention to the city's crime rate was scaring people away.

Then Michael Eisner decided that the Disney Co. needed Broadway and walked into the open arms of Rebecca Robertson, who needed Disney in Times Square.

Eisner, who was born in suburban Westchester, was a successful movie executive when he was recruited to take over the ailing Walt Disney Co. by Roy Disney, the brother of its legendary founder, and Sid Bass, Dan Doctoroff's boss at the family's private equity firm. The company had narrowly dodged several takeover attempts and was seen as rudderless, both creatively and strategically. Eisner launched an ambitious plan to revive Disney with new kinds of movies, television shows, and theme parks. He believed that establishing a foothold in live theater on Broadway was crucial for maximizing the market for his successful films and for creating new properties that could be made into films. His early efforts met with derision. A *New York Times* cultural critic dismissed his changes in early 1994 by saying, "Disney's corporate behavior has been so Mickey Mouse of late you have to wonder."[2]

Robertson, president of the 42nd Street Development Project, was desperate to find some way to jumpstart the revival of seedy Times Square that had been stalled for years by lawsuits and was now paralyzed by the collapse of the market for the office space that was the centerpiece of the revival plan. She hired the noted architect Robert Stern to come up with a plan to revitalize existing buildings, focusing on entertainment and tourism rather than building new towers. The key, she believed, was the New Amsterdam Theater on 42nd Street. Built in 1903, it had been at the center of the nightlife of the city in the Roaring 1920s. It sat 1,200, but its distinctive marble interior and classical friezes were badly deteriorated. She spent $35 million to buy it in 1992.

"Tourists were still flooding Times Square," she recalled a few years later. "Crime was getting better. The Gap had opened a retail store at the corner of 42nd Street and Broadway and was doing unbelievably good business, much to everyone's surprise." She got lucky, too, because Stern knew Eisner and convinced him to come to 42nd Street and check out the New Amsterdam. He recognized what 42nd Street could become. "Isn't it funny how outsiders always do?" Robertson said. "For New Yorkers it is sitting right in front of them. But Disney folks looked at the beauty of the theater, looked at the high pedestrian counts, and looked at the fact that the project was actually happening."[3]

For taking such a big risk, Disney wanted substantial financial help. Robertson's task was complicated, because she was also in talks to bring Madame Tussauds wax museum to the same block and to build a modern movie theater across the street. In the end, she inked all three deals. Disney agreed to invest $8 million and received a $21 million loan from the city and state at 3 percent interest. A preliminary agreement was signed the last day David Dinkins was in office. Completing the deal took a bit more time than anticipated amid doubts that Times Square and its tawdry atmosphere were the right place for family entertainment. As Eisner told the story at the celebration of the theater's opening, he took another walk down the street, this time with

Rudy Giuliani, pointing out the porn shops that still dotted the area. Giuliani fixed him with a stolid gaze, Mr. Eisner said, and repeated, "Michael, they'll be gone."[4] Giuliani kept his promise, passing tough zoning laws that drove pornography outlets from Times Square, despite strenuous objections from civil liberties groups.

But owning a theater was only one part of the equation. Disney also had to prove that its kind of entertainment would attract audiences. Some New Yorkers, especially those in the media who regarded Manhattan as more sophisticated and worldly than the rest of the country, worried that Disney would undermine what they loved about the town. Other Broadway producers were also suspicious. Disney had no ties to the club—and especially the established owner/producers, led by the Shuberts—who had long controlled what it meant to be "on Broadway." Disney's deep pockets could redraw the financial rules of the game. Its expertise in films and theme parks could raise audience expectations for what a Broadway musical could deliver. Rival producers feared that they would be unable to keep pace.[5]

Eisner chose the successful film story of *Beauty and the Beast* as his first effort on Broadway, even before the renovation of the New Amsterdam was completed. He set a budget of $11.9 million, high but not unheard-of. He hired two well-known Broadway creatives—lyricist Tim Rice and actor Terrence Mann—but staffed the production primarily with Disney people imported from Los Angeles and the theme parks. Advance ticket sales were mediocre, and on opening night in 1994, the reviews were condescending at best: "a gigantic kiddie show," "lure for tourists," "pretty tacky stuff."[6]

Luckily for Disney, no one paid attention to the critics. In that era before Internet sales, people flocked to the box office the next day. *Beauty and the Beast* broke the one-day box office record for the Palace Theater, where it was playing, in the first two and a half hours; by 5 p.m., it had shattered the Broadway record. The box office stayed open until midnight to accommodate the throngs. By the time it closed, Disney had sold more than $600,000 worth of tickets. Slightly downsized when it changed theaters, *Beauty and the Beast* played for 13 years, and its 46 previews and 5,464 performances ranked as the sixth-longest run ever when it closed.[7]

Seeking an even bigger success, Eisner suggested that the company bring *The Lion King* to the stage and hired a promising director named Julie Taymor, who had built a reputation as an innovator and had extensive experience with masks. Eisner backed her vision, and Disney's second production premiered in November 1997 to great acclaim. The *New York Times* said it was the "the most memorable, moving and original theatrical extravaganza in years."[8] Today, *The Lion King* remains one of the dominant productions on Broadway. Each week, it fills virtually every one of its seats, grosses $1.8 million, and commands one of the top-three average ticket prices.

Disney has staged six musicals since its arrival, never more than three at any one time. In all, it has sold more than 30 million tickets, and for many people, a Disney production is their first Broadway experience. No longer was New York reserved for the elite—a special place for special people, as one architect said, bemoaning the arrival of companies like Marriott and Disney.[9] Instead it was a destination for all Americans. Applebee's opened a few doors down from the New Amsterdam, and around the corner Red Lobster and Ruby Tuesday took the two most prominent locations. Disney and the others it brought to Times Square were the reason David Ringwood brought his family into the city from upstate New York every year. "Disney knows the formula, they know how to do it," he says, standing in line to get into a matinee performance of *Mary Poppins* at the New Amsterdam. "We're huge Disney fans. We've seen *The Lion King, Beauty and the Beast,* so we had to see *Mary Poppins.*" He had hoped to find discount tickets, but when he couldn't he paid full price.[10]

The Ringwoods lived close enough to make a one-day trip into the city, but most visitors needed hotel rooms at a price they could afford. Bill Bratton and Ray Kelly made it possible to build hotels anywhere in the city's five boroughs.

Bratton's policing strategies were so innovative and powerful that the department continued to drive down crime even under his flawed successors. Bloomberg's decision to return Kelly to the post he held under Dinkins could have signaled a major shift in strategy. Bratton had disparaged many of Kelly's actions, especially in his book *Turnaround,* and Kelly has responded from time to time with criticisms of Bratton. Yet when Kelly became commissioner, the key Bratton policies—Comp-Stat and the emphasis on preventing crime rather than arresting crimi-nals—remained at the center of police strategy. Community policing, as trumpeted in the Dinkins era, did not return. Instead, Kelly put new em-phasis on technology and revamped the department to meet the threat of terrorist attacks.

Despite the loss of some 5,000 officers as the city's budget was re-duced, crime declined in every year of the Bloomberg administration, with murders falling to 471 in 2009, the lowest number since 1963. In 2010, the number increased to 532 murders, but the overall crime rate declined 2 percent.[11] The mayor and Kelly constantly reiterated that New York was the safest big city in America. They did more than make tourists feel safer. The decline in crime also meant that visitors were happy to stay in outlying neighborhoods and even other boroughs be-cause they could travel back and forth to Manhattan no matter what the hour.

The struggle to expand the footprint of the hotel industry was long and difficult. In the early 1990s, outer-borough developer Joshua Muss proposed a hotel and office complex for downtown Brooklyn. If Brook-lyn were a city, its 2.3 million people would make it the fourth largest in the country, he explained. It boasted 60,000 businesses and excellent subway connections to Manhattan and Queens. No one bought it. He was constantly told that "a hotel in Brooklyn is a piece of pork to a ko-sher butcher shop."[12]

Finally, when the city gave him a deadline in 1995 to come up with the financing or lose the site, he put together the bank loans he needed for the $230 million project.[13] The 384-room hotel (a Marriott, of course) opened in mid-1998, the first large hotel in Brooklyn in 68 years. It was supposed to attract travelers doing business in Brooklyn and tourists on a budget, since its rooms were about 20 percent cheaper than in Manhattan. To most people's surprise, another market mate-rialized—people coming to Brooklyn to visit family for weddings, Bar Mitzvahs, and other occasions. In retrospect, it seemed so obvious: a city that big, especially one that saw such population turnover, would not only generate business like weddings; they would be big ones with many out-of-town guests. Only two years after the doors opened, Muss and Marriott proposed adding another 280 rooms. Occupancy was averaging 93 percent, Bill Marriott's threshold for success.[14]

Brooklyn was only one of many places that attracted hotels. The Meatpacking District, located at the western edge of Greenwich Village, was a place where meat was cut and packaged by day and a hangout for prostitutes, especially transvestites, at night. *Crain's* publisher Alair Townsend, who moved to the area in 1982, once wrote a column about having to walk past the condoms on her sidewalk in the morning, castigating the unique breed of New York politicians who defended the rights of prostitutes to ply their trade. This was not a place tourists were likely to feel comfortable. Gradually, the crackdown on quality-of-life crimes in the Giuliani administration made the area safe. Hotels soon began arriving. One of the first was the 16-story, 200-room Greenwich Village Hotel. The 13-story Hotel Gansevoort followed in 2004.

The hotels that popped up in the Meatpacking District were primarily high-priced boutiques. Other developers—notably an ambitious immigrant from Taiwan—took advantage of the decline in crime to move into out-of-the-way places with lower land prices to build budget hotels for cost-sensitive travelers.[15] Sam Chang had come to the United States in 1977 to work in his parents' hotel in Los Angeles, and two years later he embarked on a cross-country trip in his new car with a friend. After eight months, he drove into the city through the Lincoln Tunnel, looked at the skyline, and was smitten, just as Dan Doctoroff was on his late-night ride up the FDR Drive.[16]

Twenty years later, he had amassed enough capital to begin his real estate career, snapping up a small parcel near the convention center and building a moderately priced Comfort Inn. In the next decade, he built more than 25 such hotels, most of which had fewer than 300 rooms, in less desirable areas of Manhattan and the other boroughs. His partner John Lam struck out on his own in 2004 and quickly amassed a portfolio of some 20 similar hotels. The Financial Crisis hardly dented their momentum.[17] About 40 percent of the hotel rooms built between 2008 and 2010 were in the outer boroughs, according to the tourism agency

NYC & Company.[18] At one point, 40 hotels were on the drawing board for Brooklyn. The rates at these hotels were often half that of the major properties in Midtown. When the Marriott Marquis opened, New York could count 46,000 hotel rooms. Today, the total is approaching 90,000.[19]

City officials had helped tourism projects when they were seen as real estate investments, as was the case with the Marquis, the New Amsterdam Theater, and the Brooklyn Marriott. They were ambivalent about more direct aid. Ed Koch adamantly refused to put city money toward luring tourists, saying that if the hotel owners wanted to advertise the city, they should raise money themselves. David Dinkins reduced money for the Convention and Visitors Bureau when he cut the budget, restored it when there was an outcry, and defended the high taxes the city levied on hotel rooms. Rudy Giuliani undermined the push for an improved convention center and used the convention bureau as a refugee for high-level deputies he wanted to move elsewhere. Ironically, the politicization of the tourism agency actually served to raise its stature with government officials.

September 11 cemented the ties between government and tourism. Only two days after the attacks, during a press conference updating the estimate of the number of people killed, Rudy Giuliani told the worldwide audience watching on television that if people really wanted to help the city, they should go to a Broadway show. He then virtually ordered the producers to reopen by the next day.[20] They did. Soon the tourism industry and the city joined forces in a campaign called New York Rising, designed to show that New York was still a good place to visit. Much of the effort was focused on media, with scenes of tourists arriving in New York. Ads were quickly shot and received hours of airtime, much of it donated. The decline of the industry was reversed.[21] By March 2002, the 27 shows open on Broadway were filling 90 percent of their seats. Hotels were doing better as well.[22] Traditionally, hotels were at peak occupancy on Tuesday nights, filled with business people. Now they were booked solid on Saturday nights with weekend travelers. Even today, hotel occupancy is at its highest on Saturday nights.

The tourism rebound picked up speed in 2003, as the city's economy regained its footing. In 2006, Bloomberg installed ad executive George Fertitta at NYC & Co. and gave the agency $15 million to spend on advertising and marketing. Each year after 2001, the number of visitors rose, except for the small decline in 2009 following the Financial Crisis. It is poised to exceed 50 million people a year, 40 percent more than in the year after September 11. These additional tourists can find beds because of all the new hotels that had been built, and they can afford them because the increased supply kept a lid on room rates. The average room rate in New York City topped $300 a night in 2007. Amid the Great Recession, prices were slashed to under $240 a night in 2009. Even today, increases have been small because of all the new budget rooms flooding the market.[23]

Some New Yorkers remain ambivalent about the benefits of the tourism industry. The acerbic website Gawker highlighted a 2010 picture of a sidewalk divided in half, with the word "tourists" painted on one side and "New Yorkers" on the other. "While we want visitors to NYC to have a wonderful and comfortable time, spend lots of money and tell their friends to come too, we also want them to get out of our way and not make our lives a living hell," wrote one columnist.[24] The same year a poll on another local website, Gothamist, incredulously found that 65 percent of those voting preferred the pre-Disneyification Times Square, although it wasn't clear if the young people participating had any idea of the crime, fear, and sleaziness it had featured.[25]

Mayor Bloomberg is troubled by no such doubts. Every speech he gives on the economy contains at least one acknowledgment of the sector's importance. Each January he finds an attractive backdrop, usually in a borough other than Manhattan, to announce the latest tourism total, stress the number of jobs created, and take as much of the credit as possible. He deserves credit, of course, but so do Bill Marriott, Michael Eisner, and a long list of others. Just five years after the Marriott opened its doors in 1985, the Convention and Visitors Bureau estimated that the tourism sector accounted for 143,600 jobs. Today, NYC & Co. puts that number at more than 310,000. The gain of 160,000 jobs is almost enough to replace the 184,000 factory jobs lost in the same period.

Cultural institutions of all kinds thrive on tourists. Visitors purchase 63 percent of Broadway tickets.[26] They account for more than half the attendance at museums like the Metropolitan Museum of Art. These arts-motivated visitors see about three cultural venues on each trip, and many extend their stays to take in enough of the cultural offerings. Many restaurants rely in large part on tourists.

Retail has been transformed as well. Twenty million tourists a year visit Macy's flagship store on 34th Street. The impact is most apparent in Times Square. In just the two years between 2008 and 2010, average per-square-foot retail rents in the area almost doubled, to $1,700, as teen-oriented retailers like Forever 21 and American Eagle built their largest stores virtually side by side. Forever 21, which is paying more than $20 million a year in rent, is open from 8 a.m. to 2 a.m., contains 151 fitting rooms and 32 cash registers, and employs 500 workers. The company can justify the rents because it expects annual sales to top $100 million and for the tourists who come to New York to take their enthusiasm for the merchandise back home.[27]

No visitors are more prized than those who come from abroad. They stay longer than tourists from within the United States and spend more as well. The weak dollar has been a particular draw since it, as well as the lack of value-added taxes that inflate retail prices at home, makes it almost possible to finance a visit on the savings from purchases alone. International tourists total about 10 million, or one-fifth of the total. The United Kingdom and Canada historically provide the most, although emerging powerhouses in Asia like China and India as well as resurgent countries like Brazil are sending millions of people to replace traditional stalwarts like the Japanese.

The visceral reaction of many New Yorkers to the tourists—feeling displaced—is misguided. Without them there would be many fewer shows on Broadway, not nearly the number of restaurants and higher prices at those that remain, and a sharp decline in the number of cultural organizations, which also would have shorter hours and many fewer exhibits.

Proponents of government support for industrial jobs argue that tourism is an inadequate replacement for manufacturing. In an impassioned plea for more city support for manufacturing in the book *What's Next for New York City's Economy,* Adam Friedman pointed out that manufacturing jobs pay about $52,000 on average—anywhere from 49 percent to 21 percent more than the average retail and restaurant jobs.[28] This broad brush misses how jobs in those sectors directly related to tourism pay much better than the average, in large part because they are unionized. "In major hospitality markets, such as Miami and Houston, where union density is low (less than 20 percent) the vast majority of hotel workers earn wages in the $7–8 hour range, with little if any benefits," says Peter Ward, the leader of the hotel workers union, in *What's Next for New York.* "However, where union density is higher, workers have been able to achieve significant improvements. Union density is highest in New York City and San Francisco, in the 70–80 percent range. Hotel workers in those cities are able to earn middle class incomes, with wages starting at $18–20 hour, high-quality healthcare, and defined-benefit pension plans."[29]

Nonunion hotels like the Marriott Marquis match the union pay scale, in large part to avoid the work rule requirements that drive up costs and limit management flexibility. The waiters at high-end steak houses like Smith & Wollensky can make $100,000 in a good year. The guards and other workers at museums, owned by the city, are unionized. Unions dominate Broadway, and even stagehands on long-running shows earn more than $70,000 a year.

Meanwhile, many of the manufacturing jobs that do exist have changed dramatically. Wages are high precisely because the work that remains is highly skilled. At the Brooklyn Navy Yard, Ferra Designs produces impressive metal staircases and other architectural products, many of which go into the apartments and townhouses of famous actors like Robert De Niro. The people who make these products are not unskilled immigrants, but college graduates from schools like the Pratt Institute of Technology, trained designers who like to work with their hands.[30]

The factory jobs that have migrated overseas would no longer provide for a middle-class lifestyle. Consider the now ubiquitous iPhone, a symbol of Chinese dominance in manufacturing. Workers in southern China in 2010 were paid only about $1 an hour to assemble the phone, and the total value of the labor involved amounted to only about 7 percent of the $600 cost. The same is true for the workers who assemble the garments once made in New York. In the top two sources for apparel imported into the United States, the minimum wage for a Chinese worker is 93 cents an hour, and in India the figure for a skilled worker is 68 cents. Wages in Central America aren't much higher, approaching $2 an hour.[31] Even if such work returned to the United States, the best workers could hope for would be minimum wage.

In every way, tourism has replaced manufacturing in the city's economy. It provides diversification and a counterweight to Wall Street. It generates many middle-class jobs. It employs immigrants and unskilled workers and speeds them up the economic and social ladder far better than factory work. It is especially hospitable to women. It makes few demands for tax breaks and other city incentives.

Its importance is too little appreciated by most New Yorkers.

CHAPTER 13

TRICKLE-DOWN ECONOMICS

EVEN AS FEAR GRIPPED THE CITY AMID THE DEEPENING Financial Crisis, the elegant Rose Main Reading Room at the New York Public Library was filled, on the first Monday night in November 2008, with many of the most important people in New York. The room, long the heartbeat of the famous building, was as big as two city blocks—78 feet by 297 feet—and its long oak tables were covered with cloths for the annual Library Lions Benefit. Author Toni Morrison served as master of ceremonies, and the event honored playwright Edward Albee, essayist Nora Ephron, and novelist Salman Rushdie. Mayor Michael Bloomberg made it clear how important the evening was in the city's social and philanthropic calendar. He not only came to deliver a short speech; he stayed for the entire dinner.

The library raised almost $3 million that night, as the event showcased the connection between Wall Street and the rest of New York. Catherine Marron, the chairwoman of the library's board, welcomed the throng. She was the wife of Donald Marron, longtime chief of PaineWebber, whose fortune was ensured when he sold the company in the 1980s. Library President Paul LeClerc noted that all the costs of the dinner itself had been covered by the steering committee, which included venture capitalist Lionel Pincus, financier Felix Rohatyn, Lehman Brothers' Richard Fuld (who didn't attend), and buyout specialist Stephen Schwarzman. The cost of the remaining tickets went directly to the library's programs. LeClerc also noted that a few months before, Schwarzman had pledged $100 million for the library, and the building would soon carry his name, albeit discreetly.

In some ways, the dinner marked the end of the fourth great Wall Street boom in modern New York. This time Wall Street had found a way to make money on an unprecedented scale and to pay itself sums that made the bonuses of the 1980s seem paltry. It had lifted the city and its institutions, like the library, as well. But the question on everyone's mind that night was whether they would also be the ones to ruin the city's economy once again.

Wall Street's post-9/11 recovery began as early as 2003, even as the media and regulators began to expose the seamy side of the Internet boom. New York attorney general Eliot Spitzer led the way, exposing the dubious practices of Henry Blodget and his fellow analysts and investment bankers, eventually extracting multimillion-dollar settlements from securities firms and driving Blodget out of the business. Structural reforms were instituted to separate research and investment banking presumably to protect investors from advice merely designed to facilitate investment banking transactions. As had happened in every previous Wall Street downturn, some experts claimed that the securities business had been fundamentally changed. Goldman Sachs and Morgan Stanley seemed to suggest they might be right. In 2002, their investment banking revenues were only half of the $10 billion they had collected in 2000. Two firms that had avoided the worst Internet excesses, Bear Stearns and Lehman Brothers, were expected to falter as interest rates rose.[1] The number of jobs on Wall Street had fallen by 35,000, or a little more than 20 percent, between the peak in 2000 and 2003. Total wages and bonuses plummeted as well, declining by $11 billion or about the same percentage. Still, Wall Street accounted for 20 percent of all the income in the city.[2]

In many ways, the turnaround began with the decision by Google, which had emerged as the dominant company on the Internet, to go public.[3] The news generated great excitement and revived interest in initial public offerings. At the same time, and more important, traders began making larger profits as they committed more of their firms' capital. Goldman Sachs borrowed $18 billion in 2003 for its traders, and it generated $9.9 billion in revenue, a one-third increase over the previous year. Meanwhile, investment banking provided only $2.7 billion of the firm's revenue. Goldman didn't break out the earnings for each group, but everyone knew where most of the firm's profits came from.[4]

The bond houses didn't falter, either. The Federal Reserve Board had cut interest rates in the aftermath of the Internet implosion and September 11 to keep the economy from a severe recession, which helped the bond market. Bear Stearns and Lehman thrived in that environment and even after interest rates rose modestly. The decades-long drive to increase homeownership had led to relaxed standards for mortgages, setting off an explosion in home prices and lending. Like Salomon in the 1980s, Bear Stearns and Lehman Brothers' expertise in bonds allowed them to capture much of the business as housing loans were packaged and resold in collateralized mortgage obligations, three words everyone in America learned in the coming years. Goldman entered the business in a big way, and Merrill Lynch and Citigroup tried to join the crowd in the middle of the decade.

Meanwhile, the man who would become the most important banker in the Financial Crisis returned to the city to take over J.P. Morgan Chase. Chase was the product of a dizzying series of mergers with other banks, both within New York and across the nation, but by the early years of the decade its profits trailed many of its peers, and it was often tagged as a mediocre bank. In July 2004, the bank completed its merger with Banc One of Chicago, a deal designed to broaden its geographic reach and bring Banc One CEO Jamie Dimon back to New York from exile in Chicago. A longtime protégé of Citigroup CEO Sanford Weill, Dimon had been ousted by his mentor after clashing with Weill's daughter. He had fixed the troubled Chicago bank, and now he turned his attention to doing the same at J.P. Morgan Chase, whose profits were only a third of Citi's, although they were close in size, with about $1 trillion in assets.[5]

As the recession bottomed out and the shock of the September 11 attacks receded, Wall Street's rebuilding gained momentum. Merrill Lynch added more than 1,000 people to its ranks in 2004 as it moved into fast-growing areas like energy and electronic trading.[6] Postings for securities jobs at Baruch College's business school jumped 70 percent that year, and twice as many new Baruch MBAs landed positions as the year before.[7] Bonuses rose a startling $8 billion. In part, the increase in compensation reflected the changing nature of the business, especially in New York. The number of secretaries fell by 15 percent in the three tough years, and the ranks of clerks were pared by 20 percent as firms embraced technology to handle their work.[8] When Wall Street began hiring again, the additions were all well-paid professionals—bankers, traders, and salespeople—which raised compensation expenses for the firms dramatically.

Just as Salomon had dominated the 1980s, Goldman Sachs towered over its rivals in this era. In many ways, that was fitting. Salomon had been the first major securities firm to go public; Goldman was the last. Salomon had given a face to Wall Street greed as John Gutfreund's $3.1 million pay for 1986 attracted enormous attention, especially in Michael's Lewis landmark book, *Liar's Poker.* Lewis believed that the 1980s would be an anomaly—a historical curiosity—in the steady and predictable ways of making money. Goldman Sachs proved him wrong.[9]

The firm had been founded by a German immigrant, Marcus Goldman, in 1869, and Sachs was added to the nameplate when his son-in-law joined him. Always headquartered in Lower Manhattan, the firm pioneered the use of commercial paper and was one of the leaders in the early IPO market. In 1930, Sidney Weinberg became its senior partner and pushed it into more prestigious investment banking work, which gave it its imposing reputation, solidified by its role in leading Ford Motor Co.'s initial public offering in 1956. Ironically, it underwrote more Internet IPOs than anyone else in the tech boom, but it escaped the opprobrium heaped upon Merrill Lynch, Morgan Stanley, and Frank Quattrone's various employers.

For much of the 1990s, co–chief executive Jon Corzine tried unsuccessfully to persuade his partners to go public. While many were happy with the millions they took home each year, Corzine was a trader, and he knew the company's profits were limited by the lack of capital and because partners were reluctant to make the riskiest bets when it was their own money at stake rather than the money of their shareholders. Finally, in 1999, he won over a majority of the partners, in part by elevating investment banker Henry Paulson to equal status as co-chief executive. The two men did not mesh. When Goldman traders lost $650 million after Russia defaulted on its debt, Paulson pushed Corzine aside.[10] Many thought the move would symbolize an end to Goldman's obsession with trading. They were wrong.[11]

In early May 1999, the firm was ready to sell stock, and strong demand allowed it to increase its target price. It launched the IPO at $53 a share, and investors pushed the price up to just over $70 by the end of the first day's trading, making the partners richer than they had ever imagined. The value of Paulson's stake in the company, for example, soared to $315 million. When he needed to fly to New York on short notice in the treacherous days of September 2008, he merely put the cost of a private plane on his personal credit card. Corzine's stock was valued at $335 million, and he used a small portion to finance successful campaigns for the US Senate and governor of New Jersey, as well as an unsuccessful attempt to be reelected for a second term as governor.[12]

Partners weren't the only people who cashed in. Every other employee received stock valued at half their take-home pay in the previous year, plus a bonus for longevity. A secretary who had worked for the firm for five years and made $40,000 received shares worth $25,000 at the expected offering price. By the end of the first day's trading, that secretary's holdings were worth more than $30,000.[13] By October 2007, each share was worth more than $228, almost five times the offering price.

Much of the new capital—almost $4 billion was raised in the IPO— was handed to the traders, led by Lloyd Blankfein. He had made his mark a few years earlier. Frustrated by the back-and-forth in a meeting trying to dissect recent trading losses, he stormed out of the session to prove the mettle of the traders by placing a multimillion-dollar bet that the dollar would increase in value against the yen. It was his first trade ever with the firm's own capital, and it paid off handsomely for Goldman.[14]

Like so many traders, Blankfein did not come from a connected family or a fancy prep school. He grew up in New York City housing projects and put himself through both Harvard and Harvard Law School. He was rejected by Goldman for a job in investment banking and had to settle for a position as a gold salesman at its J. Aron subsidiary. Like Salomon's Lou Ranieri a decade earlier, his personal style attracted attention—he wandered the trading floor without shoes, at least until a promotion in 2003. He pushed his traders to be more and more aggressive. In 2004, when he was promoted to co–chief executive alongside Paulson, the average amount Goldman could lose in any single day reached $71 million, more than double the amount it had been willing to lose in one day in 2000. Morgan Stanley, Goldman's main rival, tolerated only a $40 million daily bet.[15] When Paulson decided to accept an offer as George Bush's Treasury secretary in 2006, Blankfein became sole chief executive.[16]

True to its reputation, Goldman was the best on Wall Street in investment banking, arranging mergers and corporate stock and bond sales. It was a powerhouse in the mortgage securitization business, packaging and selling increasingly dubious mortgages and other consumer loans. Most importantly, its traders were feared on Wall Street because they were unmatched in their ability to time markets. As others continued to believe that housing prices and mortgage bonds would rise, Goldman took a major bet that the market was headed for trouble even as it sold such bonds to longtime clients. In 2006, Goldman's profits hit an unprecedented $10 billion, about 40 percent of the $26 billion earned by all big securities firms, which itself was a record. The next year, benefiting from its bet against housing and against its clients, Goldman's earnings jumped another 22 percent to $11.6 billion.[17]

It was fitting that Blankfein became the highest-paid CEO on Wall Street and maybe even appropriate that he was the highest paid ever. However, the amount is stunning, especially compared with Gutfreund's pay two decades earlier. In 2005, Goldman handed Blankfein $38 million. The next year, he received a 42 percent increase to $53 million.[18] And then, ignoring the developing crisis, Goldman's board paid Blankfein $68.5 million in cash and stock for his work in 2007. His two top lieutenants did almost as well. Forty-seven-year-old Gary Cohn and 48-year-old Jon Winkelried each received a $66.9 million bonus, putting their total compensation only $1 million behind their boss's.[19]

If Gutfreund's outrageous $3.1 million pay two decades earlier were adjusted for inflation, it would have amounted to $7.8 million in 2007. Blankfein was paid almost nine times what Gutfreund had made. Even then, Goldman wasn't the most lucrative place to work on Wall Street. In this Wall Street boom, big securities houses like Goldman couldn't compete with the money generated by private equity firms and hedge funds.

A Salomon alumnus and former Treasury secretary, William Simon opened Wall Street's eyes in the 1980s to the possibilities of private equity and its major tool, the leveraged buyout (LBO). Private equity firms amassed a pool of cash, which they used to purchase public companies whose stock traded at a discount to their potential value, often because their managements were comfortable with the status quo. Firms like Simon's Wesray then loaded up the firms with debt, installed new management to make them more profitable, and then resold the companies to the public, often realizing windfalls many times their investment. Another New York private equity firm named Kohlberg Kravis Roberts (known as KKR) dominated the business in the late 1980s and 1990s, most notably winning a heated competition for RJR Nabisco.[20]

KKR remained a major force in private equity, but the leading firm of the era was the Blackstone Group, founded in 1985 with $400,000 by Stephen Schwarzman and Pete Peterson, the Lehman investment banker who forced the company's sale and refused to give up his special bonus without compensation.[21] By 2007, it was by far the world's largest such firm, with $28 billion in private equity funds, $17 billion in hedge funds, $13 billion in real estate funds, and $6.5 billion in bond funds.[22] That year it won a bidding war for the portfolio of office buildings controlled by Equity Office Properties Trust, paying $39 billion in what was the largest LBO ever.[23] Blackstone's 2006 earnings were $2.3 billion, and its investors, primarily large institutions including public pension funds, profited as well.[24] Annual returns since its founding were 30.8 percent

before Blackstone's fees and a still impressive 22.8 percent after Blackstone's hefty take off the top.[25]

Now Schwarzman and Peterson decided to secure their future by
taking Blackstone public. The irony was obvious. Private equity firms
thrived because the stock market failed to value companies appropriately and because companies could be run better if they didn't have to
meet the short-term demands of stockholders. Nevertheless, the payoff
for Blackstone's leaders was irresistible. Peterson, who retired with the
IPO, received $1.9 billion and retained a 4 percent stake in the com-
pany. Schwarzman sold shares worth more than $600 million, and his
24 percent of the public company was worth $7.7 billion the day Black-
stone went public at $31 a share.[26] That made the $400 million he paid
himself in 2006 seem like almost small change. KKR followed suit with
its own IPO.[27]

If Lloyd Blankfein's $68 million had provoked anger, Schwarzman's
bonanza and lavish lifestyle sparked outrage. A *New York* magazine
columnist described him as "a perfect poster boy for this age of greed,
sharklike, perpetually grinning, a tiny Gordon Gekko [the famed trader
of the Oliver Stone movie *Wall Street*] without the hair product."[28]
Schwarzman was reputed to dine on $400 crabs. His wife invited 1,500
people to his 60th birthday party early in 2007, and some of those invited, like General Colin Powell, admitted they barely knew him. Held
at the Park Avenue Armory, it featured singer Rod Stewart, who was
reported to charge as much as $1 million for such events. Congress in-
troduced bills to hike taxes on private equity gains, perhaps inspired by
his indiscretion.[29]

But alongside his conspicuous consumption, Schwarzman assumed
a leading position in the arts and cultural world. In 2004, he became
chairman of the Kennedy Center for the Performing Arts in Washington.[30] Two years later, New York's Frick Museum invited him onto its
board in an effort to tap into the newly emerging wealth in the city.[31]
And in early 2008, his gift of $100 million to the New York Public
Library became one of the largest gifts ever to a New York cultural
institution.[32]

His gift was designed to jumpstart fundraising for an ambitious strategic plan to bring the landmark on Fifth Avenue and 42nd Street into the twenty-first century and to make it a hub of reading and book borrowing as well as research. In return, the building would be named for the buyout king, with inscriptions in the marble stone at its main entrances. Library President LeClerc sought to deflect criticism by noting that virtually every room in the facility had been named for a donor and that the names of the library's three famous founders—John Jacob Astor, Samuel Tilden, and James Lennox—were also inscribed on the building, although only in one location.[33] Schwarzman embraced the library's ambitions. "This was an absolutely first-class, professional, practical strategic plan and it deserved to be supported," he said. "The library helps lower- and middle-income people—immigrants—get their shot at the American dream."[34]

The library benefited far more than Blackstone's new investors. Its stock rose only modestly on its first day of trading, soon slipped below the offering price, and was hurt badly in the Financial Crisis.

Hedge funds became as important as private equity firms and equally lucrative for their founders and the city. Whereas private equity firms buy, improve, and then sell companies, hedge funds specialize in trading, using their own capital in aggressive and risky maneuvers. The first hedge fund was founded in 1949, but they came into prominence in the early 1990s when George Soros made more than $1 billion in a famous bet that the English pound would drop dramatically. He defied the efforts of the British government to support the currency, a sign that governments could not always defeat the power of players like hedge funds.

These firms became attractive career alternatives for the best traders on Wall Street, who chafed under the restraints of heavily regulated companies and what they regarded as unfair restraints on their compensation. Neal Berger spent half his life working for the biggest names on Wall Street, such as Morgan Stanley and J.P. Morgan Chase, before opening his own fund. Thirty-six years old and unmarried, he spent every moment looking for small price discrepancies to exploit. "My goal is to make as much money in any given year as George Soros pays in taxes," he said in 2005, a few years after opening his doors.[35]

In a way, the game was fixed. Hedge fund managers received an annual fee of approximately 1.5 percent of the assets and kept about 20 percent of any trading profits. Their expenses were small compared with their assets; Berger's firm employed only 23 people, which was typical. Originally designed for wealthy individuals, who were told they had to be prepared to lose all the money they invested, hedge funds now drew their capital from institutions, including public pension funds, just like private equity firms.[36]

Many hedge funds were tracked avidly, including Tudor Investments, started in 1980 by Paul Tudor Jones II. His long-term returns—26 percent a year since the start date—were so irresistible that he was managing $19 billion by 2007, compared with $125 million in 1986. His star status allowed him to charge more than most other hedge funds. He took 4 percent of assets as his basic fee—almost $800 million a year—and 23 percent of all profits.[37]

Like Schwarzman and many other hedge fund billionaires, he put some of that money toward good causes. Jones founded the Robin Hood Foundation, which supported more than 200 organizations fighting poverty in the city. Its annual benefit headlined the society news. The dinner in 2007 raised $71 million, a one-third increase from the previous year. One attendee, probably a hedge fund manager himself, paid $1.3 million so that he and nine friends could have dinner with star chef Mario Batali. Justifying the excess, another hedge fund manager and Robin Hood board member claimed that "there was a feeling of social responsibility and philanthropy in the room that was palpable. It was overwhelming."[38]

In the decade between 1998 and 2008, the number of hedge funds tripled, and assets under management increased tenfold to $2.2 trillion. In 2007, the funds accounted for 30 percent of all stock trades in the United States, 55 percent of all trading in emerging market bonds, and 35 percent of all derivative action. While some hedge funds had located in suburban Greenwich, the city was home to more than a third of all hedge funds in the world with assets of more than $1 billion. London was a distant second, with 75 funds of that size.

Wall Street's impact on the city during the Bloomberg era cannot be overstated. Using the broadest measure, New York City securities jobs peaked at 190,000 in October 2007, about 10,000 below the 2000 record. Yet pay had risen so dramatically that the sector accounted for 28 percent of all the wages in the city, the highest figure ever. The average salary exceeded $400,000, or seven times the average for everyone else working in the city. From 2003 to 2007, Wall Street salaries had increased 76 percent; everyone else's pay had risen less than 20 percent. Cash bonuses hit $33 billion in 2006 (they declined slightly in 2007) compared with $10 billion in 2002. In all, said the annual report on the industry from the state comptroller, each job on Wall Street created another 3.2 jobs elsewhere in the economy—2 in the city and 1.2 elsewhere, mostly in the suburbs.

The industry directly provided 20 percent of state and 13 percent of the city's tax revenues, without counting for indirect payments through the property tax. Personal income and business income taxes from the sector gave the state $12 billion in 2007. The enormous size of the city budget was dependent on Wall Street in two ways. Its own progressive income tax and business taxes provided billions directly, and the amount Wall Street sent to Albany allowed the state to increase aid to education and spending on health care in the city even as it diverted some of the money to other, less well-off areas of New York.

Wall Street was the main fuel of the boom; tourism provided a significant additional boost and prosperity rippled through the city. In 2004, the Zagat Survey found that 226 restaurants had opened in the city, the most since 2000.[39] The numbers kept growing as the economy improved. Jobs were so plentiful that 34-year-old John Chasteen received a 30 percent raise in late 2005 to join the top-rated Sea Grill in Rockefeller Center. A 26-year-old actor named Robby Sharpe got a waiter's job the very first day he arrived in the city from Newfoundland, Canada, and was pleasantly surprised when his tips totaled $150 a day. Barbara Jacobs, who admitted only to being in her 60s, landed a job as a prep cook after taking courses at a cooking school. A survey showed that executive chefs averaged $85,000 a year.[40]

Retail thrived as well. Home improvement stores like Home Depot and discounters like Target had long steered clear of New York, convinced that exorbitant rents, higher labor costs, and hefty taxes made it impossible for them to make a profit. Home Depot realized that this assumption wasn't true when its new store in Elmont, Long Island, just a short distance from the Queens border, was so successful that it became the chain's top-grossing store, with annual sales of $100 million. The clientele was so extensive that the store stayed open 24 hours day. The Atlanta-based company decided to blanket the city with stores, starting in Queens. Soon virtually every national chain was represented in the city.[41]

The realization that New York had too few stores to serve so many people—both the 8 million residents and the tourists—spurred activity in the boroughs. The depressed area in Brooklyn called Red Hook, home to several public housing projects, was fertile territory first for Target and then for the Swedish retailer IKEA. In Manhattan's SoHo shopping district, homegrown retailers gave way as names like Apple and Bloomingdale's offered landlords much higher rents to establish destination stores. Banks aggressively took corner locations in Manhattan and surged into the boroughs. After all, Brooklyn had one branch for every 8,600 people. Minneapolis had one branch for every 4,100 people.[42] Retail jobs soared and by June 2006 set a record, with more than 286,000 people working in stores.[43]

Competition pushed up wages, too, with the median hourly wage hitting $10.59.[44] The increase was welcomed, but economists noted that retail pay was both below the average for the city and insufficient for a family to aspire to anything resembling a middle-class lifestyle. While retail wages were low, building all those stores added higher paying construction jobs, and the economies of Staten Island, Brooklyn, Queens, and the Bronx outpaced even Manhattan's in the early years of the recovery.[45]

As Wall Street money cascaded through the city, its financial engineering inflated the economy as well, although mostly in commercial real estate. The ravages of subprime lending were confined to a few neigh-borhoods in Queens and Brooklyn where middle-class minority families owned their own homes and were lured into high-risk loans. The rest of the city was spared, since New York's residential market was so tilted toward renters and because co-ops demanded large down payments and blocked exotic loans.

Securitized loans did provide a steady stream of money for large residential projects, and building permits jumped to nearly 34,000 in 2007, the highest total since the city started keeping records in 1964.[46] Construction activity was so intense that every available union trades-man was at work. Unions, which controlled hiring under their contract, imported 1,000 workers from elsewhere in the country to try to meet the demand.[47] They preferred that approach to training more workers, espe-cially the minorities who had long been shut out of the lucrative trades, since they doubted the level of work would continue. The unions were right when the Financial Crisis shut down the flow of construction loans and nongovernment construction dried up.

Low interest rates, easy money from banks, and the commercial mortgage securitization market sent the value of buildings soaring. Harry Macklowe showed how to play the game when he bought the GM building on Fifth Avenue for a record $1.4 billion in 2003, beating out many rivals. He updated the building, including luring the city's first Apple retail store, and refinanced it twice, including once in late 2007, when the property was valued at $2.7 billion. Many others followed in his wake—buying, refinancing, and flipping buildings at big profits. The most famous was Blackstone's $39 billion purchase of the Equity Office Properties Trust collection of 573 office buildings, which it immediately began flipping to other landlords.[48] Macklowe, seeking to duplicate his success at the GM building, bought seven buildings in New York for $7 billion using short-term debt.[49]

The rapid run-up in building prices was based on the sharp increase in commercial office rents. The New York City office market is inelastic. The lack of available sites and intense competition among various users for them inflates land prices. The tight hold of union construction work-ers and the difficulties of building in such constricted spaces make the cost of construction exorbitant. When companies expand, rents move up sharply because there is no way to increase the supply of space. The reverse happens in downturns. Rents fall sharply because landlords need to make deals at whatever price to keep their cash flow high enough to meet debt and operating costs.

As Wall Street recovered, rents moved up in 2004 and 2005, especially for the buildings with large enough blocks of space for financial firms. Rents pushed past $60 a square foot in late 2005, a 20 percent jump in just two years.[51] Those prices were modest compared with what hedge funds were willing to pay. With their small staffs and huge margins, the cost of real estate was inconsequential for hedge funds. The right address to impress their clients mattered much more, and hedge funds concentrated in a few of the best buildings. Harry Macklowe's GM building was at the top of the list, and in 2005 and 2006, hedge funds were fighting over spaces despite asking rents that reached $125 a square foot.[52]

The combination of strong demand from financial firms, hedge funds with no limit on what they would pay, and growth in law firms and other business service firms riding Wall Street's momentum led to dizzying increases. In late 2005, many deals for new space went for more than $70 a square foot. The $100 barrier was breached by more and more hedge funds, and even a traditional bank, Wachovia, paid an average of $100 a square foot to add 75,000 square feet to its existing lease at the Seagram building.[53] The GM building was demanding $150 a square foot and getting it.

Interestingly, this time the rapid rise in rents did not spur a wave of relocations out of the city. In part, this was a reflection of the change in the workforce, especially at financial firms. Few low-paid back-office jobs existed anymore, since technology now handled the work such people had previously performed. In their place, financial firms had hired thousands of skilled professionals, and for them, New York had become so desirable that moving elsewhere was unthinkable. If a cost-conscious CEO did decide to leave, there were many other companies ready to hire the disaffected. Goldman Sachs discovered that in 2004 when it tried to move traders to its new tower across the Hudson in Jersey City; the traders simply said they wouldn't go, and Goldman was able to fill only a portion of its new building. In 2007, the average rent at the most important buildings in the city reached $104 a square foot. The average for all of Midtown was just shy of $80 a square foot.

Charities and city government benefited as much as real estate, if not more. In 2006, a benefit for the New York University Child Study Center raised more than $6 million. The Guggenheim Museum and Samuel Waxman Cancer Research Center galas took in more than $4 million. *Crain's* publisher Alair Townsend counted more than 20 nonprofits that raised at least $1 million from their fund-raising parties and suggested, only half in jest, that anyone not attainting that level keep the amount secret to avoid embarrassment. Total tax collections increased 74 percent between 2002 and 2008, reaching $37.5 billion. John Lindsay's progressive income tax played a crucial role. Personal income tax receipts doubled in that period to $8.8 billion.

In all, the city added 262,000 jobs between 2003 and 2008, a 7 percent increase. The number was just shy of the 1969 record. There was so much wealth that it made many New Yorkers uncomfortable. Incomes that would be envied in virtually every other city seemed hopeless inadequate.

Writer Penelope Trunk moved to New York in the mid-1990s seeking to make a name and cash in on the Internet boom. Ten years later, she had achieved some recognition as a columnist and blogger and was making more than $200,000 a year, a figure that put her in the top 10 percent of household income in the city. Nevertheless, she abandoned Brooklyn's Park Slope for Madison, Wisconsin. "The birthday parties were killing us," she said, feeling there was no way to compete with the family that rented a ship for their young child's big day. "It was a super interesting life, but interesting doesn't make you happy."[54]

Trunk's experience reflected a city of widespread inequality. New York always seemed to have more poor people than it should have, especially in good times. In 1999, a survey by the Community Service Society of New York found that one in four New Yorkers were below the poverty line, despite the roaring economy. Clearly, many residents, especially those with little education, were unable to get ahead no matter how hard they worked. Of course, the rate also reflected the continuing tide of immigration, since new entrants to the city were almost always poor. Most immigrants moved up the economic ladder, especially by the second generation, while new arrivals continued to replenish the ranks of the poor.[55]

But even considering the impact of immigration, no one could deny the widening gap that was so stark by 2007. The top 1 percent of households in the city accounted for 44 percent of the income in New York, more than triple the 17 percent in 1987. The bottom 90 percent accounted for 34 percent, compared with 59 percent two decades earlier. Wall Street's three-decades-long obsession with greed accounted for most of the increase, although the city's revival also lured many other rich people to New York. The growing gap between the rich and everyone else was a national problem—the top 1 percent of households in the United States earned 23 percent of total income, about twice the percentage as in 1987—but no other large city showed such extremes as New York.[56]

The fourth Wall Street boom, this time with an assist from tourism, had made New York and some New Yorkers richer than they had ever been. The Financial Crisis sent the city's economy reeling once again, and the end to the real estate bubble led to the largest real estate failure in history, which served yet again to entrench the city's rent regulation laws.

CHAPTER 14

THE BIGGEST
CRASH OF ALL

IN THE SUMMER OF 2000, *NEW YORK TIMES* COLUMNIST
Paul Krugman was intrigued by a story in the paper about the travails
of apartment renters in San Francisco, where "there are never enough
apartments . . . horror stories of elderly longtime tenants being forced
out . . . tales of barely inhabitable rooms for $1,000 a month." The next
day the noted economist, then in his second year as a regular columnist,
called the report interesting but flawed. "And yet there was something
crucial missing," he wrote, "specifically two words that I knew had to be
part of the story. . . . To an economist or for that matter a freshman who
has taken Economics 101, everything about that story fairly screamed
those two words, which are, of course, 'rent control.'"

Rent control is one of the best-understood issues in all of economics, he explained. Controls on rents reduce the quality and quantity of
housing and send the cost of living in uncontrolled apartments sky-high
because desperate renters have nowhere else to go. Construction is depressed because landlords fear that controls will eventually be extended
to their new units. Relations between tenants and landlords grow increasingly acrimonious, spurring a political arms race to tilt the game
toward one side or the other. Rent control pits people against each other,

he noted, quoting a San Francisco official who said no one in that city seemed to trust anyone anymore.[1]

It wasn't just San Francisco, of course, where the economics of rent control caused such undesirable consequences, nor was it the only place where reporters sidestepped the issue when writing about housing and ignored the question of who benefited and who was hurt. Krugman's column applied to New York as well.

The system of rent regulation that New York kept in place after wartime controls were ended elsewhere—and that John Lindsay saved and extended in 1969 as he ran for reelection—took firm root in the city. There were periodic adjustments that sometimes tightened the rules and sometimes loosened them and transferred control of the system between the city and state. Every two years when the law came up for renewal, Democrats backed tenant demands for more protections and Republicans sided with landlords seeking relief, resulting in a standoff that was resolved only in the last days of the legislative session in June. The result was usually a simple extension, in large part because Republican state senators from the city sided with the tenants and Democrats.

Landlords had enough by the early 1990s. In 1992, real estate interests funneled more than $350,000 to Republican legislative campaigns compared with only about $50,000 for Democrats.[2] Most of the money went to GOP state senators. The state's Conservative Party and a new group called Change-NY threatened to recruit primary challengers to any Republican who backed rent regulation. New studies picked up the theme of Ken Auletta in *The Streets Were Paved with Gold,* which showed how rich people paid below-market rents as well as poorer people. Newspaper editorial writers throughout the state supported changes as well.

Republicans coalesced behind luxury decontrol, designed to end benefits for those with higher incomes. Knowing the political clout of the people who lived in the almost 1 million regulated apartments, city politicians rushed to beat back any weakening. It was predictable that Democrat Mayor David Dinkins, locked in a tough reelection campaign, sought the spotlight as he traveled to Albany to lobby for the laws' extension without being weakened. It was more of a surprise that Republican Rudy Giuliani arrived on the very same day as his rival to proclaim his support of a simple extension. Giuliani had flirted with reforms that would have made wealthy New Yorkers pay market rates, but with his campaign gaining momentum, he came out firmly for extending the rent rules without changes. His campaign advisers insisted that anything less than an unyielding pro–rent rules position was political suicide.[3]

Democrats worried that Republicans might actually allow the laws to expire. So a compromise was struck. Apartments that rented for more than $2,000 a month would no longer be protected when they became vacant, and landlords could rent them for whatever the market would bear. Any apartment that rented for more than $2,000 a month where the tenants' household income exceeded $250,000 for two consecutive years could also be decontrolled. Tired of confronting the issue so frequently, legislators made this version effective for four years.[4]

As 1997 approached, the political climate in New York as well as the nation had shifted sharply to the right. Rudy Giuliani was aggressively cutting back city government, attacking crime, and trying to curtail social programs like welfare even if he continued to support rent regulation. An unknown state senator from suburban Westchester, George Pataki, had pulled off a stunning upset in 1994, denying Democrat Mario Cuomo a fourth term. He had voted against rent regulation as a legislator and publicly pointed out its flaws during his campaign. And Joe Bruno, a pugnacious former boxer, now led the Republicans in the state senate. He clearly abhorred rent control and knew that preserving GOP control of the senate in an increasingly Democratic state required huge campaign funds. There was no more reliable source of that cash than real estate interests.

Landlords were ready to do their part. Their major associations contributed more than $700,000 to legislative campaign funds in 1996, with most of the money going to Republicans. Individual owners gave hundreds of thousands more. Tenant advocates portrayed this as a fight between greedy real estate barons and poor New Yorkers who would be thrown out of their homes. The reality was much more complicated. Bruno's most enthusiastic supporters were small landlords, who scrambled to keep their buildings maintained and eke out a small profit under rent rules. When Bruno spoke to an enthusiastic business audience in early 1997, the front of the room was packed with well-known business leaders in expensive suits and ties. In the back were gathered the small landlords in short-sleeved cotton shirts, with no ties or jackets, desperate for changes that would help them.[5]

Bruno had opened the debate the previous December when he announced that he would allow the rent laws to expire unless Democrats agreed to a plan to permanently phase them out. Anticipating Paul Krugman's column a few years later, Bruno said rent regulation "is the best example of government at its worst that I can point to in this state." It discouraged construction, he said, worsening the housing crisis. It paradoxically drove up rents for residents of unregulated apartments, who in effect subsidized those in regulated ones.[6] Pataki said he, too, favored changes, but he wasn't more specific, positioning himself to be the savior who engineered a compromise. Giuliani said he opposed Bruno's plan, although he came under criticism for not doing enough to preserve the current laws.[7]

Tenant advocates mobilized repeated demonstrations against Bruno and Pataki. Fire broke out in a building where Bruno kept an office, which he blamed on his opponents. Republican senators from New York City broke with their leader. By June, the debate had crystallized over Bruno's fallback position. All vacant apartments would be deregulated, which would fundamentally alter the system from one in which the regulation affected a specific apartment to one that benefited a specific tenant. Most places in the country that had maintained rent regulation employed some version of this arrangement—vacancy decontrol.[8]

Pataki inched away from Bruno's position. Isolated politically, Bruno gave up on his biggest ambitions. Instead of vacancy decontrol, he accepted a deal in which landlords could automatically increase rents by 20 percent when a tenant moved out, up from the previous rule of 16 percent. An extra $100 was allowed on vacant apartments costing less than $300 a month. The income level that would allow immediate decontrol of units renting for $2,000 a month was lowered to $175,000. Other provisions allowed landlords to boost rents when they rehabilitated apartments. Outraged tenants gathered in front of the governor's office to denounce the agreement, carrying signs that read, "Vacancy

Decontrol Equals Evictions." Bruno was subdued. "I am happy but not ecstatic," he said. "I am happy because we're getting where we need to be, which is a place where we are approaching the market on vacancy."[9]

The original 1993 changes had little impact; not that many apartments rented for more than $2,000. The provisions affecting wealthy individuals had very little effect; few landlords wanted to engage in efforts to prove that their tenants exceeded the income limits. Over time, however, as rents rose, an increasing number of apartments rented for more than the deregulation threshold. Landlords increased their renovation spending as apartments became empty to push still more units above $2,000. As the economy boomed in the years after 2004 and with Wall Street eager to lend money on absurdly easy terms, some of the city's biggest landlords saw an opportunity to make billions investing in regulated apartment complexes. The result was the biggest real estate debacle ever. That story begins with Robert Moses.

⊷ ⊶

FACED WITH THE RETURN OF HUNDREDS OF THOU-SANDS of veterans at the end of World War II, Robert Moses began exhorting insurance companies to help build the housing they would need. He steered the civic-minded Metropolitan Life Insurance Co. to an 80-acre neighborhood of gas tanks, industrial buildings, and run-down apartments on the East Side known as the Gashouse District. With the help of government condemnations, property tax breaks, and an agreement that the insurer would limit its profits, Met Life built more than 11,000 apartments there in two complexes, one called Stuyvesant Town after the first leader of Dutch New York and the second named Peter Cooper Village after the inventor of the steam engine who created a free engineering school in the heart of the city. The complexes were for whites only at first; a smaller version called Riverton was constructed for African-Americans in Harlem. Eventually, lawsuits eliminated the racial barrier.[10]

When Met Life decided to sell the complex in 2006, the company itself was undergoing a transformation spurred by its decision to convert from a mutual owned by its policyholders to a publicly held company. It was in the process of shedding many of its New York real estate holdings to increase profits. It sold its iconic headquarters building not far from Stuy Town and Peter Cooper, and it moved several thousand employees across the river to Queens. (Eventually, it decided that it couldn't recruit employees to that facility and leased a major office tower on 42nd Street to give it a headquarters befitting such an important company.) It had deregulated more than 3,000 units at the two complexes. It had undertaken an extensive renovation program designed to speed the process by rehabilitating units and increasing rents.[11]

News of the sale was slow to grab public attention. When it did, Stuy Town and Peter Cooper became synonymous with the middle class and supposedly a textbook example of the benefits of rent control. "It's really sad," said 17-year resident, historian, and filmmaker Suzanne Wasserman about the pending sale. "New York has always attracted people who aren't just interested in money—people interested in culture and poetry and music and dance and those young people who are the creative capital of the city. They aren't going to have a place here and probably really don't already."[12]

The reality was more complex. The young people Wasserman thought would be the victims of deregulation actually had little chance of landing a rent-regulated apartment because longtime residents wouldn't give them up. In 1985, the start-up staff of *Crain's New York Business* gathered in the Peter Cooper apartment of one of the paper's senior executives for a party. The executive had divided his two bedrooms into three and renovated the kitchen. Editors and reporters who had recently moved to New York were dumbfounded. Why would anyone spend money to renovate a rental apartment? Elsewhere in the country, when someone wanted more bedrooms or a better kitchen, they simply moved. Eventually, the out-of-towners learned that rent regulation provided the answer. The system required landlords to renew leases; otherwise they could abuse the system. So tenants in practice acted as if they owned the apartments and benefited from the cut-rate rent even if their incomes soared. The *Crain's* senior executive also owned a house in the Hamptons, purchased in part because his rent in the city was so low that he wouldn't even discuss what he paid.

More than 100 potential bidders looked at the initial offering documents in September. The next month, 16 of them made first-round offers. Many dropped out as the price escalated, including the LeFraks, long experienced in big residential properties in the city. Others were deterred by the growing public clamor that the sale would be a threat to middle-class New Yorkers. In the end, Tishman Speyer and the Apollo real estate group were in a race to top each other's proposals. Tishman won with its offer of $5.4 billion, a record-shattering price. Only the sketchiest financial details were revealed at the time, but Tishman put in only $112 million of its own money. The rest came from its partners, including many public pension funds. CalPERS, the giant California pension fund, contributed $500 million; its counterpart in Florida invested $250 million. Most of the money was borrowed. The interest payments and the costs of operating Peter Cooper and Stuy Town would exceed the income in the next few years, so a reserve was established until revenues could be increased.[13]

Jerry Speyer and his son Rob, who had spearheaded the deal, assured residents that they would be respectful of the role the complexes played in the city. The Speyers had achieved success and enormous profits with other landmarks like Rockefeller Center and the Chrysler Building by improving the properties. The same general idea would work at Stuy Town and Peter Cooper. The difference was that the huge debt they took out on the property meant that they would need to raise rents quickly on the market-rate units and deregulate thousands of other apartments as soon as possible. While they had firsthand experience with the ups and downs of the city's economy, the prospects for the next few years seemed bright. They expected to be able to handle the political opposition. Jerry was a friend and loyal ally of Mayor Bloomberg. The mayor supported rent regulation, as quietly as possible, but no one believed he really believed the system was good for New York. The mayor stayed out of the issue. Deputy Mayor Dan Doctoroff said limited city resources needed to be used elsewhere to create affordable housing.[14]

Signs that the Speyers had misread the market came early. They hiked rents sharply in late 2006 and early 2007. For example, a two-bedroom apartment was raised to $4,450 a month, from $3,250 just two years before. Even the young people flocking to work on Wall Street and in the city's law firms couldn't, or wouldn't, pay that much. The Speyers had also misread the properties' location; by New York standards, it was too far from the subway, at least four long blocks. Many people moved out.[15]

The Speyers didn't intend to violate the law, but they did intend to end the passive approach of other landlords. They hired investigators and lawyers to find people who actually lived elsewhere, violating the rule that a rent-regulated apartment had to be a tenant's principle residence. There would be hundreds if not thousands of such illegal residents, they believed. After all, everyone in New York knew people who moved out of cheap regulated apartments and illegally sublet them to make a little extra income.

While the Bloomberg administration did remain neutral, other politicians railed against the efforts to find those violating the rent laws. In the forefront was Dan Garodnick, the local councilperson, who lived in a regulated apartment in the complex. To the Speyers' surprise, the *New York Times* took up Garodnick's cause. In its most important story, published in May 2008, the *Times* sympathetically chronicled the travails of those who had been targeted, emphasizing the time and legal fees that they incurred to fight back. One of those residents was Edward Stanley, a 53-year-old retired police detective who had spent $5,000 in legal fees after he was accused of actually living in the home he owned on Long Island. The story didn't say where on Long Island, although the exclusive Hamptons seemed a good guess.

An exasperated Rob Speyer, obviously frustrated by the *Times,* said plaintively in that story, "We want a community of people who really live at the property. We don't understand the effort to protect the rights of people who live there illegally." Like the 2000 story that Paul Krugman had found interesting, the *Times* left out something important. Nowhere in the story was the issue raised of whether it was good public policy to allow some lucky renters, whose below-market rents were subsidized by their landlords and by those who paid higher rents in the unregulated market, to buy second homes.

The Speyers realized that the plan wasn't working. Some insiders speculated that their decision to walk away from the Hudson Yards showed that they knew trouble was brewing. Soon the new owners ended the long-standing prohibition of pets, attempting to broaden the market of potential tenants. Then they began cutting the rents. Revenues fell in 2007 instead of rising, and the cost of fighting legal challenges upset the financial plan as well. The biggest blow came when the courts ruled that many of the units had been decontrolled illegally. The complex had taken advantage of a special tax incentive for improvements. Reversing years of practice, the courts ruled that using the tax benefit meant that the apartments remained regulated. The Speyers faced two disasters. Not only would they have to cut rents even more, they would not be able to deregulate units.[16]

The tenants who had brought the suit on the tax incentive said they were attempting to preserve affordable housing. Those who received the rent cuts were not needy; they were the people who lived in market-rate apartments. Most were professionals like political consultant Lauren Bierman, who had chosen to move in with a roommate because the rent and location made sense to them. After the court ruling, she received a reduction in her monthly rent. But when the recession hit, there were better and less expensive places to live, and she left to be replaced by someone just like her.

Each setback for the Speyers added to the pressure as the complex exhausted its $890 million reserve and soon was no longer able to pay the interest on the debt. In the depths of the Financial Crisis, some experts put the value of Stuy Town and Peter Cooper at as little as $1.9 billion. Tishman Speyer decided not to put any more money into the losing venture and in January 2010 surrendered the property to its creditors. All those who had put up equity lost their entire investment. Junior creditors were wiped out, too. One loser was the government of Singapore, whose investment fund had lent $575 million as well as contributed $200 million in equity. No one knew how much would be recovered on the $3 billion first mortgage. The government-owned Fannie Mae and Freddie Mac held a portion of that loan.[17]

What Tishman Speyer did was called a strategic default—walking away from an asset that was under water—meaning that its debt exceeded the amount its property would ever be worth, even though it had the financial resources to meet its obligations. At the time it defaulted, homeowners around the country in similar situations were told it was their patriotic duty not to attempt a strategic default and that they had a moral obligation to continue to pay their mortgages if they could. If they did not, the housing market would slide further, endangering the national economy.

Legally, homeowners were obligated to pay because their mortgages were recourse loans, meaning lenders had access to their income and other assets. Tishman Speyer was not legally obligated to do so because its loans were non-recourse, meaning the lenders had access only to the revenues of Stuy Town and Peter Cooper. In all other ways, the situations were identical. Homeowners who defaulted or filed for bankruptcy found their credit ruined for years. Some real estate experts said Tishman's reputation would be tarnished. Instead, Tishman Speyer was soon able to borrow on favorable terms to make other purchases.

Other rent-regulated complexes similar to Stuy Town and Peter Cooper were acquired in similar deals, often led by private equity firms. In all about 90,000 units were involved, and most failed to pay off, including the purchase of the Riverton complex in Harlem.[18] The failure of the Speyers' effort was attributed to greed and easy money. That was the easy lesson to draw. The more important conclusion was what the failure showed about the system that allowed it to happen. Rent regulation had depressed the value of Peter Cooper and Stuy Town and yet was home to many well-off New Yorkers who could afford to pay higher rents. Vacancy decontrol provided a tool for an ambitious landlord to capitalize on that disparity by raising the rents and the value of the property. The money it invested would also revitalize an important housing asset for the city and increase the property taxes it collected. When political opposition and the Financial Crisis upset the Speyers' plan, the result was more than just the biggest real estate failure ever. It meant that vacancy decontrol would not be sufficient to speed the demise of rent regulation.

AMID THE STUY TOWN CONTROVERSY, the Citizens Budget Commission (CBC), the group that had exposed virtually every reckless financial maneuver that had led to the Fiscal Crisis of the 1970s, set out to do the same for rent regulation.

"The Citizens Budget Commission had last studied and written about rent regulation in 1991 and its recommendations influenced the 'luxury' and vacancy decontrol adopted in 1993," recalls CBC president Carol Kellerman. "Twenty years later, with the debate on renewal of the rent regulation law looming in 2011, we decided to investigate the current state of rent regulation in New York City. It was the first major effort to examine the impact of vacancy decontrol and to document who benefits from the system and its consequences for residential real estate in the city."[19]

Released in June 2010, the report was titled *Beyond the Rhetoric*. The CBC found that rents in regulated apartments were reduced by an average of 31 percent, or $5,500 a year. The CBC focused on how "poorly targeted" the subsidy was. About 12 percent of the people in regulated apartments had household incomes above $100,000, meaning they were in the top fifth of all households in the city. The biggest benefits were in Manhattan, where the gap between regulated and unregulated units was the widest, and the biggest savings went to those with the highest incomes.[20]

Outside Manhattan, many people in rent-regulated apartments received no benefit because market rents were the same or even lower. Despite rent regulation, poor families were forced to spend more on housing than they could afford. Millions of poor and middle-class people lived in the unregulated market anyway. The CBC also tackled one of the clearest examples of rent regulation's unintended consequences. In the rest of the country, as families see their children strike out on their own, they move to smaller units, freeing up large apartments for younger families. In New York, the economics are reversed. It is less costly for an elderly couple to stay in a three-bedroom apartment even after their children leave than to seek a more appropriate unit. This drives up the cost of large apartments for growing families that need more space and contributes to the flight of families from the city.

The CBC broke with Krugman on one point. It did not believe that regulations deterred new construction, because such units were exempt. It reiterated the findings of other studies that landlords defer maintenance on regulated properties either because they don't have the money to do repairs or because there is no incentive to do so. And while landlords bear the biggest financial burden, taxpayers suffer as well. Using economic models that showed that rents and therefore property values would rise modestly overall if all regulations were ended—since the value of regulated units would rise while rents and values of unregulated units would fall—in the end the city would collect an additional $300 million a year in property taxes.

CBC president Carol Kellerman publicized the findings in a series of op-eds. The *New York Observer* and *Crain's New York Business* wrote stories on the report. Politicians studiously ignored it.

+⤙ ⤚+

REAL ESTATE INTERESTS CONFRONTED a new political environment in 2010 as they plotted a strategy for the fight over renewing the law. Stuy Town's troubles had sullied the reputation of one of their most important figures and intensified the usual demonization of landlords. Democrats had regained control of the state senate in 2008, and it was only the internal splits among them that prevented the legislature from enacting a series of harshly anti-landlord bills. There would also be a new governor. Attorney General Andrew Cuomo, who seemed certain to win election, had a long history of supporting government intervention in housing. As Bill Clinton's secretary at the Department of Housing and Urban Development (HUD), he had been one of many HUD officials to push for lower standards for mortgages, contributing to the subprime crisis. He had worked in real estate before winning election as attorney general, and real estate tycoon Andrew Farkas was the finance chairman of his 2010 gubernatorial campaign. He said he supported tenants and wanted to strengthen the rent law, although he never specified how.

The city's leading real estate group, the Real Estate Board of New York, decided that it needed to hedge its bets. It amassed a $3.5 million war chest for the legislative elections, which it spread among Republican senators and a select group of suburban Democrats who it thought might support their rent positions. A second group that represented smaller landlords, the Rent Stabilization Association, put all their money behind the Republicans, calculating that the best way to protect their interests was to make sure the Republicans regained control of the senate.[21] The party's leader in the Senate, Dean Skelos, would know that the money he needed to keep a majority depended on how he dealt with rent regulation.

The two groups were divided on more than strategy. While the smaller landlords at worst wanted to preserve the status quo, the big landlords wanted the legislature to overturn the court decision that had crippled Tishman Speyer. They also wanted the legislature to force Mayor Bloomberg to lower property taxes on rental apartments, the only type of housing that wasn't given a break. The big owners were willing to trade an increase in the threshold for luxury vacancy decontrol for those provisions.

Both groups miscalculated. Governor Cuomo had broken with Democratic orthodoxy by cutting spending, opposing tax increases even on the wealthy, demanding concessions from public employee unions, and capping local property taxes. Business groups led by real estate developers amassed $10 million for advertising to support his positions. But Cuomo meant what he said about rent regulation. Skelos, who had aligned himself with the governor on most other issues, was not prepared to risk a confrontation. He agreed to raise the threshold for luxury vacancy decontrol to $2,500 and to make it more difficult for owners to use rehabilitation expenses to raise rents. The big landlords' other requests were ignored. Real estate interests said little publicly, but they fumed privately that all the money they had given to the Republicans resulted in so little help.[22]

Nevertheless, tenant advocates were furious at Governor Cuomo, even though the proposal would clearly slow the deregulation of apartments. They had convinced themselves that he would dismantle vacancy decontrol. Michael McKee, the public face of the Tenants Political Action Committee, called the deal an "unmitigated disaster," saying, "This is not real rent reform. This is continuing the phase-out and elimination of the entire rent regulation system."[23]

Nothing had really changed in 50 years. Neither Ken Auletta's *The Streets Were Paved with Gold,* nor Paul Krugman's column, nor the determined effort of the CBC had changed the framework of the debate, which continued to be presented as a fight between greedy landlords and middle-class and poor New Yorkers. The issue of including a reasonable income or needs test as the key basis for occupying a rent-regulated apartment never became part of the discussion. Government programs ranging from welfare to Medicaid to student loans impose an income test. Programs like Social Security and Medicare are available to all at a certain age. The benefits of rent regulation do not depend on need, but rather on whether a person is resourceful enough to obtain a regulated apartment.

One major reason for the lack of serious debate was the change in attitude at the *New York Times,* still the most influential media voice in the city. In 1987, the paper's editorial page delivered a stinging critique under the simple headline, "End Rent Control." "There's probably nothing that so distorts a city worse than rent regulation," it said. "It accelerates the abandonment of marginal buildings, deters the improvement of good ones and creates wondrous windfalls for the middle class—all the while harming those it was meant to help, the poor. . . . The single soundest step the State Legislature can take on behalf of housing is to return to free market incentives."[24] In 1996, the paper reiterated its view in calling for gradual elimination: "Mr. Bruno is right to call for decontrol. Rent regulation has not served New York well."[25] In 2011, the *Times* stood with the tenant groups. While it never tackled the issue exclusively, its editorials on Albany issues supported the demands of tenant advocates.

The almost two-decade experiment with reforming the system had modest results. It had allowed some landlords to make a lot of money and others to lose enormous sums. It had spurred some increase in the money spent rehabilitating aging housing. In the end, the CBC study showed, only a little more than 200,000 apartments had been deregulated in the 14 years since 1993. That was far too few to change the political equation that led even mayors like Rudy Giuliani and Michael Bloomberg to support it. A system that created winners and losers without regard for income and that clearly hurt the new arrivals to the city remained entrenched.

CHAPTER 15

THREE SECTORS
TO THE RESCUE

EVER SINCE THE 1960S, NEW YORKERS HAVE BEMOANED the disappearance of the city's middle class. At first, the problem was attributed to white flight and the decline of manufacturing, since people assumed that factory jobs equaled middle-class lifestyles. Wall Street's enormous success, which produced such wealth for a few, raised the expectations of what it took to be middle class and made many feel that they simply couldn't live well in New York. Today, the belief that the middle class is declining is based on studies like the one from the Fiscal Policy Institute that show big gains in wealth by the rich and the erosion of income for the rest of New Yorkers. Other experts claim that all the growth in the economy has come from low-paying sectors like retail, which pay so little few families can do more than survive.

Like so many strongly held views about New York, the disappearance of the middle class is greatly exaggerated. The city's fast-growing tourism sector provides a road to the middle class for immigrants and others with limited education, just as manufacturing did for so many decades. For those with college degrees, three emerging sectors are creating tens of thousands of good jobs—higher education, film and television production, and a revived tech sector powered by companies creating

Internet businesses. All three are thriving because so many young people find the city's allure irresistible. Government plays a role as well. Higher education needs government to clear obstacles so it can build the class-rooms, research facilities, and dormitories required to expand. The TV and film business needs direct government help in the form of a tax break to make New York competitive with other locations. The Bloom-berg administration is moving to help Internet companies by trying to lure a world-class engineering school to the city in hopes of increasing the inadequate size of that job pool.

Not unexpectedly, New York's two most prestigious universities— New York University (NYU) and Columbia (and the lawyers who led them for more than a decade)—have spearheaded the emergence of higher education into one of the most promising sectors of the city's economy. It lures students from all over the country, an increasing per-centage of whom remain in the city to fuel its crucial industries. It at-tracts billions of dollars in outside investment. It is adding jobs at one of the fastest rates of any part of the economy.

NYU had been long consigned to the ranks of big commuter schools, but its trustees decided on a bold gamble in 1985. Worried that the num-ber of New York–area high-school graduates was in a long-term decline, they diverted money intended for the school's small endowment into hiring more and better-known faculty. Upgrading the school's reputation would lure students from elsewhere in the country, they thought. Re-cruiting prestigious researchers would pay off in grants and attract more generous benefactors. To achieve those goals, NYU launched a building program at its Greenwich Village campus to add housing for out-of-state students and give the school a sense of community that it had lacked.[1]

By the 1990s, NYU was gaining in stature. As crime declined, par-ents were willing to send their precious offspring to the heart of the city, more confident that they would be safe. The booming city's economy offered an unmatched opportunity for students to get internships. In 2001, undergraduate, graduate, and professional students numbered a little more than 31,000, and NYU received more than 30,000 applica-tions for 4,000 spots in the freshman class. Average SAT scores had risen to an impressive 1337 out of a possible 1600. At that point, the trustees entrusted their ambitions to the dean of the law school, 58-year-old John Sexton, an outgoing administrator known for his hugs and fund-raising ability. After overcoming the financial squeeze created by the September 11 terrorist attacks, he announced a $200 million campaign to improve the school of liberal arts.[2] His sights were set on Ivy League schools like Harvard. "The ambition here is to live out what it means to be a first-class university," he said.[3]

His biggest problem was in his own backyard, where relations with the community were at a nadir. While a few people recognized that NYU's presence bolstered the area, most clung to the outdated notion that the village was a center of bohemian life with an eclectic mix of townhouses and tenements and artists, writers, and folk singers. "Today, N.Y.U. is looked at as the enemy by anyone who lives in the Village," said Barry Lewis, an architectural historian who lectured at a local design school. Added the head of the local community board, "It isn't our job to recognize their educational objectives, which I am sure are worthy. Our concern is to keep the look of the village."[4]

Over the next few years, NYU built and purchased more buildings, tried to lessen opposition by consulting with the community, and in 2008 agreed to move some of its operations elsewhere in the city. Looking at the growth of the world economy, Sexton broadened his sights and decided to open a campus in oil-rich Abu Dhabi, paid for mostly by the government, as well as Shanghai and elsewhere. Yet he made his biggest commitment to New York, where NYU had a paltry 160 square feet per student, compared with 326 at Columbia and 866 at Yale. Sexton unveiled a 20-year plan to increase NYU's space by 40 percent. It would continue to decentralize where it could, expanding an engineering school in Brooklyn and even saying it was interested in a satellite campus on a small island located between Brooklyn and Manhattan. The key remained the Village, where it would add 3 million square feet of classrooms, dorms, and offices and build yet another large tower.

The loudest voices in the Village dug in for a fight. "NYU seems to have worked on their P.R. machine quite a bit," said Andrew Berman, executive director of the Greenwich Village Society for Historic Preservation, "but the reality of what they are doing—which is taking over more and more of the neighborhood—doesn't seem to have changed much." His solution: NYU should expand someplace else.[5]

Sexton's response was to link his plan to the needs of the city. "For New York to be a great city, we need NYU to be a great university," he said. "We need space to run our academic programs, to have the faculty that teach in these programs, to have the students who attend these programs, to create not only carriers of knowledge but ambassadors of New York for the future."[6] In his first ten years, he had increased the student body from 31,000 to 37,000 and its full-time and tenured faculty from 2,600 to 3,900. Its total employment now stood at almost 18,000, up 25 percent, and he had raised $3.9 billion. If Sexton could expand as much as he wanted, the number of students, most of whom would come to New York from elsewhere, would pass 46,000. The economic benefits would be enormous.[7]

The issues were similar uptown in the West Side neighborhood that Columbia called home. The school had made its own gains in the 1990s as President George Rupp rebuilt its prestige and popularity, increased the endowment to $4 billion, put up a new student center, and raised already high admission standards. To succeed him, the trustees tapped 55-year-old Lee Bollinger, a Columbia Law School graduate with a national reputation in constitutional law and a sterling record as president of the University of Michigan.[8]

Columbia had always offered a well-defined campus, unlike NYU, but it, too, was space constrained. It considered building a second campus to the south on the site owned by Donald Trump along the Hudson River. Bollinger scotched that idea. Columbia already operated separate facilities in northern Manhattan where its medical school was located, and he knew the difficulties of operating two campuses from his time in Ann Arbor. A second campus outside the city was an option but an undesirable one. He turned his attention to an underutilized area just north of the campus in west Harlem and began drawing up the biggest expansion in 75 years to dramatically increase the school's campus, broaden its arts and sciences offerings, and build the kind of modern buildings needed for students, faculty, and especially research. "Columbia is one of the great institutions in the world and it can be

greater still," he said. "When you look at what the university's standing was in the 1950s, we are not there yet. But we can again define
what greatness is."[9]

Money was not a problem. The university's endowment was the
eighth highest in the country and its credit rating a stellar AAA. Neither
was demand. If it wanted to expand the student body, it could.[10] Applications had doubled since 1995 and the acceptance rate cut in half.
History was Bollinger's problem. An effort to build a gymnasium on a
park in 1968 had sparked an angry racial conflict that portrayed Columbia as an elite institution for whites ignoring the needs of its mostly
minority neighborhood and had tarnished the university's reputation for
decades.[11]

Columbia faced echoes of the 1968 fight as activists attempted to
portray the school's plans as a similar encroachment. The area was different, though, primarily a run-down collection of warehouse and light
industrial uses. Columbia was far more adept this time, buying up much
of the land in advance and using lucrative offers to persuade the 300 or
so residents to leave. But it faced numerous challenges to its plans from
recalcitrant commercial property owners who didn't want to leave. It
also encountered resistance from local groups clinging to the idea that
the area should be used for manufacturing. Local politicians demanded
guarantees of jobs at the university and benefits for the community. The
plan inched through the city's approval process for four long years as
the Bloomberg administration provided only behind-the-scenes support.
Finally, in 2007, the city council gave its approval. A few landowners
still blocked the plan until the courts finally agreed that eminent domain
could be used to evict them.

The work now under way at the site will cost $7 billion and result in
a new neighborhood of technologically advanced glass buildings housing a center for research on the brain and the schools of the arts and
business. Housing for graduate students and faculty and more lab space
will follow. Bollinger claimed that the ambitious agenda had led to an
outpouring of gifts. In 2006, it raised more money than any other Ivy
League school or similar rivals like Stanford. It could restore Columbia's
reputation to the unmatched level of the 1950s.[12]

The stories of NYU and Columbia—and their impact on the economy—were repeated at the city's other colleges and universities. Seattle native Charlie Klein knew he wanted to come east and looked at schools in Boston and New York. He was lured to St. John's in Queens by a relentless marketing campaign by the private Catholic school, which emphasized its more intimate feel, easy access to the best of the city, and especially the internships its students could land.[13] In 2008, applications jumped by 27 percent to more than 35,000. Another Catholic school, Fordham, lured more students to its Bronx campus but found especially strong demand for its Lincoln Center campus on the West Side of Manhattan.[14] Built for 3,500 students, it now educated more than 8,000 in several divisions, including its highly ranked law school. It, too, endured the city's painful land-use process to win approval for a rebuilding project that would allow it to increase the student body to 11,000. The New School boosted enrollment by 37 percent in the decade, many of them drawn to its Parsons School of Design by the hit cable show *Project Runway*, which was filmed there.[15] Even the City University of New York, a once-proud institution felled by the Fiscal Crisis and the elimination of admission standards, staged a remarkable turnaround under a new chancellor and began attracting students from elsewhere.

The Bloomberg administration seized on these developments and started calling New York "College Town USA." The mayor's third deputy mayor for economic development, former Goldman Sachs partner Robert Steel, pointed out that New York's 600,000 college students, who attended 110 institutions, were more than the entire population of the city known most as a college town, Boston.

In 2009, higher-education jobs exceeded factory jobs for the first time ever. In a little more than a decade, the number of jobs in postsecondary education increased by more than a third to around 100,000, and the total understated the impact since it didn't include adjuncts and other similar freelance workers. These new jobs included professors with salaries that ranged from $60,000 to $150,000, administrators, and staff people, especially technology experts to run computers and assist with new classroom teaching methods. The boom produced blue-collar positions, too, in food service, maintenance, and security. Most of these jobs were unionized, paid decently, and offered health benefits. In other words, they were middle-class jobs.

SITTING IN HER OFFICE IN SILVERCUP STUDIOS practically under the Ed Koch Queensboro Bridge, Ilene Landress is planning the production of *Girls,* a new HBO show about a 20-something trying to carve out a living in New York. It's fitting, for that is exactly what Landress has done over the past 25 years.[16]

Wanting to spend a year in New York after graduating from upstate Union College in the early 1980s, Landress enrolled in a master's program in health issues. Acceptance to medical school followed, but the ten-year timetable to become a doctor seemed too long. So she landed a job on a television show called *The Equalizer.* While movies often came to New York for location shots, it was unusual for a television series to be based in the city. "The title was parking production assistant," she says. "We invented that job on *The Equalizer.* My job was to scout out and protect the parking space the trucks would need when we went out on location."

Today, Landress is one of the city's top television producers, with credits that include the hit HBO series *The Sopranos.* And she has a different problem. So many television shows are shooting in the city that unless one is cancelled, she may not be able to book studio space for *Girls.* Something else is different, too: some 100,000 people work in the film business, most of them in well-paying middle-class jobs.

The film industry essentially began in New York, and in the 1920s, silent film stars like Gloria Swanson and Rudolph Valentino shot their movies in a studio in the Astoria neighborhood in Queens. The industry soon decamped to Los Angeles because of the weather. The army shot training films at the facility during World War II, but by 1970, the facility was abandoned. In 1980, developer George Kaufman approached the Koch administration with a proposal. The city would acquire the property from the federal government, and Kaufman would revive it as a studio. Koch agreed, and Gloria Swanson came to help unveil the plan.[17]

Others fell into the movie business much like Landress. Real estate developer Harry Suna bought the Silvercup Bakeries plant in Queens to consolidate two small manufacturing businesses he owned. When his plans for expansion didn't work out, the businesses were sold, and he and sons Alan and Stuart began considering what to do with the facility. When they received an inquiry from people in the ad business looking for some place to shoot commercials, they realized that the former bakery's open floors and high-ceilings were well suited for the film and TV business as well.[18]

The early years were a struggle and mirrored the industry's travails in the city. John Lindsay attempted to encourage the industry by creating a specific film office in city government, with limited success. Movie studios boycotted New York in the early 1990s, tired of recalcitrant unions and high wages and other costs. Even after the settlement of a bitter strike, producers would agree to shoot in New York only when unions provided special concessions. Many shows set in New York were actually shot in Toronto, where friendlier union leaders and a cheap Canadian dollar made the economics irresistible.[19] The crime wave and the fallout from the 1989–1993 recession made matters worse. "We almost went out of business then," says Alan Suna.

One producer remained loyal to New York. Dick Wolf created the television series *Law & Order* to show how the police and district attorneys worked together to bring criminals to justice. His were stories ripped from the headlines—usually of the tabloid *New York Post*. He wouldn't shoot anywhere but New York. The light was wrong in California, he claimed. Shows that were set in New York but filmed elsewhere betrayed their lack of authenticity in every scene, he insisted. Only New York actors would get it right, he believed. "There is a different type of actor in Manhattan than Los Angeles," he said. "Manhattan actors are primarily stage actors. They are used to looking at the totality of the shows rather than just their scenes." Even though he won concessions from the unions, each episode of *Law & Order* in the early years of the 1990s cost $250,000 more than if he had moved to California. But he told the bean counters, as he called them, that he wouldn't relocate.[20]

Law & Order was shot in Manhattan. Two HBO series made Silvercup famous—*Sex and the City,* which began filming in 1998, and *The Sopranos,* the most successful series ever on cable television, which debuted in January 1999. Even with the new work, the industry was troubled. The year *The Sopranos* premiered, the number of feature films shot in the city declined sharply because of high costs. As other states and cities began to imitate Toronto and offer tax breaks to producers, more work was moved elsewhere.[21]

New York finally decided to meet the competitive challenge in 2004, offering a 10 percent tax credit on production costs, excluding salaries for the leading actors, writers, and directors. The legislature allocated $25 million a year, and the city chipped in with a 5 percent credit as well. The effect was almost immediate, as the film industry added thousands of jobs. Demand was so great that funds for the credit sometimes ran out. Other times the credit lapsed amid long-drawn-out budget fights in Albany. Every time that happened the number of productions fell. In 2010, the legislature approved a 30 percent tax credit that would provide $1.2 billion over five years. The benefit was so lucrative that the city was able to drop its own incentive without much opposition.[22]

The tax incentive made New York competitive financially, and the city itself did the rest. Its talent pool was so extensive that only Los Angeles could rival it. It offered locations that couldn't be matched anywhere else. Living in New York had become so fashionable that many of the most important actors, directors, and writers now made the city their home. Like everyone else, they preferred to sleep in their own beds at night and chose to work in movies and TV shows shot nearby.

Just as the pieces seemed to be in place, the city faced a potentially crippling blow. NBC cancelled *Law & Order* after a 20-year run. How would the show ever be replaced? many asked. It had provided jobs to some 4,000 people, the city's film office figured out. It pumped $79 million a year into New York, and its total impact in two decades was something on the order of $1 billion. Hundreds of actors in New York had appeared in the series—many had become big stars, like Chris Noth and Sam Waterston—and mayors had been happy to show up for cameos as well.[23]

The answer came from across the East River in Brooklyn, where another HBO series called *Boardwalk Empire* had just begun production for its first season. Home base was Steiner Studios, which had been built in the Brooklyn Navy Yard for $128 million, including $28 million in infrastructure spending by the city. Its five enormous soundstages were the biggest in New York. Famed director Martin Scorsese spent some $18 million on the pilot, double the norm, and the budget for the first year reached $65 million. It provided work to 1,200 people plus roughly 2,000 extras. Its 12 episodes took 200 days to shoot, and it hired some 500 companies to provide equipment, props, and food.[24]

Not only was there a show to replace *Law & Order,* but also there was more than enough business for all the studios. The following year, a record 23 television series were shot in New York. The Bloomberg administration counted another 140 news programs, talk shows, and reality series at work. The number of feature films reached 200.[25] Ilene Landress scrambled for space and for people. "It's so busy in New York, if you have seen a movie you can get hired to work on one," she says.

While Landress exaggerated, the value of the movie and TV business to New York is obvious on any studio set. Carpenters are building backdrops. Electricians are wiring lights. Teamsters are hauling equipment. Writers are reworking scripts. Hairdressers, makeup artists, and costume assistants are everywhere tending to the actors. There are also accountants to manage the books and gofers of every sort. And there are caterers bringing an endless supply of food for this army of workers.

Unlike traditional jobs, workers in the film and TV industry are essentially freelancers, moving from production to production. They work very long hours—at least 12 hours a day—and have periods without employment. Yet, reflecting the impact of unionization, an electrician who works 100 days a year makes more than $60,000. A hairdresser who works that much cracks $70,000. If they find work for 150 days a year, or a little less than a schoolteacher puts in, they make about $100,000. Even a lowly production assistant earns $40,000 for about 100 days.[26]

The size of the tax breaks given to the industry has attracted critics who denounce them as corporate welfare that merely fattens the profits of film studios. They imply that New York should eliminate its incentive even if other states don't. However, each time the credit has lapsed, production has declined sharply. The money clearly results in large numbers of jobs. An analysis by the state comptroller and the city puts employment in the film and TV production business at about 100,000.[27] Like higher education, film and TV production is now helping produce a new middle class.

THE IDEA OF LIVING IN NEW YORK had been in the back of Chris Maliwat's mind ever since his high-school drama club from suburban Kansas City visited the city on a school trip. Instead, he decided to go to school on the West Coast after he was accepted by Stanford.[28] When he earned a degree in symbolic systems, or the science of building technology that solves people's problems, the doors in Silicon Valley opened. His early jobs involving implementing e-commerce platforms for companies like Levi's and Harley-Davidson. He put in a stint at eBay and developed a specialty in personalization while working at Netflix. He had thought about New York from time to time, but all the jobs he saw seemed to be about implementing technology at established companies. The work was not very exciting especially compared with the Bay Area, where technology is the company, not merely one of many tools used to execute the firm's strategy.

Then he was cold contacted in 2010 appropriately through LinkedIn by Gilt Groupe, the online flash sales retailer founded by DoubleClick veteran Kevin Ryan. Maliwat's reading convinced him that this was a technology company and that many others like it were being established in New York. He noticed that venture capital investment in New York start-ups was rising sharply as well. "This time New York made sense," he says. "I had to mitigate personal risk and New York had developed to the extent that was possible. If the company I joined faltered, I would be able to find a new job. I wouldn't have to move back to the West Coast or down to DC."

The tech sector, or more precisely the Internet sector, was staging a comeback and had become broad and established enough that companies like Gilt for the first time could lure people from Silicon Valley. It was also creating thousands of good jobs in the city again.

Ryan was one of a handful of Internet veterans not sullied by the
boom and bust of the 1990s. He had left DoubleClick when the board
had sold the company in 2005 over his objections because he believed
the price offered by a private equity firm was too low.[29] Within three
years, he had created a mini-empire of six new Internet companies. He
teamed up with his Yale classmate Henry Blodget on a news website that
soon became known as the Business Insider, covering a wide range of
industries. Another company provided a shopping guide, a third music,
and a fourth was an early entrant to cloud computing. The most promising, though, was Gilt.

He had come across a similar company called Vente-Privee on one
of his many visits to France. Stores in France can discount prices only
during government-regulated sales periods. The rules didn't extend online, however, and Vente-Privee exploited the loophole to build what
soon became the largest flash-sales site in the world. As any New Yorker
would recognize immediately, Vente was simply an online version of the
sample sale in which clothes are available at steep discounts for a few
hours, which knowledgeable New Yorkers had long thronged in search
of great bargains. Gilt showed such promise that Ryan soon dismantled
his holding company and became CEO of Gilt.

Growth came quickly, and he easily raised money, including $138
million from Goldman Sachs and others in early 2011, which gave the
company a valuation of $1 billion, larger than any other Internet com-
pany in the city. Competitors emerged quickly on the flash-sales front, so
Ryan expanded into full-price apparel and gourmet food and travel. He
soon had more than 800 people working for him, claimed revenues of
half a billion dollars, and shrugged off the idea that he had yet to make
a profit.

He didn't have the spotlight to himself, however. A 34-year-old
snowboard enthusiast and entrepreneur, Dennis Crowley, moved into
the social media scene with Foursquare, which allowed people to check
in and tell their friends where to meet them. He raised $20 million, at-
tracted 7 million users, and hired more than 50 people. He linked up
with American Express and other companies to offer discounts as well
as networking.[30]

Former investment banker Barry Silbert created SecondMarket, an online trading platform for banks and others to exchange illiquid assets. New York had long been home to software companies serving Wall Street. Now technologists and securities firm refugees sought to move trading and other financial activities to the Internet. SecondMarket was among the most successful, as revenues quickly passed $30 million.[31]

A few companies that prospered were survivors of the dot-com bubble. LivePerson, which developed software to allow companies to provide customer service online, went public in April 2000 at $8 a share amid the weakening technology market. Only a few months later it faced bankruptcy, avoiding that fate by slashing staff and conserving cash. It regained profitability in 2003, and with so much business conducted online, it built its client roster to 8,500 and boosted revenues to $130 million in 2011.[32]

The center of the city's Internet sector remained advertising, the industry that had lured DoubleClick's founders from Atlanta in the first place. Many were application companies. Brian O'Kelley, who built the online ad firm Right Media and sold it to Yahoo for $850 million in 2007, founded AppNexus to allow real-time bidding for ad space. Pontiflex created technology to allow advertisers to target consumers on websites related to their products. And then there was Google.[33]

Google sent its first salesperson to New York in 2000, installing him in a Starbucks. Its 2007 acquisition of DoubleClick for $3.1 billion gave it hundreds of employees in New York. It just kept buying New York start-ups. In 2009, it paid $750 million for AdMob, a top seller of banner ads on iPhones and web pages. The following year it took over Invite Media, which delivered ads across websites. In 2011, it shelled out $400 million for Admeld, which helps publishers sell display ads in real time. Google soon was by far the largest Internet company in the city, with more than 2,000 staffers, and it made clear that it had plans to grow even more when it paid $1.8 billion in cash to buy a 3 million-square-foot building on the West Side near the Meatpacking District. About half the people who worked at Google were engineers and other technology specialists. Most of the others were ad salespeople; no city had more of them than New York. This melding of technologists with talent from the city's more traditional industries was a key to New York's Internet growth.[34]

Gilt, for example, recruited tech specialists like Chris Maliwat, whose title was vice president of product management. It married them with scores of people from the city's fashion, retail, and consumer products companies. The résumés of its executives included stints at LVMH, Gap, and J. Crew. Its merchandising assistants came right out of the Fashion Institute of Technology and other similar schools. "They come because we are cool," says Melanie Hughes, who had been Ryan's top human resource executive at DoubleClick and rejoined him at Gilt. "We have some of that West Coast coolness with a New York edge. Gilt is a grown-up version of what we had at DoubleClick."[35] Her observation applies to the city's entire Internet sector.

In 2010, the city attracted $2.2 billion in venture investment, up a third from the previous year. The state labor department counted 50,000 jobs, up 20 percent in five years and almost certainly understated as the statisticians struggled to keep track of all the new companies.

Unlike universities and TV and film production, Internet companies didn't need much direct help from the city. Office space was costly, but it wasn't exactly cheap in Silicon Valley, and talent actually could be somewhat less expensive than in the Bay Area. The two balanced out, entrepreneurs said, although in the end, New York was more costly because taxes were so much higher. They said tax breaks would be nice but didn't really push the idea. The Bloomberg administration did see one way, however, to speed the growth in the tech sector.

Seth Pinsky, a Doctoroff aide who had risen to become president of the city's Economic Development Corporation, took some time off after Lehman Brothers failed. He walked around the city and talked to people about the impact of the downturn. Everyone expected him to be working furiously to help the city survive the coming economic storm. What he was actually doing was implementing the Doctoroff agenda as if he were head of the Real Estate Development Corp. rather than the Economic Development Corp. He decided that a new strategy was in order.[36]

At first the administration launched a series of initiatives designed to help the many people expected to lose their jobs in the downturn, in large part by helping them start their own businesses. Incubators were established and entrepreneurship classes offered. As important as he thought these would be, Pinsky searched for an idea he called a game changer. The best one, he decided, was a new, world-class engineering school. Internet executives had made it clear that they believed the lack of engineers was the primary barrier to faster growth. So Pinsky championed a plan that the city offer land and up to $100 million in infrastructure improvements to a top engineering school willing to establish a division in the city. His new boss, deputy mayor Steel, rescued it from bureaucratic inertia and announced it in his first major speech.

The proposals attracted enormous attention, and several schools prepared final bids, including two of the most highly ranked engineering schools in the country: Maliwat's alma mater, Stanford, and Ivy League Cornell, whose world-famous medical school had long called New York home. Both said winning the New York competition was one of their most important priorities. Stanford claimed it would spend $2 billion over ten years on its New York campus.

The enthusiasm of Stanford and Cornell was one of several signs that this Internet boom might be more permanent than the last one. Venture capitalists like Fred Wilson and John D. Robinson IV had amassed decades of experience with investments. Recent college graduates no longer could raise millions of dollars; the executives who headed these companies were now in their 40s and were on their second, third, and even fourth start-up. Even the employee rosters were older. At Gilt, the average age is in the mid-30s; in its rapid-growth era, the average age at DoubleClick was only 26. Most significantly, these were companies with substantial revenue in the hundreds of millions of dollars, not start-ups with capital and no customers.

Yet two parallels with the new media boom were unsettling. Many of the most prominent Internet companies' strategies were unproven. Gilt, facing a rapidly shifting competitive environment, entered new niches at a furious pace, looking for a big payoff. Foursquare's location technology faced competition from social behemoth Facebook, and it wasn't clear how it could make money off its audience. Many companies were losing money. Finally, for all the self-congratulation, New York had not produced a Google or a Facebook, which is why the mayor's speeches on the Internet resurgence usually featured Google. There was simply no hometown favorite that would resonate equally with his audience.

+— —+

HIGHER EDUCATION, TV AND FILM PRODUCTION, and the Internet sector together had created almost 300,000 jobs in the city, rivaling tourism in size and diversifying the economy as well. They attracted educated professionals from around the country. They provided the kind of middle-class jobs many lamented could no longer be found in New York.

CHAPTER 16

THE END OF THE NEW YORK ERA?

PICTURE A CRAGGY MOUNTAIN RANGE WITH HIGH peaks and valleys, some shallow and some deep. This is the landscape of the economy of modern New York when measured by the number of jobs, the most reliable statistic tracking the city's ups and downs. A picture of Wall Street's ups and downs would be virtually identical. One of the national economy would be radically different.

A long, steady ascent begins at the left side of the picture. This is the 1950s and 1960s, when New York benefited from the long national postwar economic expansion, superheated in the first Lindsay term by the Go-Go Years on Wall Street. The first peak is the highest in the picture—the jobs total reached 3,797,700 in 1969—and is followed by a steep plunge. This is New York's Great Recession—which lasted eight long years from 1969 to 1977—and cost the city 620,000 jobs. While the end of the 1960s Wall Street boom played a significant role in the downturn, the precipitous plunge in manufacturing caused the most damage, as the long-term flight of factories from the city accelerated in part because of the burdensome effects of Lindsay's 1966 business tax overhaul. The loss of 800,000 people in the 1970s also devastated neighborhoods and eliminated thousands of retail jobs. The city's near bankruptcy created a paralyzing pessimism about New York's future, further dampening business activity. This economic crisis contributed enormously to the Fiscal Crisis, which is largely ignored in the standard histories of the era.

The valley eventually turns into another gradual climb. The city's recovery began with the election of Ed Koch in 1977 and a new attitude toward the economy and business. From the time of the revered Fiorello La Guardia, New York mayors believed that the city's business sector was primarily a source of revenue of the government. The new mayor, a liberal from Greenwich Village, reversed that outlook: business and especially development was the most important factor in the health of the city. While Koch's contributions were vital, the greatest fuel for the 1980s boom came from Wall Street, where Salomon Brothers showed how much money could be made in fixed-income securities once interest rates were deregulated. This was the decade when Wall Street discovered greed and how good it could be for the people who worked in the securities business and for the city itself, although in retrospect the supposedly exorbitant pay of the late 1980s looks modest.

This mountaintop isn't as high as the first one and turns into a plateau before plunging again. New Yorkers understood by the mid-1980s how the city had become inextricably linked to Wall Street, and they feared the effects of the stock market crash of October 1987, only to become complacent when the city seemed to hold its own. Securities firms and other businesses began retrenching almost immediately after the crash, but those losses were offset by growth in city jobs as Koch rebuilt the municipal workforce and government-funded jobs in social services and health care increased as well. When tax revenues started to decline, public sector jobs had to be cut, too, and then the city suffered again through a long recession that lasted four years and eliminated 325,000 jobs. Doubts about New York's viability rivaled those of the late 1970s because of a rising crime epidemic that seemed uncontrollable.

The next rise begins as a gradual slope that turns abruptly skyward to another high mountaintop. Rudy Giuliani took over as mayor in 1994 just as improving markets revived Wall Street. His decision to appoint Bill Bratton as his first police commissioner was a master stroke or a piece of extraordinary luck, for Bratton revolutionized policing by convincing cops that their job was not to arrest criminals but to prevent crime. The resulting decline in crime reshaped the city, making it safe for tourists to venture beyond Manhattan and for parents to send their children to colleges in the city. Many have tried to belittle the reduction under Giuliani as the result of national trends or a police buildup initiated under his predecessor, David Dinkins. The critics ignore the decisive break in strategy between Dinkins and Giuliani. They also fail to give credit for how much more crime fell in New York than anywhere else in the country.

The upward thrust reflects the Internet's boost to Wall Street and the city's new media industry. Wall Street became more profitable and paid its employees bigger bonuses, and the new media industry created more than 50,000 jobs. The downturn began with the Internet bust in March 2000. The recession was well under way when the terrorists attacked the World Trade Center on September 11, 2001, and the economic dislocations from that attack were mostly short term. This downward slide doesn't last long, and the valley isn't deep.

Beginning at a higher elevation, the final climb is steep and nearly matches the first peak. The markets improved quickly, Wall Street discovered new businesses like housing securitization, and new players like private equity firms and hedge funds found ways to profit from markets on a scale never envisioned before. Now Wall Street's greed knew no restraint. Average pay soared past $400,000, six times the average of the rest of the city's workers. Goldman Sachs CEO Lloyd Blankfein was paid $68.5 million one year, nine times the compensation that made Salomon Brothers' John Gutfreund such a controversial figure in the 1980s, and that is after adjusting for inflation. Yet $68.5 million paled when compared with the money earned by private equity titans like Steve Schwarzman or successful hedge fund managers like Paul Tudor Jones. Wall Street accounted for 28 percent of all the income in the city at the peak. In the 1970s, the figure was 3 percent. Even in the 1980s, it was only 10 percent.

The last slide is the shortest and ends at the highest elevation, to the surprise of virtually everyone. New York—the home of Wall Street—was at the epicenter of the Financial Crisis that began in 2008, and most people thought Wall Street was solely to blame for the nation's economic woes. New York should have been among the areas hurt the most; instead it was among the areas affected the least. The nation lost 8.4 million jobs, or about 6 percent, in the recession that lasted 27 months, the longest since World War II. New York saw jobs decline by about 140,000, or 3.5 percent, and its downturn lasted 15 months. It was the second mildest recession of modern New York.

Certainly, much of the credit goes to the bank bailout known as the Troubled Asset Relief Program (TARP). President Bush's Treasury secretary, Henry Paulson, a former chief executive of Goldman Sachs, and Federal Reserve Board chairman Ben Bernanke decided that they could not allow the nation's financial institutions to fail without causing a global economic meltdown. After all, the big banks and Wall Street firms were indispensable—allocating capital and lending the money that fueled economic activity. So they bailed out Wall Street instead of Main Street despite the political consequences.

New York's major financial institutions received $197 billion in capital injections under TARP. The money saved some firms like Citigroup, which clearly would have just gone out of business. It meant much smaller layoffs at others. Bernanke may have helped even more than TARP. He pushed rates so low for the likes of Goldman Sachs and J.P. Morgan Chase that they could borrow from the Fed at zero interest rates. The firms took the money and invested it in the safest place possible, US government bonds. It was a simple trade and a lucrative one. Wall Street profits in 2009 soared to more than $61 billion, three times the record of 2006. Under intense public pressure, the firms reduced their pay and bonuses but not nearly as much as they would have if their profits had collapsed.

In the end, Wall Street shed about 35,000 jobs, about the same number as it did after the tech crash of 2000. The fallout was not as severe as in the past. The Financial Crisis and Great Recession of 2008–2009 showed that New York was very diversified. Despite the global recession, tourists continued to pour into the city, especially once hotel prices plunged. Visitors to the city declined by only 4 percent, and hardly any jobs were lost. Structural changes to the city's economy helped as well. No industry is more cyclical than manufacturing. That sector accounted for only a little more than 2 percent of the jobs in New York. Few industries are less cyclical than education and health care, which together now account for the largest number of jobs among the major categories tracked by the statisticians.

＋—   ＋—

WHAT TITLE SHOULD BE GIVEN TO THIS PICTURE? "A Study in Futility," some would say. New York has never been able to match, much less exceed, the number of jobs it counted in 1969, and its population has grown by more than 300,000. The nation added more than 60 million jobs since then, an increase of 78 percent. Since 1975, the earliest available comparable data, the Dallas metropolitan area almost doubled its employment total, adding 1.8 million jobs.[1] At 6.3 million people, Dallas is nearly the same size as New York. Conservatives say this is New York's own fault because its high taxes and burdensome regulation strangle business activity. Liberals argue that this is the result of the Koch–Giuliani–Bloomberg pro-business policies that failed to help the vast number of low- and moderate-income New Yorkers. Whatever the merits of that debate, it overlooks two crucial points. It is impossible for a mature, densely populated city like New York to match the growth of a place like Dallas. And, since 1969, New York has replaced 750,000 manufacturing jobs. It has generally done so with much higher-paying jobs, which has led to a sharp increase in incomes. This transformation has also allowed the population to increase at a rate no other mature Eastern or Midwestern city can match. It is an impressive accomplishment.

If political figures debate the meaning of the city's peaks and valleys, economists frequently misunderstand the dominant forces guiding the economy. They say that the city's economy tracks the nation's or that the trajectory of the US economy is the most important factor in determining the city's path. It simply isn't true. Consider New York's Great Recession. The nation experienced a slight downturn in 1970 and a more difficult recession later in the decade, but neither rivaled the disaster that engulfed New York. A decade later, the 1982 Reagan Recession devastated parts of the country, and unemployment soared past 10 percent. New York barely noticed, losing a minuscule 40,000 jobs because financial services were not much affected. Conversely, the nation quickly shrugged off the 1987 stock market crash, whereas it caused havoc in New York. And the last downturn was the Great Recession That Wasn't. New York's economy is so big that it is driven by its own dynamics, of which by far the most important is Wall Street.

Wall Street also dictates the ebb and flow of city government, whose size and mission was greatly expanded by John Lindsay and then cut back by his successor during the Fiscal Crisis. With the city so shaken by its brush with bankruptcy, Ed Koch followed a strict policy of fiscal rectitude. He met targets for restoring the city's financial stability early because he so disliked state oversight. He added back workers only when he was sure that the city could afford it. When the economy improved, however, he was unable to resist using the revenue to speed the restoration of city services, which meant hiring more people. He even relented on the hiring freeze he imposed after the 1987 stock market crash when the economy did not weaken immediately.

The story repeated itself in the 1990s. Rudy Giuliani came to office as a dedicated conservative with a mission to reduce the size and scope of city government permanently. He proceeded to do that in his first few years, using the leverage of the financial squeeze that resulted from the recession. Then, like Koch, Giuliani allowed a rapid increase in the budget—and the number of city employees, beginning as he prepared to run for reelection in 1997 and continuing for his second term. He, too, could not resist spending the billions a booming Wall Street poured into the city coffers. By allowing the public sector to track Wall Street, these mayors exacerbated New York's already pronounced cyclicality.

Giuliani's successor had no qualms about the size of the city's government as long as it was affordable. In June 2005, the day his dream of a West Side stadium died, Michael Bloomberg met with the publisher and top executives of *Crain's New York Business* for a photo op to celebrate the publication's special twentieth-anniversary issue. Taxes seemed to be on his mind. "Everyone complains about taxes," he said. "I love it when I write a big check to the government. It means I made a lot of money."

The mayor had been a Democrat before changing his registration, a tactical move because he knew he couldn't win a Democratic primary for mayor. He believed in the social safety net and that government should do as much for its less well-off citizens as it could as long as it was as efficient as possible. In his first year in office, he abandoned his campaign vow not to raise taxes and pushed through the largest property tax increase in the city's history. The city's fiscal health was paramount, he said, and anyone who believed that the city could cut its budget to accomplish that simply didn't know what he or she was talking about. Soon the administration embraced the idea that it was the quality of life that was crucial to the city's economic success, a way to justify the city's tax burden—double the average of the nation's nine other largest cities, according to the Independent Budget Office.[2]

When the economy improved, the mayor saw no harm in spending the windfall. Projections for his remaining budgets put the total increase in his 12 years in office at 82 percent, with the total reaching $73 billion. If he had merely tracked the inflation, the figure would be more like $60 billion. Much of the money went to the city's workers. He equated pay with talent; salaries at Bloomberg L.P. were always higher than at its competitors. He agreed to big pay increases because it was politically expedient and he thought it was right. Teachers got the biggest raises because he was determined to improve results in the classroom. He didn't completely understand the consequences of this strategy. Because city employees receive pensions determined by their salaries, the pay increases meant that the city would be required to put more into the pension fund each year. When Bloomberg took office, the annual bill was $1 billion. Today it exceeds $8 billion and eats up an ever-increasing percentage of the budget.

In his third term, the mayor changed his mind on taxes—again—and what kind of government New York could afford. New York taxes had become just too high, he said in 2010, and any increase even on just the wealthy would send people and businesses elsewhere. With the surplus he had built in good times exhausted, the city payroll would have to be trimmed, although his preferred method was by attrition. He claimed that he would maintain the quality of life by using technology to improve services, but many mayors before him had made the same promise with little to show for it.

——

BARRING ANOTHER MELTDOWN OR TERRORIST ATTACK, the New York that Michael Bloomberg will turn over to his successor on January 1, 2014, will be prosperous, safe, sound, and a magnet for the rest of the nation, if not the world. The recession had only nicked New York, and its employment is nearing the 1969 peak even with a too-high unemployment rate. His police commissioner, Ray Kelly, has continued to drive down crime for almost 12 years, employing technology to offset a decline in the number of police. It is a magnet for ambitious professionals from around the country and the world.

It will be a city that is not growing as quickly as the mayor proclaimed. He had expected the 2010 Census to show New York at a record 8.4 million people, on its way to 9 million in the year 2030. When the Census found only 8.175 million people, he yelled foul and claimed that it had missed at least 50,000 New Yorkers. Even if he was right, the number is well below his projection. The most likely explanation for the missing 200,000 people was that immigration has slowed. Immigrants were attracted to New York because there was so much opportunity and because there were many run-down neighborhoods where housing was cheap. The four periods of prosperity have led to gentrification in every borough and almost every neighborhood. For example, the once-downtrodden and dangerous Bed-Stuy area of Brooklyn drew thousands of upscale whites who integrated this once almost exclusively African-American neighborhood. Newcomers to the United States were simply headed to cheaper places.[3]

It is a city where the myth of manufacturing clings to life. In February 2007, at a *Crain's* business forum, Planning Commission chairwoman Amanda Burden said she would tackle Ed Koch's outdated zoning restrictions in the garment center, where dilapidated buildings were shunned by most businesses. "The garment center has perhaps the most anachronistic zoning in the entire city," she said, promising action within a month.[4] Nothing happened. Several times the Bloomberg administration floated ideas for preserving some manufacturing space while lifting the zoning. Zealots determined to protect the dwindling number of apparel manufacturing jobs, which numbered less than 3,000 in the area, refused to compromise. Bloomberg shunned a public fight, and the neighborhood continued to languish. In a great irony, the failure to lift the zoning rules became the biggest threat of all. Apparel companies that supposedly needed the manufacturers protected by the rules fled to other neighborhoods where the buildings were modern and amenities kept their workers happy.[5]

Most important, New York will be a city that can grow. When the recession struck and the big development projects stalled, the mayor turned to a series of small efforts based on the idea of spurring entrepreneurship—a tiny venture capital fund, incubators for various sectors that provided space for a handful of companies each, and programs to help people become business owners. In all, the administration claimed more than 60 new initiatives. During his reelection campaign, they showed that he cared about blunting the impact of the economic downturn. Afterward, they continued to provide excuses to hold press conferences and other media events to send the same message. They were good politics if little else.

When those efforts fade away, the legacy of Dan Doctoroff will remain. The city had approached the 1969 employment peak three times, and it faltered even before Wall Street collapsed because there was nowhere to put the professional and white-collar jobs being created. Instead, gleaming office towers went up across the Hudson, in other suburbs, and in other cities to house those people. Doctoroff's ambitious agenda had finally broken through the chains of the manufacturing myth, and now the city had many places, most of them along the waterfront, to build the commercial and residential space to keep the jobs in New York and allow the population to grow. Whether they will be built, however, may depend on the fate of Wall Street.

ROBERT CARO'S *The Power Broker* served as Doctoroff's primer on how power was exercised in the city. *Gotham,* by historians Edwin Burrows and Mike Wallace, was his text on the city's history. He read each chapter carefully, underlining key passages. The book convinced him that New York had become a great city because of repeated periods of financial innovation. That assumption was the bedrock of his confidence in the city's future. Doctoroff had taken a leap to reach that conclusion. *Gotham* ends in 1898 with the consolidation of New York and Brooklyn.

His successor, Robert Steel, took a different lesson from his own time on Wall Street. Steel had spent more than two decades at Goldman Sachs and stood at Treasury Secretary Paulson's side during the height of the Financial Crisis. Asked by a group of young journalists about the future of Wall Street, he noted that the great success of Wall Street in the last three decades occurred as capitalism was embraced around the world. Wall Street orchestrated the transition of many countries to a market-based economy. No such task remained for the investment bankers and traders of tomorrow. The future wasn't bleak, he insisted, but neither would it be so expansive and profitable.

Neither explanation fits the turmoil on Wall Street since the early 1960s. Each of the four great Wall Street booms since then brought important financial innovations and reckless speculation, manipulation, and often criminal behavior. The democratization of markets in the 1960s was clearly beneficial, allowing many more people to participate in markets, especially through often less risky mutual funds. The absurd conglomerates created in that era cost many huge sums when they collapsed. The bond boom of the 1980s created new financing mechanisms that allowed many companies to grow and prosper. It also led to excessive leverage through junk bonds, devastating corporate bankruptcies, the worst insider trading abuses ever, and the market manipulations of Michael Milken. The Internet boom did create companies like Amazon.com, Henry Blodget's famous stock pick that helped jumpstart the mania, which changed businesses like retailing in ways that benefited consumers. Most of the companies were mirages, and untold billions were lost when they crashed. The securitization of debt, the development of derivatives, and the rise of hedge funds all added liquidity to the markets. Private equity firms became a force to improve corporate performance. Hedge funds delivered large profits to their investors. Whatever the value of those innovations, the result was the Financial Crisis and a terrible recession that harmed hundreds of millions of people.

The true genius of Wall Street in modern New York was figuring out how to make itself rich. Whatever Wall Street created between the late 1980s and the last boom could not justify Goldman's Lloyd Blankfein being paid nine times more than Salomon's John Gutfreund. Nor could they justify the billions of dollars Steve Schwarzman took from creating Blackstone or Jones's wealth amassed from his hedge fund. The irony, of course, is that it was this innovation that made New York so rich. Wall Street's ability to pay so much for office space and investment bankers' ability to spend unlimited sums on apartments made real estate developers and landlords wealthy. Its bonuses supported luxury retail. Its philanthropy made New York the home of so many nonprofits. The taxes it paid allowed city government to grow so large and to pay its own workers so well.

Wall Street's ability to continue to support the city remains in doubt. Its rescue from the Financial Crisis may have been only a temporary reprieve. The Dodd-Frank law passed by Congress to ensure that there is never another Financial Crisis ordered a sweeping change in the structure of Wall Street. For example, firms like Goldman Sachs and J.P. Morgan must sell off or shut down their proprietary trading units on which they came to rely on for such a large percentage of their profits. Regulators are insisting that financial institutions build up their capital in the belief that the bigger cushion will make them better able to survive financial shocks. It is the opposite approach—borrowing more instead of amassing capital—that made the firms so profitable. Even if the political pressures to reduce compensation ebb—and they have had only a modest impact—lower profits will mean that the firms themselves will cut their pay and bonuses.

Economists and politicians believe that the solution is to diversify the economy so New York is not so dependent on Wall Street. The last recession shows that goal has already been achieved. It won't save New York. If Wall Street is permanently restructured, New York will be much less wealthy. No industry will pay its people so well that they will be able to generate two other jobs in the city. No industry will pay so many billions of dollars in taxes. The effects will be wrenching. If financial firms can no longer pay $80 a square foot for office space, building values will decline. No new construction will take place until land prices drop. Both will mean big losses for real estate people. The same will be true for workers. Construction unions will have to accept a sharp decline in their wages and benefits to make new building possible. The financial squeeze will radiate throughout the city. Without young investment bankers to support the market, apartment prices will decline. The ranks of luxury retailers will thin. Nonprofits will find fund-raising much more difficult, and many will close their doors. The public sector will feel the most pain. Wall Street still accounts for 9 percent of all city tax revenue and 15 percent of state revenue, which allows Albany to send so much money to the city.

Bloomberg himself has contributed to the illusion that New York can afford whatever it wants, especially when, like Koch, he made deals to win approval for his big development schemes. When the city council approved the rezoning of Greenpoint-Williamsburg, the mayor agreed that about 20 percent of the housing would be set aside for low- and moderate-income people.[6] He also agreed that any high-rises must use union doormen and other workers. Raising the prices on other units finances affordable housing. The higher wages for union doormen mean that renters and condo owners pay higher rents or maintenance charges. When Willets Point was approved several years later, Bloomberg agreed that 35 percent of the units would be for lower- and moderate-income people, and that prevailing wages—which means union wages—would be paid to construction workers, building service workers, and even the people who staff retail stores.

He also saddled the city with an enormous increase in its debt burden, nearly doubling the amount the city owes to $105 billion from $55 billion when he took office. In a less wealthy New York, the city won't be able to afford its pension or debt burden or all the commitments to affordable housing and other amenities in its development projects.

The inability of the mayor to pare the public sector shows the difficulty. For most of 2011, Bloomberg insisted that the city would have to lay off several thousand teachers for the first time in more than a decade. It was a reasonable step to close the big deficits that New York faces in future years. The teachers mounted a vigorous campaign against the job cuts, and the city council sided with them. In the end, Bloomberg agreed that there would be no layoffs. Some jobs were eliminated through attrition, and the union made concessions that provided some savings. The bulk of the money came from simply increasing his estimate for tax collections. Carol Kellerman, president of the Citizens Budget Commission, said the result just postponed the day of reckoning. She felt as frustrated as had her predecessors in the decade leading up to the Fiscal Crisis as they railed against reckless financial maneuvers.[7]

The likely candidates in the 2013 mayoral election not only do not accept the mayor's view that some cutbacks in city government are necessary, they pose a formidable challenge to the fundamental Koch–Giuliani–Bloomberg philosophy of putting the economy and the businesses that make it work at the center of policy.

To Democrats, the last 20 years have been an accident. Rudy Giuliani was elected in 1993 only because their candidate was a weak and indecisive incumbent who had been blindsided by a bad recession and a soaring crime rate. Giuliani's reelection four years later demonstrated merely the power of incumbency, especially in good times. Bloomberg's narrow election in 2001 was the unfortunate consequence of the enormous political dislocations stemming from the September 11 terrorist attacks. His reelection again showed the power of an incumbent coupled with his willingness to spend $100 million on his own campaign, dwarfing the ability of any Democrat to compete. The mayor's office was the anomaly, since Democrats maintained a lock on other city offices and in the city council, which led to only more frustration because New York gives the mayor enormous powers to control the direction of city policy.

By the beginning of Bloomberg's third term, however, his opponents began coalescing around a series of economic issues. The stark inequality in the city, the high unemployment rate that stemmed from the recession, and the enormous growth in mostly low-paying retail jobs led to the formation of a coalition determined to use city government to improve the lives of those left out of the city's great prosperity. The efforts were sparked by labor unions and the organizations they financed like the Fiscal Policy Institute, the Working Families Party, and other traditionally liberal groups.

The first issue to gain traction concerned paid sick leave. A bill introduced in the city council originally required any employer with more than ten workers to provide at least five paid days off for illness. The idea had been adopted in San Francisco and Washington, was pending in a few other large cities, and was approved in nearby Connecticut. Proponents argued that it was a simple matter of health and fairness. Small business regarded the bill as a threat to their very existence. With small margins and a need for great flexibility, they believed that the bill would be enormously costly.

The second measure would require most employers to pay a living wage, usually defined as $10 an hour with benefits and $12 without. Some proposals would impose this higher minimum wage only on companies that did business with the city, but both supporters and opponents believed that the living wage would eventually apply to virtually all companies in the city. This idea was as much anathema to small firms as paid sick leave, and it attracted the ire of larger businesses as well. Developers in particular worried that it would hurt their ability to attract national retailers, which would not be willing to pay higher wages at a store in New York City compared with their operations in nearby suburbs. Unions and their allies also pushed a third initiative, higher taxes on the wealthy by making the city's income tax even more progressive.

All three issues are based on the idea of New York as a special place for special people—different from the rest of the country, and even from the suburbs that surround it. The controversy over whether to allow Walmart to open stores in New York showed the clash of these differing visions.

Walmart had scoured the boroughs for years looking for a perfect site to open its first store in the city. It abandoned the effort in 2006. Like other national retailers in the 1980s, Walmart simply didn't see how its business model could work given high land and construction costs. It didn't help that the Bloomberg administration's wouldn't offer much public support. Walmart revived its search for sites a few years later, because it had no choice. Its sales growth in the country was minuscule, in large part because it had saturated most of the United States. It took on and won a bruising political fight to open outlets in Chicago and decided to push ahead in the three large cities that remained beyond its reach—Washington, Boston, and, most important, New York.

This time the mayor would be on Walmart's side because he thought keeping Walmart out of the city was simply foolish. His view became clear when Joyce Purnick published her biography of him in 2009. "Everyone leaves to go to Nassau County or Westchester (to shop at Walmart)," he told her. "Shirley Franklin, the mayor of Atlanta, she laughed at me in the face. They just got the biggest Wal-Mart in Atlanta—she was thrilled. Only we can turn victory into shit."[8] At a *Crain's* breakfast forum just before the election, he promised that this time his administration would publicly back the retailer.

The fight against Walmart was led by the retail workers union, which had the most to lose since supermarkets were one of its remaining strongholds in the city and Walmart had crippled unionized supermarket chains elsewhere in the country. The retail workers union had also been battling Walmart for years. It was aided by the company's reputation for paying rock-bottom wages and for discriminatory employment practices. Politicians who opposed Walmart argued that it was simply a renegade company and that it would devastate small businesses, as it had in many small towns. Walmart itself stressed the jobs it would create and how much the city already was losing as thousands of New Yorkers traveled to its suburban stores to shop. Walmart's position was bolstered by the new retail order in the city, which had been blanketed by similar stores like Home Depot and Target. They too were nonunion. They paid no more than Walmart and offered no better benefits. Walmart's wages easily met the terms of the living wage bill; the unionized supermarket contract did not.

The debates over sick leave, living wage, higher taxes, and Walmart came as the clout of the city's business community declined precipitously. Two decades had elapsed since an organization called the New

York Chamber of Commerce had faded into oblivion. The New York City Partnership, founded by David Rockefeller as a broad business-union group to influence policy in the aftermath of the Fiscal Crisis, was the most visible advocate of business interests. It had evolved into the representative of the city's most important corporations in finance, business services, and real estate. The Real Estate Board of New York, whose membership overlapped some with the Partnership, appeared powerful, too, and looked out for the interests of landlords and developers. They were allies on most issues but not all. In fact, their clout primarily came because of their alliance with the mayor. Small businesses were virtually powerless. Historically, the chambers of commerce in each of the boroughs represented them, but none commanded much attention. The sick leave and living wage bills so worried these firms that they formed a 5 Boro Alliance to fight the measures. They received some help from the Partnership and Real Estate Board but struggled for influence.

A decade earlier, real estate and finance executives had made sure that their views were considered through large campaign donations to key council members. Since the most ambitious council people aspired to citywide office, they courted business leaders because they knew they would have to ask them for money for expensive campaigns. Over time, the city enacted ever-smaller limits on the amount any individual could give. It introduced a taxpayer-financed system that provided city money that matched only small contributions. Finally, Mayor Bloomberg agreed to a sweeping restriction on contributions from executives whose companies did business with the city.

By essentially eliminating business contributions, the city had empowered labor unions because they could still give money and they could mobilize workers for campaigns. The election of city council members depended almost exclusively on whom the unions supported, either directly or through the Working Families Party, a union-created political party. Of the 51 members, only one was a businessperson. The council moved sharply to the left, especially when compared with the Dinkins era, when the council fought higher taxes and reflected the values of the city's middle class.

The leading Democratic candidates for the 2013 mayoral race all embraced the challenge to the Koch–Giuliani–Bloomberg philosophy.

All three—comptroller John Liu, the first Asian-American elected to the council, public advocate Bill de Blasio, and council speaker Christine Quinn—were elected with strong Working Families Party support. Quinn positioned herself as the most moderate and blocked the sick leave bill, although she did so not because it was bad policy but because the economy was too weak to impose it on small businesses. She was vociferous in her opposition to Walmart.

The idea that New York voters—where registered Democrats outnumber Republicans 2–1—support these positions may be flawed. Poll after poll showed that voters wanted Walmart stores in the city. The first Quinnipiac Poll showed that 57 percent supported Walmart, and as the fight intensified, the figure rose to 63 percent.[9] Three-quarters believed that Walmart's lower prices would benefit New Yorkers even though they also agreed that Walmart would hurt small businesses. A quarter said they already shopped at the giant retailer.[10]

It is unclear whether a Republican or independent candidate will emerge to capitalize on that sentiment as Giuliani had in 1993 and Bloomberg in 2001. The lack of such a candidate in 2009 contributed to Bloomberg's decision to run again. If the city faces another economic or fiscal crisis, businesses executives will try desperately to find a candidate. If the economy continues to recover, they may decide to make the best of whoever wins the Democratic primary, as they did when David Dinkins beat Ed Koch and they kept their distance from Rudy Giuliani in his first campaign.

Wall Street may save the city again as it has done so often in modern New York. The investment bankers, traders, hedge fund executives, and private equity specialists may concoct another financial innovation that propels the markets and sends their own pay and bonuses soaring. If Wall Street does that, New York will be rich again, tax revenues will be plentiful, and the political disputes over handing out the spoils affordable. If not, the next mayor will face the daunting task of leading New York into a future much less prosperous than its present. Or the next mayor could ignore those forces and push New York into a new era of expansive government, as Lindsay did. The result could well be another economic and fiscal cataclysm.

ACKNOWLEDGMENTS

THE STORY OF *MODERN NEW YORK: THE LIFE AND ECONOMICS of a City* told in these pages has also been written in the weekly print editions of *Crain's New York Business* and on the website Crainsnewyork.com. I am indebted to the 100 or so talented reporters and editors who worked for me while I was editor and whose journalistic skills provide so much of the foundation for this book. My thanks to Alair Townsend, the best boss any editor could ever want, and to Publisher Jill Kaplan and Editor Xana Antunes, who continue the mission of Crain's with such accomplishment.

My biggest debt is owed to Steve Malanga and Elizabeth MacBride. Steve was the No. 2 editor at Crain's for 14 years, and the point of view in this book was formulated in our daily, often hourly, discussions of the news, the people, and the issues. After Steve left Crain's, Elizabeth assumed his role as the person who challenged my point of view and kept me from disastrous detours both as my managing editor and as a friend in the years since.

About 100 students at CUNY Graduate School of Journalism have taken my class on Covering the NYC Economy and Business, and they have contested my point of view and helped me refine how to write this story, as have the public policy students at the New School and Baruch, who have studied the issues with me. They all have my thanks.

This book would not have been written if I had not found a home at the J School, which has turned out to be so much like Crain's in the late 1980s and 1990s, a feisty and innovative upstart competing against more established brand names. To Dean Steve Shepard and Associate Dean Judy Watson who make the J School such a challenging and fulfilling place for my new career, my thanks. My gratitude goes most of all to Professor Sarah Bartlett. I wouldn't be at the J School without her. She hired me as an adjunct and is the consummate colleague.

My favorite book on journalism is the *Wall Street Journal Guide to Feature Reporting,* which explains the concept of wise men and women. These are the people journalists rely on for guidance, to test theories, and to understand difficult concepts. Unlike most sources, they do not do so in return for the publicity they might get. In fact, they are rarely quoted. Instead, they help journalists because they believe that the truth needs to be told. I relied on four wise men and women in the writing of this book. They will go unnamed, of course. This is my public thanks.

I appreciate all the efforts of my editors at Palgrave Macmillan, especially Emily Carleton, and to my agent, Robert Guinsler of Sterling Lord Literistic, who believed in a book many others thought was too parochial. I could meet the deadline for this book only because of the help of my research assistants at the J School—Cesar Bustamante, Madhura Karnik, and Azriel Relph—and the freelance help of Emily Laermer.

Last, but probably first in importance, is Joann Molloy, who convinced me to write it. During our many and probably tedious conversations about the need for a post-Crain's career, she would ask, "Why don't you write a book?"' And I would answer, "I can't write a book." Eventually, one day, I began that conversation by saying, "I think I will write a book."

NOTES

A NOTE ON SOURCING

This book is the product of historical research, my reporting and writing on New York business, economic, and political issues since 1985, and original reporting specifically for the book.

The historical research for each chapter is sourced in the endnotes. When a book or study underlies a significant section, that is described and the source cited in the endnote.

I oversaw Crain's coverage of the vast majority of the topics covered in this book and wrote about many of them as well in editorials and columns. Contemporaneous accounts, primarily in *Crain's New York Business* and the *New York Times,* provided specific facts, examples, and quotes. They are sourced in the endnotes.

I also conducted new interviews with some of the most important people in this book, beginning with the final years of the Koch administration. Those interviews were often only the latest of a series of discussions on the issues. For example, many of the people quoted or profiled in the book discussed the city's economic, business, and political issues in the hundreds of editorial board meetings held at *Crain's New York Business* over the time period of this book. Virtually all the important political and governmental figures were featured at the Crain's Breakfast Forums I moderated for more than 20 years. A significant number also were guests at my classes on New York City at the CUNY Graduate School of Journalism. In only a few cases did the editorial boards or forum appearances result in transcripts (primarily in video) or published stories. Nevertheless, they left lasting impressions. This book represents information from all of those encounters, which is why many of the interviews are not dated. In particular, incidents and quotes from my colleagues at Crain's have been drawn from hundreds of discussions we had during the time we worked together.

Some of the anecdotes in this book I witnessed personally, such as the opening scene at the Crain's Future of New York conference or the Lions dinner at the New York Public Library as the Financial Crisis escalated. I have tried to make it clear in the text when that is the case.

In a few cases, interviews were on a not-for-attribution basis, which I have handled in the traditional newspaper way by describing the source as specifically as possible without naming them.

In some cases, quotes used in the book appeared in truncated form in published accounts that years later no longer are clear. Where possible, I have contacted the source and clarified the quote. I have corrected grammatical errors.

The employment numbers in this book unless otherwise cited come from the New York State Department of Labor. The department furnished me with a file containing job numbers starting in 1958. Information from 1990 is available on its website. A similar file tracks Wall Street compensation as a percent of the total compensation in the city.

The city's Independent Budget Office furnished the tax revenue numbers. The city employment figures were compiled by the Citizens Budget Commission and are adjusted for the various changes to the way the city payroll was counted.

CHAPTER 1: THE CITY TOO BIG TO FAIL

1.　Portions of Jamie Dimon's February 6, 2009, speech to the Crain's Future of New York Conference are available at http://media.crainsnewyork.com/title,2be748da,J_P__Morgan_CEO_discusses_the_future_of_NYC
2.　From an audio file provided by the mayor's office to the author.
3.　Lisa Fickenscher, "Occupancy Drop Forces Layoffs at Hotels," *Crain's New York Business,* January 12, 2009.
4.　Lisa Fickenscher, "Taking off the Ritz," *Crain's New York Business,* April 6, 2009.
5.　Patrick McGeehan, "Mayor Sticking by Tourism Projections Despite Dropoff in 2009," *New York Times,* January 5, 2010.

CHAPTER 2: LINDSAY AND THE GREAT RECESSION THAT WAS

1.　Vincent J. Cannato, *The Ungovernable City* (New York: Basic Books, 2001), 22.
2.　Barry Gottehrer and Marshall Peck, "The Businesses Come—But Mostly Go; City's Study Report, Still No Action," *New York Herald Tribune,* February 3, 1965.
3.　Ibid.
4.　Leonard Sloane, "New York: Business Capital of the Nation," *New York Times,* January 11, 1965.
5.　John Brooks, *The Go-Go Years* (New York: A Truman Talley Book, 1973), 183. Unless otherwise noted, the section on the 1960s stock market boom is based on *The Go-Go Years.*
6.　Leonard Sloane, "New York Is Bullish on Merrill," *New York Times,* October 26, 1972.
7.　Robert Alden, "City Hall Is Seen Leaning Strongly to 2% Income Tax," *New York Times,* January 21, 1966.
8.　Robert Alden, "Medicine for City's Ills," *New York Times,* January 25, 1966.
9.　Robert Alden, "Lindsay Offers Income Tax Plan, Asks 50% Increase in Stock Levy; Exchange Threatens to Quit City," *New York Times,* March 4, 1966.
10.　Ibid.
11.　Robert Alden, "26 Top Executive Reject Tax Plan Sought by Major," *New York Times,* April 5, 1966.
12.　Robert Alden, "Mayor Denounces 2 Business Groups Fighting Tax Plan," *New York Times,* April 6, 1966.
13.　Cannato, *The Ungovernable City,* 106.
14.　Charles R. Morris, *The Cost of Good Intentions* (New York: W.W. Norton & Company, 1980), 141–2.
15.　David K. Shipler, "Lindsay Orders a Rent Rollback for 600,000," *New York Times,* February 9, 1969.
16.　"Politics and Rent Control," *New York Times,* February 18, 1969.
17.　Franklin Whitehouse, "News of Realty: Landlords Balk," *New York Times,* March 26, 1969.

18. Charles G. Bennett, "Council Rent Until to Cut 15% Rises Backed by Mayor," *New York Times,* April 11, 1969.
19. David K. Shipler, "Rent Rise Limits of 10% and 15% Voted in Council," *New York Times,* April 25, 1969.
20. Ken Auletta, *The Streets Were Paved With Gold* (New York: Random House, 1979), 42.
21. Ibid., 43.
22. Brooks, *The Go-Go Years,* 342.
23. Gottehrer and Peck, "The Businesses Come."
24. Auletta, *The Streets Were Paved With Gold,* 65.
25. Michael Sterne, "Unexpected Woes Slow Beame Plan," *New York Times,* August 15, 1976.
26. Michael Sterne, "A Plan to Revitalize New York's Economy Is Offered by Beame," *New York Times,* December 21, 1976.
27. Will Lissner, "Bienstock Sees an Upsurge in City's Economy in 80's," *New York Times,* April 5, 1976.
28. Auletta, *The Streets Were Paved With Gold,* 16.

CHAPTER 3: GREED IS GOOD
1. Editor, "The Death of Equities," *Business Week,* August 13, 1979.
2. Ibid.
3. Michael Lewis, *Liar's Poker* (New York: Penguin Books, 1989).
4. Michael Blumstein, "Morgan Stanley Fights for No.1," *New York Times,* April 1, 1984.
5. Lewis, *Liar's Poker,* 136.
6. Anthony Bianco, "The King of Wall Street," *Business Week,* December 9, 1985.
7. Kenneth B. Noble, "Wall St. Bonuses: Fewer This Year," *New York Times,* December 22, 1981; Thomas J. Leuck, "Wall St.'s Bountiful Bonuses," *New York Times,* December 15, 1982.
8. Kenneth N. Gilpin, "Bonuses on Wall Street May Be the Fattest Ever," *New York Times,* December 13, 1986.
9. Lewis, *Liar's Poker,* 24.
10. Jonathan Miller, author interview, Spring 2011.
11. Ken Auletta, "The Fall of Lehman Brothers: The Men, the Money, the Merger," *New York Times,* February 24, 1985.
12. Sandra Salmans, "New Yorkers & Co.; The Street's Well-Paid Upstarts," *New York Times,* March 31, 1986.
13. A. O. Sulzberger, Jr., "Job Growth Since 1976 Is Mostly in Manhattan," *New York Times,* October 6, 1981.
14. Richard J. Meislin, "Poll Finds a Mixture of Pride and Worry for City's Future," *New York Times,* December 21, 1981.
15. Martin Gottlieb, "A Decade After the Cutbacks, New York Is a New City," *New York Times,* June 30, 1985.
16. Joyce Purnick, author interviews, Spring 2011.
17. Damon Stetson, "Labor Study Finds Economy of City Now 'More White Collared Than Ever'," *New York Times,* March 13, 1982.
18. Martin Gottlieb, "New York Leading Other Cities in U.S. in Population Gain," *New York Times,* August 21, 1985.
19. William R. Greer, "Surge in Jobs in All 5 City Boroughs," *New York Times,* November 2, 1984.
20. Martin Gottlieb, "A Decade After the Cutbacks, New York Is a Different City," *New York Times,* June 30, 1985.
21. Ibid.
22. Jonathan Miller, author interviews, Spring 2011.
23. "Developers; New Kids on Block: A Formidable Duo," *Crain's New York Business,* October 16, 1989; Albert Scardino, "Record Price for Skyscraper," *New York Times,* December 17, 1986.

24. David W. Dunlap, "Back-Office Tenants Slipping Out of Town," *New York Times,* April 22, 1984.
25. Blake Fleetwood, "As Rent Go Up, Some Merchants Say They Must Shut Their Doors," *New York Times,* December 27, 1980.
26. Mark McCain, "The Bold Take on Euclid Hall as Renewals Unsettle a City," *Crain's New York Business,* September 1, 1986.
27. Robin Pogrebin, "New Leader Seeks Stronger Voice for Art Society," *New York Times,* December 29, 2009.
28. Jane Gross, "2 Big West Side Projects Fuel Anti-Development Sentiment," *New York Times,* November 29, 1987.

CHAPTER 4: THE MYTH OF MANUFACTURING
1. Ric Burns, Director, *New York: A Documentary Film,* 2001.
2. Thelma Fate, "Garment," in *The Encyclopedia of New York City,* eds. Kenneth T. Jackson and others (New York: Yale University Press, 2010), 493.
3. Eric Gural, author interviews, Summer 2011.
4. Martin Gottlieb, "Development Plan for Times Sq. Wins Unanimous Backings of Estimate Board," *New York Times,* November 9, 1984.
5. Ibid.
6. Ibid.
7. "Manhattan in Change: The Future of the Economy," *New York Times,* July 14, 1982.
8. Frank Sommerfield, "Zoning May Hurt Garment Center," *Crain's New York Business,* September 22, 1986.
9. Carl Weisbrod, author interviews, 2011.
10. J. W. "'Bill" Marriott, author interview, January 13, 2011.
11. Cindy Rich, "Growing Up Marriot," Washingtonian.com, http://www.washingtonian.com/print/articles/6/173/3836.html (accessed March 14, 2011).
12. J. W. "'Bill" Marriott, author interview, January 13, 2011.
13. Ibid.
14. Ibid.
15. Linda Moss, "Marriot's Risky Hotel Bids, for Broadway Stardom," *Crain's New York Business,* August 19, 1985.
16. Jon Tisch, author interviews, Spring 2011.

CHAPTER 5: STRUCTURAL NOT CYCLICAL
1. Julie Johnson, "New York City's Jobless Rate Falls to 17-Year Low," *New York Times,* October 3, 1987.
2. Mark McCain, "Deals Proliferate in Softer Manhattan Office Market," *New York Times,* November 2, 1986.
3. Mark McCain, "Condo Glut Unleashes a Ticking Time Bomb," *New York Times,* April 14, 1986.
4. James Sterngold, "Contraction Is Wall Street Theme as Industry Plans for Major Cuts," *New York Times,* November 2, 1987.
5. Thomas J. Lueck, "Stock Impact Feared Grave in New York," *New York Times,* October 29, 1987.
6. Sterngold, "Contraction is Wall Street Theme is Industry Plans for Major Cuts."
7. Gary Belsky, "Wall Street's Ills Means More Firings, Cutbacks," *Crain's New York Business,* January 29, 1990.
8. Anise C. Wallace, "More Job Cuts Seen for Wall Street," *New York Times,* September 5, 1988.
9. James Sterngold, "Infighting Is on Rise at Troubled Firms After Stocks Plunge," *New York Times,* February 4, 1988.
10. Steve Malanga, "Three Months After Crash, Badly Rattled, New Yorkers Cutting Back," *Crain's New York Business,* January 11, 1988.
11. Thomas J. Lueck, "New York Area Not Badly Hurt by Stock Plunge," *New York Times,* April 19, 1988.

12. Alison Leigh Cowan, "'Soft Landing' for New York City," *New York Times*, October 19, 1988.
13. Lueck, "New York Area Not Badly Hurt by Stock Plunge."
14. Thomas J. Lueck, "New York Vacancy Level Is Highest Since 70s," *New York Times*, April 13, 1988.
15. Dena Kleiman, "New York Restaurants Struggle," *New York Times*, May 24, 1989.
16. Theresa Agovino, "An Unwelcome Sign: N.Y. Tourism Drops Off," *Crain's New York Business*, August 14, 1989.
17. Richard Levine, "Vital New York Taxes Lag, and Economy Is Blamed," *New York Times*, October 11, 1989.
18. Steve Malanga, "Speak Softly and Carry a Light Wallet; New Yorker's Mood Indigo," *Crain's New York Business*, October 17, 1988.
19. Doug Muzzio, author interviews, Summer 2011.
20. Kurt Eichenwald, "Eerie Quiet on Wall St. as Business Tumbles," *New York Times*, April 24, 1990.
21. Peter Grant, "Drexel Shock Waves Rattling N.Y. Economy," *Crain's New York Business*, February 19, 1990.
22. Kurt Eichenwald, "Wall Street Cutting Muscle Now," *New York Times*, November 9, 1990.
23. Kurt Eichenwald, "Troubled Times on Wall Street: As the Beat Wanders, an Industry Remakes Itself; Wall Street Paring Down to the Basics," *New York Times*, January 2, 1991.
24. Steve Malanga, "AIDS, Crime Haunt Christopher Street; Merchants Fight to Preserve Strip," *Crain's New York Business*, August 6, 1990.
25. Peter Grant, "Law Firm's Failure Exacts Big Toll on Troubled Landlord," *Crain's New York Business*, December 16, 1989.
26. Sarah Bartlett, "Tax Delinquencies in New York Rising Again," *New York Times*, August 9, 1991.
27. Steve Malanga, "Deepening Downturn Stalls Rebound Until Fall," *Crain's New York Business*, December 17, 1990.
28. Donatella Lorch, "Record Year for Killings Jolt Officials in New York," *New York Times*, December 31, 1990.
29. Karen DeWitt, "Tourism in New York City Is Down After 80s Boom," *New York Times*, August 24, 1990.
30. Todd S. Purdum, "Dinkins in Accor on Financing Plan for Hiring Police," *New York Times*, December 6, 1990.
31. Alan Breznick, "N.Y. Business Rejects Dinkins' Grim Budget," *Crain's New York Business*, May 13, 1991.
32. Alan Breznick, "N.Y. Tax Packing Is Too Taxing; How It Hurts Store, Co-op, Office," *Crain's New York Business*, May 6, 1991.
33. Sarah Bartlett, "The Budget Battles; New York Taxes Batter Middle Class," *New York Times*, July 2, 1991.
34. Steve Malanga, "Vanishing Act; Even Venerable Firms Can't Make It This Time," *Crain's New York Business*, January 27, 1992.
35. Ibid.
36. Alan Finder, "Lock Step With New York City Economy, Budget Treads Path of Booms and Busts," *New York Times*, May 3, 1992.
37. Ibid.
38. Catherine Rampell, "Comparing This Recession to Previous Ones: Job Losses," *New York Times*, November 6, 2009.
39. Catherine S. Manegold, "Balance-Beam Politics; Giuliani's Second Try," *New York Times*, May 23, 1993.
40. Catherine S. Manegold, "Plan Offered by Giuliani on Reducing Hotel Taxes," *New York Times*, August 19, 1993.
41. Ibid.

42. Alan Finder, "Dinkins Outlines Plan for Future Economic Growth," *New York Times,* September 22, 1993.
43. Alan Finder, "New York Poll Sees Grim View of Life in City," *New York Times,* October 8, 1993.
44. Steve Malanga, "'94 Job Gains Spur Outlook for Economy," *Crain's New York Business,* December 13, 1993.
45. Judy Temes, "Wall St. Salaries Soar; N.Y. Sees Trickle Down," *Crain's New York Business,* April 12, 1992.
46. Ibid.
47. Peter Grant, "Wall Street Is Increasing Space, Finally," *Crain's New York Business,* August 22, 1993.
48. Joseph Berger, "The New York Region; Immigrants Jam Schools, Invigorating a System," *New York Times,* April 26, 1992.

CHAPTER 6: MAKING NEW YORK SAFE FOR COMMERCE

1. Alan Mirabella, "Firms Ready to Invest in Rudy's N.Y.," *Crain's New York Business,* January 17, 1994.
2. Steven Lee Myers, "Giuliani Instructs Agencies to Cut Spending 1 Percent," *New York Times,* January 7, 1994.
3. Alison Mitchell, "Giuliani Seeks Concessions From Unions," *New York Times,* February 1, 1994.
4. Steve Malanga, "Rudy Kicks off Revolution; Mayor Trims Taxes That Hurt the Most," *Crain's New York Business,* February 7, 1994/February 13, 1994.
5. Douglas Feiden, "Rudy Kicks off Revolution; Businesses Enlist to Sell Bold Budget," *Crain's New York Business,* February 7, 1994/February 13, 1994.
6. Ibid.
7. Mirabella, "Firms ready to invest in Rudy's N.Y."
8. William Bratton, with Peter Knobler. *Turnaround* (Random House, 1998). Unless otherwise noted, the section on Bratton and his strategies is based on *Turnaround*.
9. Joseph B. Treaster, "Crime Rate Drops Again in New York, Hastening a Trend," *New York Times,* June 2, 1994; Garry Pierre-Pierre, "Fewer Killings Tallied in '93 in New York," *New York Times,* January 2, 1994.
10. Myers, "Mayor Says Crime Data Affirm Strategies," *New York Times,* January 8, 1995.
11. Clifford Krauss, "The Nation; New York City's Gift to Clinton: A Lower Crime Rate," *New York Times,* September 1, 1996.
12. Holman W. Jenkins, Jr., "The Weekend Interview with James Q. Wilson: The Man Who Defined Deviancy Up," *Wall Street Journal,* March 12, 2011.
13. Peter Powers, author interviews, Spring 2011.
14. Viorel Urma, "Paradox of a Kind: New York Is Violent Yet More Tourists Coming," *Associated Press Worldstream,* September 20, 1994.
15. Robin Kamen & Alan Mirabella, "Finally, Rebound Emboldens Firms; Hiring Picks up, Prices Firming, and Some Firms Set Expansion," *Crain's New York Business,* February 14, 1994.

CHAPTER 7: IMMIGRATION SAVES THE NEIGHBORHOODS

1. New York City Department of City Planning Population Division, *The Newest New Yorkers* (New York: Author, 2004). Unless otherwise noted, the figures on the 1990 census and comparison are from *The Newest New Yorkers*.
2. Mireya Navarro, "In New York, Low Count Draws Chorus of Criticism," *New York Times,* August 30, 1990.
3. Navarro, "In New York, Low Count Draws Chorus of Criticism," *New York Times,* August 30, 1990.
4. Edward B. Fiske, "U.S. Revises New York Census: City Is Growing, Not Shrinking," *New York Times,* January 25, 1991.
5. Elizabeth Cummings, "The Global City; Immigration Helped Transform New York from a Dying Industrial Giant into a 21st-Century City. Restrictions That Threaten

the Latest Wave Could Be Devastating," *Crain's New York Business*, December 3, 2001.

6. Sara Rimer, "Between 2 Worlds: Dominicans in New York—A Special Report," *New York Times*, September 16, 1991.

7. Raymond Hernandez, "Neighborhood Report: Flushing: An Asian Home Away from Home," *New York Times*, September 19, 1993.

8. Claudia H. Deutsch, "Commercial Property/Flushing's Chinatown; A Chinatown With a Polyglot Accent," *New York Times*, October 2, 1994.

9. Celia W. Dugger, "Queens Old-Timers Uneasy As Asian Influence Grows," *New York Times*, March 31, 1996.

10. Clifford Levy, "Race for City Hall: The Council; Incumbents in Most Races Fend Off the Challengers," *New York Times*, September 10, 1997.

11. Somini Sengupta, "Bringing Asian Voice to the Council; Three Candidates in Flushing Want to Become the First," *New York Times*, March 30, 2000.

12. Laura Vanderkam, "Where Did the Korean Greengrocers Go?," *City Journal*, Winter 2011; Ruby Danta, "Korean Small Businesses in New York City," *Asian American Centre*, April 1991.

13. Lee A. Daniels, "U.S. Report Faults Mayor on Boycott," *New York Times*, February 28, 1992.

14. Danta, "Korean Small Businesses in New York City."

15. Vanderkam, "Where Did the Korean Greengrocers Go?"

16. Sam Roberts, "New York City Drawing Fewer in Need of Aid," *New York Times*, April 12, 1994.

17. Jonathan Bowles & Tara Colton, "A World of Opportunity," *Centre for an Urban Future*, February 2007.

18. Elaine Pofeldt, "Seizing Window of Opportunity: Risky Move Into Wholesaling Pays off for Queens Manufacturer," *Crain's New York Business*, June 14, 1999; Stephen Gandel, "No Welcome Mat, No Workers," *Crain's New York Business*, December 3, 2001; Victoria Rivkin, "Window Company Defies the Odds; Crystal Builds Bug NY Factory; Chinese Market Is Next Target," *Crain's New York Business*, January 8, 2007.

19. Amy Waldman, "New Yorkers & Co; From a Flaky Foundation, a Food Empire," *New York Times*, April 26, 1998; Valerie Block, "Eatery Chain Hopes Spice Is Right: But Franchisor May Need to Supplement Ethnic Line to Reach Mainstream Market," *Crain's New York Business*, October 20, 1997; Cara. S. Trager, "Turning Mom-and-Pops Into Miniature Empires: Franchising Helps Firms Grow Quickly; But Path Is Rough, Start-Up Costly," *Crain's New York Business*, May 24, 1999; Patrick McGeehan, "Little Chains That Could . . . and Still Do," *New York Times*, June 6, 2010.

20. Daniel Massey, "Immigrants Playing a Larger Role in City's Economy," *Crain's New York Business*, January 13, 2010; "Working for a Better Life," The Fiscal Policy Institute, Chapter 4, Page 33, November 2007.

21. Julia Preston & Cindy Chang, "House and Senate Hold Immigration Hearings," *New York Times*, July 6, 2006.

CHAPTER 8: ALL THAT GLITTERS

1. Alan Mirabella, "Net Jobs Are Surf Into NY on Waves of New Media," *Crain's New York Business*, January 23, 1995.

2. Douglas Feiden, "Future of Small Business in Government's Hands," *Crain's New York Business*, April 26–May 2, 1993.

3. Judith Messina, "New Media's Hot Play: DoubleClick Infusion Largest Ever in City," *Crain's New York Business*, June 16, 1997.

4. Kevin Ryan, author interviews, various dates.

5. David W. Chen, "Wow: Cash Infusion for Internet 'Kids'; Computer Chat Room Began as Idea for 2 Students in Their Cornell Days," *New York Times*, September 19, 1997.

6. Gregg Grossman, author interviews, Spring 2011.
7. Jon Birger, "Wall St. Bonus Pay to Reach New Highs: Firms Sweetening Pot but Profits Grow Faster; Merger Specialists Win As Some Traders Lose Out," *Crain's New York Business,* October 13, 1997.
8. Laurence Zuckerman, "With Internet Cachet, Not Profit, a New Stock Is Wall St.'s Darling," *New York Times,* August 10, 1993.
9. Charles Gasparino, *Blood on the Street* (New York: Free Press, 2005), 56. The account of the tech analysts and Wall Street's Role: The internet boom is drawn primarily from *Blood on the Street.* Unless otherwise noted, the information on the Internet boom and Wall Street is drawn from *Blood in the Street.*
10. Randall Smith, "Morgan Stanley Profit Increases 33%, Lifted by Stock Underwriting, Mergers," *Wall Street Journal,* December 21, 1999.
11. Patrick McGeehan, "The Year in the Markets; The Race to Underwrite Nearly Sets a Record," *New York Times,* January 3, 2000.
12. Judith Messina, "Dash for Cash Setting off Frenzy Among NY Net Set: Firms Rush to Finish Projects, Find Allies While Cash Flows; E-Mails at 3 A.M.," *Crain's New York Business,* July 8, 1996.
13. Judith Messina, "Writing Its Ticket: Hot New-Media Firm Lures Big Investors," *Crain's New York Business,* July 29, 1996.
14. Judith Messina, "Apple Pickin' Time: Four NY Start-Ups With Cash to Burn: Venture Capitalists, Other Investors Bet on These Companies' Products, Expertise," *Crain's New York Business,* October 14, 1996.
15. Jon Birger and Judith Messina, "Up in Smoke Special Report: Silicon Alley Companies Have Burned Through $1 Billion Without Producing Any Profits or Viable Businesses," *Crain's New York Business,* November 16, 1998.
16. Birger and Messina, "Up in Smoke Special Report."
17. Janet Stites, "Industry View; The Stock Market's Gyrations Are Causing Anxiety Among Silicon Alley Start-ups That Are Planning to Go Public," *New York Times,* September 21, 1998.
18. Dow Jones Newswire, "Theglobe.com Debuts at 866 Percent Premium," *Florida Times-Union,* November 14, 1998.
19. Aaron Lucchetti, "Web Tide: Initial Public Offerings Aren't the Same in Era of Internet-Stock Mania—Globe.com Opened up 900%, Dismaying Online Buyers But Creating Media Buzz—The IPO as a 'Branding Event'," *Wall Street Journal,* January 19, 1999.
20. Lucchetti, "Web Tide."
21. Judith Messina, "Welcome to Moneyfone: AOL Offers $388 Mil. for Moviefone; Highest Price Yet for Net-Related Firm," *Crain's New York Business,* February 8, 1999.
22. Judith Messina & Mark Walsh, "IPO March Madness: 16 Silicon Alley Firms Set Offerings to Raise $1 Billion; Will They All Fly?," *Crain's New York Business,* March 15, 1999; Mark Walsh, "There's Little Privacy Left in Silicon Alley: Pressure Builds on Agency.Com, Jupiter, T3 Media to Do IPOS," *Crain's New York Business,* June 28, 1999.
23. Mark Walsh, "Once Is Not Enough for New Media Firms: Wave of Secondary Offerings Fuels Growth," *Crain's New York Business,* May 17, 1999; Judith Messina, "Insiders Unload Shares at Hot Internet Firms: They Say It's to Offset Low Salaries," *Crain's New York Business,* February 22, 1999.
24. Saul Hansell, "Gold Rush in Silicon Alley; Venture Capital Moves East," *New York Times,* February 7, 2000.
25. Mark Walsh, "Dot-coms Pay Big to Net Top Execs; More Cash in Table as Firms Seek Winners," *Crain's New York Business,* November 8, 1999.
26. Mark Walsh, "Wall Street Analysts Lust for Life on the Internet; Key Players Defect for dot-com Riches; Firms Dig Deeper to Retain Them," *Crain's New York Business,* November 15, 1999.
27. Judith Messina, "New Media's Hot Play: DoubleClick Infusion Largest Ever in City," *Crain's New York Business,* June 16, 1997.

28. Mark Walsh, "Stock Watch: DoubleClick Clique Expands As Internet's Appeal Boosts IPO: AD Firm's Red Ink Doesn't Deter Investors; In Focus," *Crain's New York Business,* February 23, 1998.

29. Judith Messina, "Double-Time DoubleClick Acquisition Strategy: Internet Ad Firm Buys Its Way to Top; Eyes 100 Targets," *Crain's New York Business,* July 19, 1999.

30. Judith Messina, "Kevin O'Connor and the Mouse That Roared; The Founder of On-line Ad Network DoubleClick Paved the Way for City's Fastest-Growing Sector," *Crain's New York Business,* May 15, 2000.

31. "DoubleClick Achieves Pro Forma Break—Even Despite Tough Advertising Environment; Q4 Revenues Up 41% Year on Year; Full Year 2000 Revenues Up 96%," *Businesswire,* January 11, 2001.

32. Peter Grant, "New York-Based Internet Media Company Signs Deal for New Headquarters," *Daily News* (NY), February 2, 1999.

33. Melanie Hughes, author interviews, various dates.

34. PriceWaterhouseCoopers, "New York New Media Association Study," March 2000.

35. "Space Hunger Buoys Downtrodden Areas; Insatiable Demand Spurs Makeovers, Driving up Prices, Forcing out Others," *Crain's New York Business,* November 29, 1999; John Holusha, "Commercial Property/Manhattan Office Space; Dot-Coms Accounted for 25% of First-Quarter Leases," *New York Times,* April 23, 2000.

36. Judith Messina, "Charities Eye New Avenue for Riches: Silicon Alley; Groups Direct Efforts at High Tech, but New Millionaires Are All Business," *Crain's New York Business,* December 20, 1999.

37. Valerie Block, "Old Media Gets a Boost From New Media Ads: Internet Firms Find Traditional Venues Best Way to Reach Customers," *Crain's New York Business,* June 7, 1999.

38. Jon Birger, "Bigger Bonuses Expected Even as Stocks Fall; Record Pay Fuels Wall St. Sprees," *Crain's New York Business,* September 27, 1999; Patrick McGeehan, "Wall St. Firms Reward Chiefs for Strong '99," *New York Times,* February 12, 2000.

39. Trip Gabriel, "In the Glare of Baubles, Bangles, Bonuses," *New York Times,* December 5, 1999.

40. Lore Croghan, "Office Rents Set Records: Leases to Soar 10% in 1998 as Corporate Expansion Squeezes NYC Tenants," *Crain's New York Business,* February 23, 1998; Lore Croghan, "Rents Soaring for Second-Tier Office Buildings: New Media Firms Discover Class B; Rents Unchanged in Best Properties," *Crain's New York Business,* June 14, 1999.

41. Emily Denitto, "Red-Hot Co-Op Market: Prices up Another 20% as Inventories Tighten and Buyers Scramble," *Crain's New York Business,* May 25, 1998; "Toniest Residents Cross the Park: Prices Soar as Upper West Side Becomes New Centre of Wealth," *Crain's New York Business,* August 17, 1998.

42. Larry Kanter, "Feeding Frenzy: 50 New Eateries This Fall; How Many Can NYC Stomach?" *Crain's New York Business,* September 20, 1999.

43. Louise Kramer, "Museums Grow to Art's Content; Buoyed by Boom; How Many Can Prosper?" *Crain's New York Business,* March 27, 2000.

44. Judy Temes, "Wages Soaring, Jobs Go Unfilled for NY Business: Hotels, Restaurant Can't Find Managers; Professional Firms Intensify Recruiting," *Crain's New York Business,* April 21, 1997; Lisa Sanders, "Boom Leaves Firms Starved for Workers: Restaurant Boost Pay, Benefits to Lure Employers," *Crain's New York Business,* August 3, 1998.

45. Charles V. Bagli, "Latest Construction Bottleneck: Shortage of Skilled Workers," *New York Times,* August 15, 1999.

46. Charles V. Bagli, "Chase to Lease Office Space in Jersey City," *New York Times,* June 2, 2000; "A Scramble for Office Space in Jersey City, Manhattan's 'West Bank'," *New York Times,* October 10, 1999.

47. Lore Croghan, "Merrill Eyes NJ Deal: Broker Will Move Workers From City, Jersey Locations to New Office Tower on Banks of Hudson River," *Crain's New York Business,* December 14, 1998; Philip Lentz, "Schumer Panel Pushes to Keep Firms

in NYC; Group of 30 to Develop Options as Space Shortage Spurs Exodus," *Crain's New York Business,* January 24, 2000.

CHAPTER 9: THE FORGOTTEN RECESSION

1. Mark Walsh, "Cool Market Threatens Alley Firms; E-tailing Sites Hit Hard; Some Firms May Merge, Fold," *Crain's New York Business,* February 7, 2001.
2. Robert Hershey, Jr., "Market Insight; A Nasdaq Correction; Now Back to Business," *New York Times,* March 19, 2000.
3. Walsh, "A Chill Hits the Alley; Plunge in Tech Stocks Shuts Down Internet Offerings; Likely to Slow Private Equity Funds, Speed M&A," *Crain's New York Business,* April 17, 2000.
4. Alexia Vargas, "Alley Icons Face Ignominy of Delisting; 24/7, iVillage, Razorfish at Risk as Shares Stubbornly Stay Below $1," *Crain's New York Business,* April 2, 2001.
5. Walsh, "Dot-Com Founders Step Aside as Pressures Grow; Seasoned Vets to Focus on Profits," *Crain's New York Business,* August 14, 2000.
6. Catherine Curan, "As Firms Fade, Staffers Collect Wages of Fear; Phases Include Denial, Anger, Acceptance," *Crain's New York Business,* June 11, 2001.
7. Jayson Blair, "Lack of Advertising Forces Theglobe.com to Shut Web Sites," *New York Times,* August 4, 2001.
8. Kevin Ryan, author interviews, class visits.
9. Brian Steinberg, "Buyout Firms Circle DoubleClick," *Wall Street Journal,* April 22, 2005.
10. Steinberg, "DoubleClick Sets Pact to Be Bought for $1.1 Billion," *Wall Street Journal,* April 25, 2005.
11. Dennis Berman, Kevin Delaney, and Robert Guth, "Google to Pay $3.1 Billion for Web Firm DoubleClick," *Wall Street Journal,* April 14, 2007.
12. Amy Harmon, "Media; Requiem for a Cheerleader: Silicon Alley Magazine Is Dead," *New York Times,* October 8, 2001.
13. Stephen Gandel, "Wall Street Hiring Rolls on Despite Market Slowdown; Firms Anticipate Rebound, Seek More Technology Bankers; Merrill a Harbinger," *Crain's New York Business,* July 17, 2000.
14. E. S. Browning, "Party On: Despite Stock Slump, Wall Street Binges on Pay and Perks—A War for Talent and a Yen for Large Headquarters Spur Warnings of Trouble—Mr. Banks' $25 Million Deal," *Wall Street Journal,* September 18, 2000.
15. Stephen Gandel, "Street Pulls More Bank Jobs; Poaching Increases as Mergers Make Executives Jittery; Lehman on Prowl," *Crain's New York Business,* October 9, 2000.
16. Stephen Gandel, "Wall Street's Bonus Babies; Record Payouts, But Nervous Bankers Are Trading the Rolls-Royce for a Vespa," *Crain's New York Business,* February 19, 2001.
17. Stephen Gandel, "Wall Street's New Rallying Cry: Cut Costs; Slumping Earnings Force Firms to Pare Wages, Trim Staff; Retails Hit Hardest," *Crain's New York Business,* February 5, 2001.
18. Susanne Craig, Charles Gasparino, and Jathon Sapsford, "Deals & Deal Makers: Wall Street Top Guns Face Layoffs, Too—Cuts Are Expanded from Lower Levels," *Wall Street Journal,* August 22, 2001.
19. Stephen Gandel, "Mack's Ax to Swing Again," *Crain's New York Business,* March 12, 2002.
20. Eric Lipton, "Mayor Persists on Stadiums in a Race to Beat the Clock," *New York Times,* April 27, 2001.
21. Philip Lentz, "Giuliani's Tentacles Pinch BID: New Rules Signal Displeasure with Grand Central," *Crain's New York Business,* April 27, 1998.
22. "NY Mayor in Senate Race Admits Link with Woman: The Admission, Coming After News of His Cancer, Sparks Speculation Giuliani Will Quit the Senate Race," *Vancouver Sun,* May 5, 2000.

23. Alan Finder, "City Hall Sues Con Edison Over 18-Hour Blackout," *New York Times,* July 16, 1999.

24. Alair Townsend, "If Budget Chief Worked for Koch, He'd Be Out Looking for a New Job," *Crain's New York Business,* January 5, 1998.

25. Alair Townsend, "Giuliani's Retribution Campaign," *Crain's New York Business,* October 25, 1999.

26. Eric Lipton, "City Officials Agree on Budget With $500 Million Tax Cut," *New York Times,* June 7, 2001.

27. Tom Fredrickson, "NYC Economy to Slow After Near-Record Year; Wall St., New Media Could Put Drag on Momentum; Business Services Stay Strong," *Crain's New York Business,* December 11, 2000.

28. Eric Lipton, "Flush With Cash, New York Gets Highest Credit Rating in 9 Year," *New York Times,* August 9, 2000.

29. Louise Kramer, "Hotels Ax Rate as Room Boom Turns to Bust; High-End Players Cut Prices for First Time in Years; New Tactics to Lure Guests," *Crain's New York Business,* August 20, 2001.

30. Tom Fredrickson, "Housing in NY Headed for a Fall; Market Could Drop 20%; Bubble Fears at Fore," *Crain's New York Business,* August 27, 2001.

31. Louise Kramer, "No Work and More Play; Lazy Economy Produces R&R," *Crain's New York Business,* June 11, 2001.

32. Michael Blood, "NYers Digging Rudy Dirt," *New York Daily News,* June 21, 2001.

33. Jonathan Hicks, "Education Is Top Theme in Campaigns for Mayor," *New York Times,* January 29, 2001.

CHAPTER 10: DISASTER STRIKES

1. Anemona Hartocollis, "New Death Toll Is Added to the Toll from 9/11," *New York Times,* June 18, 2011.

2. William C. Thompson, Jr., "One Year Later: The Fiscal Impact of 9/11 on New York City," September 4, 2002, http://comptroller.nyc.gov/bureaus/bud/reports/impact-9-11-year-later.pdf.

3. Gretchen Morgenson, "A Nation Challenged: The Overview; Wall St. Reopens Six Days After Shutdown; Stocks Slide 7%, But Investors Resist Panic," *New York Times,* September 18, 2001.

4. Lore Croghan, "Refugee Firms Race to Find New Offices; Most Abandon Financial Districts; Landlords Put Deals Ahead of Profits," *Crain's New York Business,* September 25, 2001.

5. Lisa Fickenscher, "Lengthening Shadow; After Disaster, Big Woes for Small Businesses," *Crain's New York Business,* September 24, 2001.

6. Miriam Kreinin Souccar, "Donations in Free Fall; Nonprofits Unrelated to Attack Hit Hard," *Crain's New York Business,* October 1, 2001.

7. Lore Croghan, "Firms Fleeing Take 17,500 Jobs to N.J. Suburbs; More Losses Likely From Downtown; Can Incentives Slow Defections?," *Crain's New York Business,* October 29, 2001.

8. Lore Croghan, "Developers Rush to Build Offices; Projects Fast-Tracked; City Could Gain 14 Million Square Feet of Commercial Space," *Crain's New York Business,* October 1, 2001.

9. David Barstow, "A Nation Challenged; Federal Aid; Old Rivals, but One Voice in Request for Help," *New York Times,* September 19, 2001.

10. New York Road Runners, emails, Summer 2011.

11. Stephen Gandel, "Wall Street's Lousy Year Takes a Big Turn for the Worse; Slipping Revenues Force Firms to Weigh Major Cuts; Bonuses Take $2 Billion Hit," *Crain's New York Business,* September 25, 2001.

12. Catherine Curan, "Retailers Plan Big Discounts for Lean Holiday; Take Drastic Steps to Draw Shoppers; Smaller Stores May Not Survive," *Crain's New York Business,* November 19, 2001.

13. John Sexton, author interviews, Spring 2011.
14. Lore Croghan. "After Brief Rush, Midtown Market Weakens; Displaced Tenants Backfill Space; 6.1 Million Square Feet of Sublets Available," *Crain's New York Business,* December 3, 2001.
15. Dean Murphy, "Clinton Backs Green, and Koch and Carey Give Their Support to Bloomberg," *New York Times,* November 2, 2001.
16. Philip Lentz, "Bloomberg Prepping for City Hall Race; His Political Experience Limited to Big Donations; Wallet Is Best Asset," *Crain's New York Business,* October 20, 2000.
17. Joyce Purnick, *Michael Bloomberg: Money, Power, Politics* (New York: Public Affairs, 2009).
18. James Barron, "Public Lives," *New York Times,* November 16, 2000.
19. Philip Lentz, "Citizen Bloomberg Bucks for N.Y. Mayor," *Investment News,* November, 6, 2000.
20. Adam Nagourney, "Ever-Tighter Mayoral Race Draws to a Bitter End," *New York Times,* November 6, 2001.
21. Ibid.
22. Carl Weisbrod, author interviews, Summer 2011.
23. Felicity Barringer, "The Media Business; Many at Wall St. Journal Set to Return to Manhattan," *New York Times,* October 17, 2002.
24. Stephen Gandel, "Wall Street Hit by Wave of Price Cuts; Discounting Ravages Once-Rich M&A Practices; Some Fear a Permanent Turn," *Crain's New York Business,* April 1, 2002.
25. Stephen Gandel, "Bear Trap Snags on Street's Suppliers; Securities Firms Ratchet Back Again; New York to Lag National Recovery," *Crain's New York Business,* July 22, 2002.
26. Stephen Gandel, "Wall Street Takes Ax to Whole Units; Effort to Pare Costs Reaches New Levels," *Crain's New York Business,* November 11, 2002.
27. Stephen Gandel, "Consultants Push Wall Street to Leave; Downtown's Losses Are Huge, But Some Companies Shrug Off Fears, Concentrate Workers in Midtown," *Crain's New York Business,* March 4, 2002.
28. Lisa Fickenscher, author interviews, Summer 2011.
29. Catherine Curan, "Downturn Shreds Apparel Sector; No Bottom in Sight for Garment Industry," *Crain's New York Business,* September 1, 2003.
30. Jennifer Steinhauer, "Mayor Says There's No Money to Build 2 Baseball Stadiums," *New York Times,* January 8, 2002.
31. Michael Cooper, "The Mayor's Budget Proposal; Overview; Bloomberg Seeks Cuts in Spending at Most Agencies." *New York Times,* February 14, 2006.
32. Eric Lipton and Michael Cooper, "City Faces Challenge to Close Widest Budget Gap Since '70s," *New York Times,* January 4, 2002.
33. Ibid.
34. Michael Cooper, "Bloomberg Is Considering Tax Increases," *New York Times,* October 1, 2002.
35. Jennifer Steinhauer, "Once Anti-Tax, a Mayor Changes His Thinking," *New York Times,* October 26, 2002.
36. Michael Cooper, "Bloomberg is Considering Tax Increases," *New York Times,* October 1, 2002.
37. Philip Lentz, "Business Split on Fighting Mike; Real Estate Opposes Property Tax Hike, But Others Move to Back Mayor's Plan," *Crain's New York Business,* November 18, 2002.
38. Ibid.
39. Steinhauer, "What Kind of Businessman Raises Your Taxes? A Realistic One, Bloomberg Attests, If He's Running New York," *New York Times,* December 1, 2002.
40. "One Year Later," City Comptroller, September 2002.

41. Lore Croghan, "Midtown Rent Cuts Spur New Battle of Bargains; Excess Space Going for $20 Per Square Foot; Threat to Downtown Market," *Crain's New York Business,* February 3, 2003.

42. Lore Croghan, "War Worries, Economy to Cut Rents 10% More; Landlords Begin to Feel the Chill; Tenants Expected to Start Defaulting," *Crain's New York Business,* March 3, 2003.

43. Lisa Fickenscher, author interviews, Summer 2011.

44. New York Road Runners, Emails, Summer 2011.

45. Tom Fredrickson, "Gaining by Degrees; Colleges Grow Despite Stiff Economic Headwind," *Crain's New York Business,* September 2, 2002.

46. Laura Hughes, "The Big Apple Shines; Relocation Specialists Have Been Surprised to Find that Despite the Events of Sept. 11, Executives From All Over Still Want to be in New York City," *Crain's New York Business,* June 24, 2002.

47. Catherine Curan, "Stores Takes a Risk on NYC's New Allure; Low Rents, Lease Terms Attractive Despite Economy," *Crain's New York Business,* September 2, 2002.

48. Lore Croghan, "Jersey Rush Stalling Amid Wall Street Layoffs; Financial Firms Scramble to Sublease; Owe Millions in Rent," *Crain's New York Business,* July 8, 2002.

49. Lauren Petrecca, "Boroughs Steam Ahead as Manhattan Slips; Feed on Residential Vigor, Low Crime; Modest Growth to Continue in 2003," *Crain's New York Business,* October 28, 2002.

50. Stephen Gandel, "Credit Derivatives Offer Wall Street Whiff of Success; Firms Charge into Trillion-Dollar Market, But After J.P. Morgan, Default Fears Rise," *Crain's New York Business,* September 30, 2002.

51. Aaron Elstein, "Goldman Thrives on Gambling Binge; Profits from Trading Soar; Analysts Worry About Risk," *Crain's New York Business,* April 5, 2004.

52. Aaron Elstein, "Economic Surge Rebuilds Altar of Public Offerings; Investors Worship Anew as December Brings Flock of Deals; Google in the Wings," *Crain's New York Business,* December 15, 2003.

53. Aaron Elstein, "Market's Rise Stokes Hire Hopes; Staffing Slowly Resumes; Support Workers Sought as Others Face Long Search, Low Pay," *Crain's New York Business,* September 15, 2003.

54. Joel Kotkin, "The Declustering of America," *Wall Street Journal,* August 15, 2002.

55. Federal Reserve Bank of New York, 2005.

CHAPTER 11: OLYMPIC DREAMS

1. Dan Doctoroff, author interviews, various dates.

2. Michael Cooper, "New York Cities Bid for Olympics," *New York Times,* June 23, 1996.

3. Charles V. Bagli, "New York Olympic Stadium Plan Masks Shaky Political Coalition," *New York Times,* October 2, 2000.

4. Dan Doctoroff, author interviews, various dates.

5. Charles V. Bagli, "Schumer Proposals Address Shortage of Office Space," *New York Times,* June 11, 2001.

6. Dan Doctoroff, author interviews, various dates.

7. Nat Leventhal, author interviews, Spring 2011.

8. Charles V. Bagli, "Jets, Citing Benefits to City, Detail a Stadium Plan," *New York Times,* January 27, 2001.

9. Charles V. Bagli, "West Side Plan Envisions Jets and Olympics," *New York Times,* May 1, 2002.

10. Philip Lentz & Judith Messina, "Pushing a New Frontier; Far West Side Development Plans Move Ahead Despite Criticism," *Crain's New York Business,* October 28, 2002.

11. Charles V. Bagli, "Broadway Joins Criticism of West Side Stadium Plan," *New York Times,* February 24, 2004.
12. Charles V. Bagli, "$11.5 Million Spent on Fight Over Stadium on West Side," *New York Times,* October 26, 2004.
13. Charles V. Bagli & Michael Cooper, "Bloomberg's Stadium Quest Fails; Olympic Bid Is Hurt," *New York Times,* June 7, 2005.
14. Charles V. Bagli & Jim Rutenberg, "Mayor Says Bid Was Worth a Shot, Even Long," *New York Times,* July 7, 2005.
15. Ibid.
16. Stephanie Storm, "Goldman, Sachs Group Strikes Deal for Rockefeller Center," *New York Times,* November 8, 1995.
17. Charles V. Bagli, "Biggest Building Site in Manhattan Up for Auction," *New York Times,* May 17, 2007.
18. Charles V. Bagli, "M.T.A. Toward Tishman Speyer's Railyard Bid," *New York Times,* May 22, 2008.
19. Charles V. Bagli, "New Developers Signs $1 Billion Deal to Transform West Side Railyards," *New York Times,* May 20, 2008.
20. Diane Cardell, "City Backs Makeover for Decaying Brooklyn Waterfront," *New York Times,* May 3, 2005.
21. Christopher Grimes, "New York's Mayor Vows to Hang on for a Bumpy Ride," *Financial Times,* March 14, 2003.
22. "Voices the Mayor Needs to Hear," *Crain's New York Business,* May 12, 2003.
23. Judy Temes, "Industrial Policy Has Design Flaws; Zones to Provide Low Rents, Long Leases Won't Prevent Conversions, Other Uses," *Crain's New York Business,* July 11, 2005.

CHAPTER 12: IF YOU BUILD IT THEY WILL COME

1. Constance Williams, interview with Cesar R. Bustamante, Jr. at Crainsnewyork. com.
2. Frank Rich, "Journal, Mickey Does 42d Street," *New York Times,* January 16, 1994.
3. "Reviving Time Square: An Interview with Rebecca Robertson Disney Saw 42nd St.'s Value; Outsiders Do," *Crain's New York Business,* March 27, 1995.
4. Bruce Weber, "Disney Unveils Restored New Amsterdam Theater," *New York Times,* April 3, 1997.
5. Alan Mirabella, "Broadway Fears a Mouse That Will Roar," *Crain's New York Business,* February 28, 1994.
6. "'Beast' Breaks Broadway Sales Record," *United Press International,* April 20, 1994.
7. Campbell Robertson, " 'Mermaid' Approaches, So 'Beauty' Will Close," *New York Times,* January 18, 2007.
8. Vincent Canby, "SUNDAY VIEW; 'The Lion King' Earns Its Roars of Approval," *New York Times,* November 23, 1997.
9. Charles V. Bagli, "Extending Its Reach, Room by Room; Marriott Set Out to Prove Itself in New York; Now It Dominates," *New York Times,* May 22, 1997.
10. David Ringwood, interview with Cesar R. Bustamante, Jr., August 3.
11. Colleen Long, "NYC Record 532 Murders in 2010, up from 2009," *Associated Press,* January 3, 2011.
12. John Holusha, "A Dream Grows in Brooklyn," *New York Times,* June 22, 1997.
13. Lyda Richardson, "Land Clearing Starts for Brooklyn Hotel," *New York Times,* July 24, 1996.
14. Thomas J. Lueck, "A Nice Place to Visit; A Hotel! Bus Tours! Brooklyn Hits the Tourist Map," *New York Times,* July 6, 1998.
15. Larry Kanter, "Hotel Operators Fill Vacancies in Meat District: Follow Small Art Galleries, Restaurants into Up-and-Coming Northwest Village," *Crain's New York Business,* August 16, 1999.

16. Adam Piore, "The New King of New York," *South China Morning Post,* January 7, 2007.

17. Lisa Fickenscher, "Credit Crunch Slows Hotelier's Juggernaut; Sam Chang Scrambles to Finish Projects in Pipeline," *Crain's New York Business,* April 7, 2008.

18. Lisa Fickenscher, "Hotel Check into Boroughs, Lower Room Rates Draw Visitors to Underserved Areas," *Crain's New York Business,* May 16, 2011.

19. "2011 City Facts," *Crain's New York Business,* August 29–September 11, 2011.

20. Miriam Kreinin Souccar, "Broadway's Plotting Writes a Happy Ending; Mayor's Interest, Newfound Unity Saves an Industry and Set Example," *Crain's New York Business,* March 4, 2002.

21. Cristyne L. Nicholas, author interview, Summer 2011.

22. Miriam Kreinin Souccar, "Broadway's Plotting Writes a Happy Ending; Mayor's Interest, Newfound Unity Saves an Industry and Set Example," *Crain's New York Business,* March 4, 2002.

23. "2011 City Facts," *Crain's New York Business.*

24. Brian Moylan, "A Few Rules for Tourists Visiting New York City This Summer," *Gawker,* http://gawker.com/5543792/a-few-rules-for-tourists-visiting-new-york-city-this-summer (accessed July 25, 2011).

25. Stephanie Coco-Palermo, "The Pre-Disneyfied Times Square: A Cherished Lover from the Past?" *Time Square: Cross Roads of the World,* http://www.timessquare.com/NYC__/Times_Square_History/The_Pre-Disneyfied_Times_Square:_A_Cherished_Lover_from_the_Past?/ (accessed April 29, 2011).

26. "The Demographics of the Broadway Audience," *What Goes to Broadway?,* November 2010.

27. Sharon Edelson, "Forever 21's Big Footprint in Times Square," *Women's Wear Daily,* June 24, 2010.

28. Adam Friedman, "Transforming the City's Manufacturing Landscape," in *What's Next for New York City's Economy,* eds. Jonathan P. Hicks & Dan Morris (New York: Drum Major Institute for Public Policy, 2009), 23.

29. Peter Ward, "A Case for a Pro-Worker Growth Agenda," in *What's Next for New York City's Economy,* eds. Jonathan P. Hicks & Dan Morris (New York: Drum Major Institute for Public Policy, 2009), 59.

30. Robert Ferranoi, author interviews, Fall 2010.

31. David Barboza, "Supply Chain for iPhone Highlights Costs in China," *New York Times,* July 5, 2010.

CHAPTER 13: TRICKLE-DOWN ECONOMICS

1. Aaron Elstein, "Trio to Thrive on Market Rally; Goldman, Morgan, Merrill Stand to Gain, While Bond Bonuses Could Falter," *Crain's New York Business,* June 30, 2003.

2. Aaron Elstein, "Streamlined Street Keeps the Lid on Jobs; High Tech, Low Margin Mean Cuts; Bonus-Driven Tax Revenues Still Hefty," *Crain's New York Business,* January 3, 2005.

3. Aaron Elstein, "Economic Surge Rebuilds Altar of Public Offerings; Investors Worship Anew as December Brings Flock of Deals; Google in the Wings," *Crain's New York Business,* December 15, 2003.

4. Aaron Elstein, "Goldman Thrives on Gambling Binge; Profits from Trading Soar; Analysts Worry About Risks," *Crain's New York Business,* April 5, 2004.

5. Aaron Elstein, "Dimon's Morgan Gives Chase to Citi; New Leader Brings Hope for Rebound; Share Price Rises Even s Rival's Sinks," *Crain's New York Business,* November 22, 2004.

6. Aaron Elstein, "Merrill's a Bull Again; After Cutbacks, Securities Firm Goes on Hiring, Buying Binge, Anxious Investors Get Sense of Déjà Vu," *Crain's New York Business,* October 4, 2004.

7. Aaron Elstein, "Profits Ignite Wall Street's Hiring Engine; Wanted: Bankers, Brokers, Traders," *Crain's New York Business,* May 3, 2004.

8. Elstein, "Streamlined Street Keeps the Lid on Jobs; High Tech, Low Margin Mean Cuts; Bonus-Driven Tax Revenues Still Hefty."
9. Michael Lewis, *Liar's Poker* (New York: W.W. Norton & Company, Inc., 1989), 14.
10. Susanne Craig, "House Money: How One Executive Reignited Goldman's Appetite for Risk—Outsider Mr. Blankfein Places Big Bets an Others Follow; Profiting Wit Firm's Cash—Handling Trading Blow-Ups," *Wall Street Journal,* May 5, 2004.
11. Joseph Kahn, "Vote at Goldman Approves Latest Plan to Offer Shares," *New York Times,* March 9, 1999.
12. Joseph Kahn, "Shares of Goldman Rise 33% on First Day," *New York Times,* May 5, 1999.
13. Joseph Kahn, "Even a Tiny Slice of a Big Pie Tastes Rich," *New York Times,* March 17, 1999.
14. Kahn, "Even a Tiny Slice of a Big Pie Tastes Rich."
15. Craig, "House Money: How One Executive Reignited Goldman's Appetite for Risk—Outsider Mr. Blankfein Places Big Bets an Others Follow; Profiting Wit Firm's Cash—Handling Trading Blow-Ups."
16. Susanne Craig and Randall Smith, "Bush Taps Paulson as Treasury Chief—Firm Expected to Elevate Blankfein, Underscoring A Shift Toward Trading—Mr. Inside vs. Mr. Outside," *Wall Street Journal,* May 31, 2006.
17. Bhattiprolu Murti and Kate Kelly, "Goldman, Co-Presidents Paid $67.5 Million Each," *Wall Street Journal,* March 8, 2008.
18. Jenny Anderson, "Goldman Chairman Gets a Bonus of $53.4 Million," *New York Times,* December 20, 2006.
19. Murti and Kelly, "Goldman, Co-Presidents Paid $67.5 Million Each."
20. Jenny Anderson and Michael de la Merced, "Kohlberg Kravis Plans to Go Public," *New York Times,* July 4, 2007.
21. Michael de la Merced and Andrew Ross Sorkin, "Blackstone Rival Plans Own I.P.O.," *New York Times,* June 22, 2007.
22. Andrew Ross Sorkin and Peter Edmonston, "A Titan of Private Equity May Go Public," *New York Times,* March 17, 2007.
23. Andrew Ross Sorkin and Michael de la Merced, "Behind the Veil and Blackstone? Probably Another Veil," *New York Times,* March 19, 2007.
24. Jenny Anderson, "The Logic and the Timing of Taking Blackstone Public," *New York Times,* March 23, 2007.
25. Andrew Ross Sorkin, Jenny Anderson, Peter Edmonston, & Michael de la Merced, "Blackstone Says It Plans to Go Public," *New York Times,* March 23, 2007.
26. Andrew Ross Sorkin, "A Glamorous Public Debut for Blackstone," *New York Times,* June 23, 2007.
27. Jenny Anderson, "Blackstone Founders Due Billions," *New York Times,* June 12, 2007.
28. Andrew Ross Sorkin, "In Defense of Schwarzman," *New York Times,* July 29, 2007.
29. Landon Thomas, Jr., "More Rumors About His Party Than His Deals," *New York Times,* January 27, 2007.
30. Thomas, "More Rumors About His Party Than His Deals."
31. Geraldine Fabrikant, "New Money Dances with Old Money at the Frick," *New York Times,* March 29, 2006.
32. Robin Pogrebin, "For $100 Million, a Library Card and Perhaps His Name in Stone," *New York Times,* March 11, 2008.
33. Marc Santora, "After Big Gift, A New Name for the Library," *New York Times,* April 23, 2008.
34. Pogrebin, "For $100 Million, a Library Card and Perhaps His Name in Stone."
35. Aaron Elstein, "Money-Maniacal Hedge Funders Reinvent Greed; Management Fees Provide Fastest Path to Multimillions," *Crain's New York Business,* June 6, 2005.

36. Elstein, "Money-Maniacal Hedge Funders Reinvent Greed; Management Fees Provide Fastest Path to Multimillions."

37. Landon Thomas, "The Man Who Won as Others Lost," *New York Times,* October 13, 2007.

38. Jenny Anderson, "Big Names, Big Wallets, Big Cause," *New York Times,* May 4, 2007.

39. Lisa Fickenscher, "Employers in the Soup; Restaurant Jobs Jump; Good Staff Hard to Find, Keep," *Crain's New York Business,* November 1, 2004.

40. Lisa Fickenscher, "Restaurant Staffers Are Going Like Hotcakes; Boom Feeds Demand for Top Talent, but Less-Experienced Help Wanted, Too," *Crain's New York Business,* January 2, 2006.

41. Cynthia Rigg, "Home Depot Welcome; Megastore Builds Head of Steam," *Crain's New York Business,* April 4, 1994.

42. Tom Fredrickson, "Boroughs' Bank Boom; Large Institutions, Startups Plan Sites Outside Manhattan; Poor Still Overlooked," *Crain's New York Business,* October 16, 2006.

43. Elisabeth Butler, "Good Retail Help Harder to Find; Workforce Hits Record; Hourly Wage Rise," *Crain's New York Business,* October 9, 2006.

44. Fredrickson, "Boroughs' Bank Boom; Large Institutions, Startups Plan Sites Outside Manhattan; Poor Still Overlooked."

45. Butler, "Good Retail Help Harder to Find; Workforce Hits Record; Hourly Wage Rise."

46. Tom Fredrickson, "Building Permits Jump to 34,000, Set Record; Queens, Brooklyn, Lead Surge; 421-A Rush Could Result in Decline Next Year," *Crain's New York Business,* October 15, 2007.

47. Tom Fredrickson, "Unions Bringing in Out-of-Town Muscle; Big Paychecks Draw Workers; Critics Want More Apprentices," *Crain's New York Business,* October 1, 2007.

48. Charles Bagli, "Underwater in a Big Way," *New York Times,* February 7, 2009.

49. Charles Bagli and Terry Pristin, "Harry Macklowe's $6.4 Billion Bill," *New York Times,* January 6, 2008.

50. Charles Bagli, "Macklowes Sell G.M. Building for $2.9 Billion," *New York Times,* May 25, 2008.

51. Julie Satow, "Mobbing Midtown; Big-Name Tenants Pursue Large Class A Spaces; Limited Supply Promises a Rent Spike," *Crain's New York Business,* September 26, 2005.

52. Christine Haughney, "Midtown Office Rents Picking Up; Big Tenants, Hedge Funds Fuel Rise; Trend Could Spread to Broader Market," *Crain's New York Business,* February 14, 2005.

53. Julie Satow, "Midtown Rents Surge to $100 Threshold," *Crain's New York Business,* January 23, 2006.

54. Matthew Flamm, "Get Out of Town!; Gothamites Trade in Success for Simple Life," *Crain's New York Business,* September 1, 2008.

55. Nina Bernstein, "Poverty Rate Persists in City Despite Boom," *New York Times,* October 7, 1999.

56. Daniel Massey, "The Gilded City; New York's Wealthiest Have Grown Rich Beyond Compare. Now for the Other 99%," *Crain's New York Business,* December 13, 2010.

CHAPTER 14: THE BIGGEST CRASH OF ALL

1. Paul Krugman, "Reckonings; A Rent Affairs," *New York Times,* June 7, 2000.

2. Kevin Sack, "A Test of Wills; In Albany Rent Stabilization Battle, G.O.P. Is Standing Firm on Changes," *New York Times,* June 17, 1993.

3. Kevin Sack, "Dinkins and Giuliani Go to Legislature," *New York Times,* June 22, 1993.

4. James Dao, "Compromise Is Reached on Rent Rules," *New York Times,* July 4, 1993.
5. Richard Perez-Pena, "G.O.P. Leader Urges Ending of Rent Rules," *New York Times,* December 6, 1996.
6. Perez-Pena, "The Rent Debate: The General; Bruno, in private War Room, Sees Himself as Pragmatist," *New York Times,* April 7, 1997.
7. James Dao, "Aides Say Pataki Favors Easing Some Limits on Rents," *New York Times,* March 27, 1997; "Giuliani to Step Up Pressure on Pataki Over Rent Stance," *New York Times,* May 23, 1997.
8. Raymond Hernandez, "Bruno, Threatened, Attacks Rent Groups," *New York Times,* April 12, 1997; Dao, "Vacancy Issue Becomes Focus of Rent Debate," *New York Times,* June 10, 1997.
9. James Dao, "The Rent Battle: The Overview; Tentative Agreement Reached to Preserve Rent Regulations," *New York Times,* June 16, 1997.
10. Charles V. Bagli, "Housing Complex of 110 Buildings For Sale in City," *New York Times,* August 30, 2006.
11. Charles V. Bagli, "Megadeal: Inside a Real Estate Coup," *New York Times,* December 31, 2006.
12. Charles V. Bagli, "Housing Complex of 110 Buildings For Sale in City," *New York Times,* August 30, 2006.
13. Bagli, "Megadeal: Inside a Real Estate Coup"; Bagli, "Fallout Is Wide in Failed Deal for Stuyvesant," *New York Times,* January 26, 2010.
14. Charles V. Bagli, "$5.4 Billion Bid Wins Complexes in New York Deal," *New York Times,* October 18, 2006.
15. Manny Fernandez and Charles V. Bagli, "Tenants Roiled by Challenges on Residency," *New York Times,* May 27, 2008.
16. Charles V. Bagli, "Stuyvesant Town Revenues Have Fallen, Report Says," *New York Times,* July 23, 2008; "Big Landlord Is Found to Have Wrongly Raised Rents," *New York Times,* March 6, 2009.
17. Charles V. Bagli, "Partners Near Default on Stuyvesant Town," *New York Times,* January 8, 2010.
18. Charles V. Bagli, "Mortgage Crisis Is Foreseen in Housing Owned by Private Equity Firms," *New York Times,* October 6, 2008.
19. Carol Kellerman, author interview, Spring 2011.
20. Citizens Budget Commission, "Rent Regulation: Beyond the Rhetoric," June 2010.
21. Eliot Brown, "Real Estate Flexes muscles—Industry Backing Both Democrats and Republicans in Aggressive Campaign Push," *Wall Street Journal,* October 11, 2010.
22. Eliot Brown & Andrew Grossman, "City News: Rent, Tax-Cap Deal Reached," *Wall Street Journal,* June 25, 2011.
23. Greg David, "Why Are Tenant Advocates So Upset Today?," *Crain's New York Business,* June 22, 2011.
24. Editorial Desk, "End Rent Control," *New York Times,* May 12, 1987.
25. Editorial Desk, "A Sensible Plan for Rent Decontrol," *New York Times,* December 8, 1996.

CHAPTER 15: THREE SECTORS TO THE RESCUE

1. Margaret Jaworski, "NYU Follows Syllabus For Rebirth; Along with Columbia, University Draws Top Students to City," *Crain's New York Business,* May 15, 2000.
2. Karen W. Arenson, "N.Y.U. Names Its Law Dean as President of the School," *New York Times,* May 9, 2001; NYU Department of Public Affairs, e-mails to author, Summer 2011.
3. Karen W. Arenson, "N.Y.U Begins Hiring Effort to Lift Its Liberal Arts Standing," *New York Times,* September 27, 2004.
4. Karen W. Arenson, "The Village of the Village?; As N.Y.U Edges Out and Up, Neighbors Put Up a Fight," *New York Times,* April 19, 2001.

5. Robin Pogrebin, "N.Y.U. 20-Year Plan Seeks Big Expansion in Village and Beyond," *New York Times,* March 23, 2010.

6. Pogrebin, "N.Y.U. 20-Year Plan Seeks Big Expansion in Village and Beyond."

7. NYU Department of Public Affairs, e-mails to author, Summer 2011.

8. Charles V. Bagli, "Columbia May Expand Onto Trump Riverfront Site," *New York Times,* September 15, 2000; Karen Arenson, "University of Michigan President Is Nominated to Lead Columbia," *New York Times,* October 4, 2001.

9. Aaron Elstein, "Columbia Seeks to Lead the Class; Bollinger Begins Big Push to Expand Campus, Raise More Money, Lure Top-Flight Professors," *Crain's New York Business,* October 13, 2003.

10. Ibid.

11. David Gonzalez, "In Columbia Growth Plan, Ghosts of '68," *New York Times,* August 24, 2004.

12. Timothy Williams & Ray Rivera, "$7 Billion Columbia Expansion Gets Green Light," *New York Times,* December 20, 2007; Aaron Arenson, "For a Top-Tier University, There's Now Room to Get Even Better," *New York Times,* December 21, 2007.

13. Samantha Marshall, "St. John's Blesses; Queens University's Applications Jump 27% as Recruiting Effort Pays off," *Crain's New York Business,* February 18, 2008.

14. David W. Dunlap, "Cramped Fordham Plans to Expand at Lincoln Center, Mostly Skyward," *New York Times,* February 23, 2005.

15. Amanda Fung, "New School's Growing Pains; Financially Stable University Seeks to Unify Separate Schools Under Controversial President," *Crain's New York Business,* January 26, 2009.

16. Ilene Landress, author interview, Summer 2011.

17. Gerald Fraser, "Koch Predicts Astoria Studio's Rebirth," *New York Times,* September 6, 1980; Damon Stetson, "Studios Growing to Meet City Film Industry Surge," *New York Times,* May 31, 1981.

18. Alan Suna, author interview, Summer 2011.

19. Clyde H. Farnsworth, "The Versatile City That Film Makers Like to Film," *New York Times,* April 10, 1993.

20. Dinitia Smith, "When a Hard-Nosed Producer Insists on New York," *New York Times,* August 15, 1995.

21. Miriam Kreinin Souccar, "Film Production Hits Break in Action; After an Influx of Business, Movie Industry Picture Darkens; NY-Based TV Shows End," *Crain's New York Business,* March 31, 2003.

22. Glenn Collins, "Plan to Boost Film Industry In New York," *New York Times,* August 17, 2004; Miriam Kreinin Souccar, "Tax Cuts Light up NYC Filmmaking; New Productions Headed Here, Some Firms Plan to Relocate too; Big Job Gains Possible," *Crain's New York Business,* January 24, 2005; Souccar, "TV Pilots Hit a Record in the City; Studios, at Capacity, Hustle to Expand; Production Execs Credit Tax Incentive," *Crain's New York Business,* April 18, 2011.

23. Patrick McGeehan & Patrick Healy, "A Separate but Equally Important Loss," *New York Times,* May 15, 2010; Brian Stelter & Bill Carter, "One 'Law & Order' Gets a Death Sentence, as Another Joins the Force," *New York Times,* May 15, 2010.

24. Miriam Kreinin Souccar, "Brooklyn Studio Sees Big Picture; Navy Yard's Steiner Studios Inks Movie Deal and Seeks More; Will Queens Rivals Suffer?," *Crain's New York Business,* May 10, 2004; Souccar, "Sun Rises on HBO's Boardwalk Empire; Who Needs L&O When You Have a Hit with a $65M Budget? Execs, Vendors Rejoice," *Crain's New York Business,* October 11, 2004.

25. Daniel Massey, "City's TV Industry Hits New High," *Crain's New York Business,* August 22, 2011.

26. E-mails from Carl Zucker, VP–Business Affairs, CAPS Universal Payroll, Fall 2011.

27. The Film and Television Production Industry in New York State Report by Thomas P. DiNapoli, New York State Comptroller and Kenneth B. Bleiwas, Deputy Controller, March 2010.

28. Chris Maliwat, author interviews, Spring 2011.
29. Kevin Ryan, author interviews.
30. Kira Bindrim, "40 Under Forty; Dennis Crowley, 34," *Crain's New York Business,* March 28, 2011.
31. Judith Messina, "Bold Newcomer Stables Shares; SecondMarket: The Breakthrough Idea," *Crain's New York Business,* November 8, 2010.
32. Judith Messina, "The Thriving Alley Survivor You've Never Heard of," *Crain's New York Business,* June 22, 2011.
33. Judith Messina, "People to Watch in Silicon Alley," *Crain's New York Business,* June 6, 2011.
34. Judith Messina, "Why Google Is the New Exit Strategy," *Crain's New York Business,* July 20, 2011; Charles V. Bagli, "Google Signs Deal to Buy Manhattan Office Building," *New York Times,* December 3, 2010.
35. Melanie Hughes, author interviews, Spring 2011.
36. Seth Pinsky, author interviews, Summer 2011.

CHAPTER 16: THE END OF THE NEW YORK ERA?

1. Federal Reserve Bank of Dallas, emails to authors, Summer 2011.
2. "The Caring State and Local Taxes in Large U.S. Cities," New York City Independent Budget Office Fiscal Brief, February 2007: 1.
3. Sam Roberts, "A Striking Evolution in Bedford-Stuyvesant as the White Population Soars," *New York Times,* August 5, 2011.
4. Diane Cardwell, "City Hopes to Allow More Offices in Garment Center," *New York Times,* February 15, 2007.
5. Adrianne Pasquarelli, "Fashion Firms Flee Garment District; Designers Find Other Neighborhoods More Creative, Convenient," *Crain's New York Business,* May 9, 2011.
6. Fernanda Santos, "Willets Point Project Foes Reach Deal With the City," *New York Times,* November 13, 2008.
7. Carol Kellerman, author interviews, Summer 2011.
8. Joyce Purnick, *Mike Bloomberg: Money, Power, Politics* (New York: Public Affairs, 2009), 207.
9. Daniel Massey, "Support for NYC Walmart Edges up, Poll Shows," *Crain's New York Business,* July 28, 2011.
10. Ibid.

INDEX